D1441172

Off-the-Wall Ways to Get a Job

By
Brandon Toropov

CAREER PRESS
3 Tice Road
P.O. Box 687
Franklin Lakes, NJ 07417
1-800-CAREER-1
201-848-0310 (NJ and outside U.S.)
FAX: 201-848-1727

Copyright © 1996 by Beach Brook Productions

Note: Each of the methods described in this book was inspired by an actual event; in some stories, however, to address the privacy concerns or other interests of interview and research participants—and, occasionally, to provide clarity and continuity—certain particulars have been altered.

303 OFF-THE-WALL WAYS TO GET A JOB
ISBN 1-56414-199-3, $12.99
Cover design by The Gottry Communications Group, Inc.
Printed in the U.S.A. by Book-mart Press

To order this title by mail, please include price as noted above, $2.50 handling per order, and $1.00 for each book ordered. Send to: Career Press, Inc., 3 Tice Road., P.O. Box 687, Franklin Lakes, NJ 07417.

Or call toll-free 1-800-CAREER-1 (NJ and Canada: 201-848-0310) to order using VISA or MasterCard, or for further information on books from Career Press.

Library of Congress Cataloging-in-Publication Data

Toropov, Brandon.
    303 off-the-wall ways to get a job / Brandon Toropov.
       p.   cm.
    Includes index.
    ISBN 1-56414-199-3   (paper)
    1. Job hunting—United States.   I. Title.
HF5382.75.U6T67   1996
650.14—dc20
                                                                            95-37236
                                                                            CIP

Dedication

To Mary, for giving her love unendingly.

Acknowledgments

Space does not allow me to list all the people who were kind enough to be interviewed and pass along their stories, or the stories of their acquaintances. However, a number of individuals were unusually helpful in helping me to locate some fascinating accounts; many provided important leads that led to a number of off-the-wall stories. Those good people deserve recognition here for all their help. My grateful thanks go to: Glenn KnicKrehm, without whose generous support and unending encouragement this book would never have come into existence; Leslie Hamilton; Lawrence Kaplan; Chuck Strinz; Craig Rice; Caitlyn Toropova; Judith Burros; Robert Tragert; Mary Ellen Manning; Gail Eaton; Cassandra Burros; Candace Tuttle; Donna Maturi, Nicholas McAuliffe, Fran Hagerty, Brooks Wright, Bobbie Blair, Suzanne MacLeod and the rest of the staff of the Peabody Institute Library of Danvers, Massachusetts; Steve Kennedy; David Malloy; Melanie MacLean and the entire staff of the Custom Cup Caffé, which happens to provide not only great support for writers but also the best French roast coffee on the North Shore; Arlene Olejarz; Suzanne Tragert; Tony Dias; Mel Kinnear, who rightly points out that it is God who brings all good things to life; Jon Lourie; George Driscoll; John Webster; Don Johnson; Bill Charland; Jack Burros; Dan Sullivan; Gail Eaton; Allia Zobel; Chris Fields; Michele Simos; Christopher Tragert; Mayda Schiffman; John Tragert; Anne Montagu; Matthew Tragert; Michael Scannell; Ann Marie Sabath; Denise Chapman-Weston; Kathy Tragert; and David Opton of Execunet.

Finally, for her unending patience, perseverance, encouragement, canvassing help and inspiration, I offer my thanks to my wife Mary Toropov, who could probably write a book herself about the long days that went into this one.

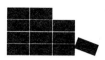

Contents

Read this first

The best introduction is a brief one, and so this part of the book will serve to pass along only one important point.

The single most critical element of any job search is the attitude of the person at the center of it. If you apply a carefully selected idea that appears in this book to your job search, do so with the attitude and certain knowledge that you will succeed. Keep fixed in your mind the notion that the people with whom you come in contact on the employment front are very lucky indeed to hear from you. Know that your aim is, in essence, already accomplished, and that you are only awaiting tangible demonstration of this fact. If you approach your job search campaign in this way, and treat temporary setbacks as learning experiences rather than as judgments upon you as a person, you may rest assured that your efforts will conclude successfully.

Shakespeare said, "All things are ready, if our minds be so."

The Buddha said, "We are what we think. All that we are arises with our thoughts. With our thoughts, we make the world."

Goethe said, "Concerning all acts of initiative and creation, there is one elementary truth: that the moment one definitely commits oneself, then Providence moves, too."

The basic idea just summarized is not new—successful men and women from all cultures, and from across the centuries, have employed it—but it is underutilized. Appropriate it for your use as you make your way through the techniques outlined in this book!

—BT

Section

Today's job market demands a little bit more from you

Important! *This part of the book features essntial information. Please read this section and the next one carefully if you want to make the most of the ideas in the pages that follow!*

This is a book about how to get a job, but it begins with three stories from Hollywood—incidents from popular films of recent years that you'll probably recognize. Two of the stories are sad; one is happy.

Do you remember when...

- In *Howard's End,* the lowly clerk Leonard Bast leaves his job after receiving an ill-advised "inside tip" that the firm he works for is about to collapse? He ends up regretting the decision to leave—and for him, the task of getting a new job seems an endless and nearly soul-crushing undertaking. In one scene, he drags himself unenthusiastically into a bank office and, in a dreary monotone, asks the manager whether there are any openings. When told that there are not, Bast sighs, turns away, and moves on to the next building, where, we somehow sense, an identical answer awaits him.

- In *Lost in America,* former advertising executive David Howard finds himself in need of a job in a small Arizona town? After getting the brush-off when applying for a position as a delivery man, he stops in at the local employment office and, after a brief and frustrating conversation, impatiently asks the job counselor where the special box containing the $100,000-per-year jobs is. When the counselor's laughter finally subsides, David learns that there is, alas, no such box on the premises.

Ready for the happy story? Remember when...

- In *Chaplin,* American film producer Mack Sennett asks English music hall comic Charlie Chaplin to journey across the Atlantic, and then across the continent, to work in motion pictures? There's a problem, though. When Chaplin arrives, he's at least 30 years younger than the middle-aged man he portrayed in the English music hall act Sennett saw. The producer, who has been searching for an older comic, briskly informs the young actor that his services won't be required after all. But Chaplin, without being asked to do anything other than leave, decides to take the opportunity to show off his comic abilities. In a few brief moments, he demonstrates half-a-dozen perfectly timed slapstick gags. He saunters. He slips. He stumbles downwards. He floats up. He smiles. He falls on his rump. He gets up and starts all over again. He makes Mack Sennett laugh. And, without pleading, fuming or complaining, he changes the producer's mind and wins the job.

Of course the obstacles faced by the characters in these movies aren't the same as those you face in trying to find the right job for you. But the three stories just outlined can help to provide you with a new and important outlook, one you may want to bear in mind as you prepare to undertake (or re-energize) your job search. The new perspective you will need to incorporate is the one Chaplin did—that of the person whose task it is to decide whether or not to extend a job offer.

Chaplin knew what his prospective employer needed...even though the prospective employer wasn't quite ready to admit it at the moment.

The producer needed someone who could get laughs. Chaplin knew he could do that. Everything else was incidental for Chaplin.

Now let's try a little exercise based on the personalities of the three people you've just read about, bearing in mind that, in today's business world, personalities are often all we have to go on. Let's pretend you're the prospective employer. How would you go about making that all-important selection of a new employee? Think for a moment about the attitudes of the three people in those stories. If you had to decide which one to take on in your organization, what would you do?

Would you ask to hear more about Mr. Bast? How do you imagine he'd react to some unexpected setback at work? Everyone encounters them; Bast has just shown you how he reacts when he's faced with one particular tough problem (the lack of a job). Maybe his downbeat attitude isn't a fair reflection of the way he approaches a typical problem during the course of the day, but, then again, how do you know that it isn't? And just as important, based on what you've just learned about him in that brief scene, how do you think he'd affect the morale of the other people in your organization with whom he'd have to work if you hired him?

Would you be interested in talking at length with Mr. Howard? Would you look forward to working with someone who expects to enter at the top level of your organization without knowing anything of consequence about what it is you actually do at your company? Based on what you know from the scene, do you think meeting him at the water cooler each morning would be a plus or a minus when it came to positively shaping your own outlook on any given work day? Can you picture him as a resourceful, team-first contributor who would focus easily and immediately on the goals your team regularly has to deliver to your superiors on a tight schedule?

Or would you rather talk to Charlie, that unflappable, inventive candidate who seems to know exactly what you need, even though he's been told to go home? Charlie, who's willing to go out of his way to demonstrate, in a compelling, instantly arresting fashion, that he has the confidence to look a tough situation straight in the eye—and the skill to make an important contribution to your current project?

Be honest. Wouldn't you pick Charlie in a heartbeat over the glum, down-on-his-luck clerk and the abrasive ad agency hotshot?

So would a lot of other people.

Now let's suppose you *don't* have a formal job opening available. Suppose you're at a party, and suppose you're introduced to each of the three applicants we just met. Suppose that each asked about the possibility of working at your company. Suppose that all three had identical formal qualifications for a job you might, just might, with a little maneuvering, be able to make room for in your next budget. With which one would you prefer to work?

No contest, right?

Do you want to hear something remarkable? Even at a time of massive economic change and career dislocation; even at a time when opportunities for career growth seem to be increasingly scarce; even at a time when whole industries suddenly and unceremoniously discharge loyal employees by the thousands; even, in other words, at a time when people are more frustrated than ever about their employment and career possibilities, and would, you'd think, go out of their way to make a positive impression with the people thinking about hiring them; even today, most prospective employers still hardly ever get to meet Charlie Chaplin.

Instead, they often find themselves sitting across the desk from applicants who give every appearance of wanting desperately to be somewhere, anywhere, else. Or people who are short on the details of how they might contribute to the organization, but long and eloquent in their desire to get one of those special jobs from that $100,000 job box.

When a Charlie Chaplin type comes along (and as a long-time manager who has perused hundred upon hundreds of resumes and interviewed countless applicants over the years, I can personally attest that that's not too often), you stop and take notice. When you find yourself forced to recognize someone who has a clear idea of what you, the manager, are trying to accomplish, who has taken on some of the responsibility for conveying his or her suitability, creativity and enthusiasm, and who is confident, upbeat and even a little funny in his or her approach to getting a job, a remarkable thing happens. You decide that you, too, really ought to think of something creative to say in response. Something other than "We'll let you know." Something other than "There aren't any openings right now." Something other than "You'd have to talk to personnel."

A recent *Time* magazine cover story bemoaned the passing of the "great American job." Every newspaper you pick up these days seems to feature an article about massive layoffs—even at some of the nation's most prestigious firms, firms that once prided themselves on long-term commitments to their employees. And, in an ironic twist, even the managers who orchestrate the layoffs may find, a few months later, that they themselves are the newest victims of a work force reduction!

Times have changed. The days have passed when we could expect to be rewarded for dutifully following the traditional channels: send standard resumes and cover letters; follow a few simple rules at the interview; win one of the expanding economy's traditional, plentiful jobs; follow a traditional, predictable career path and expect, in return for decades of traditional loyalty to the company, a reassuring measure of traditional, paternal care from a protective employer. We can remember those days fondly if we want, but they are over and it doesn't seem likely that they'll ever come back. That's the bad news.

The good news (for you, at any rate) is that the vast majority of job seekers continue to behave as though nothing has changed. They keep circling the classifieds, sending the same boring resume to hundreds of companies (apparently under the illusion that all employers want to hear the same thing) and they keep waiting for something interesting to happen, even though it very rarely does. If they somehow manage to make an appointment for an interview, they don't adequately take into account that the person with whom they'll be speaking will be also be talking to dozens (perhaps hundreds) of other qualified applicants.

In short, most of today's job seekers lose sight of the fact that, these days, half of the battle, and probably the most important half, is *being remembered in the first place.* Prospective employers don't remember all the Leonard Basts and David Howards they meet because there are far, far too many of them to keep track of. The countless applicants of the Bast and Howard variety—as well as those applicants who don't make overt errors, but instead commit the unforgivable sin of being just plain dull—can expect to get tuned out in a hurry, even if they do have something unique to offer the employer.

Not you, though. You've taken the first step toward standing out from the crowd. You've started reading this book and, in doing so, you've managed to give yourself a significant advantage over your competition. As a result, you're on your way to hooking up with a whole slew of employers who stand to benefit from meeting you. They are out there and, whether they admit it or not initially, they want to hear from people like you. Remember that producer who was sure he didn't want to work with Chaplin?

Right about now, you may be feeling a little skeptical that you can turn around someone in the same way Chaplin did in that scene. That's natural. But what this book just told you is wonderful news; so wonderful, in fact, that it's worth repeating. *The simple fact that you've picked up this book and have read this far means that you already have a significant statistical advantage over those with whom you'll be competing for employment.* You now know that you can't expect to get the job you want if you do the same things everyone else is doing, and you're ready to find out what *will* work. Congratulations! You owe yourself a pat on the back.

Stop reading right now and give yourself a small reward of some kind for having reached this important landmark. Put on a favorite piece of music, indulge in a favorite high-energy snack or call a friend and get him or her to tell you a great new joke. You deserve to give yourself a modest early dividend on the success this book is going to help you to attain.

No kidding: Stop now and give yourself a treat of some kind before reading any further!

Did you find some tangible way to congratulate yourself? Good! You deserve to be congratulated, because simply by reviewing the points covered so far in this chapter, you've already put yourself in a great position to start setting up a strategy for the career success you deserve. You've hooked up with a job search resource that's anchored in real-life results, not abstract theories.

This book offers more proven, real-world, workable stories and strategies for becoming a Charlie Chaplin-type job candidate—an on-the-ball, results-first, competition- and obstacle-annihilating candidate—than any other program you're likely to encounter. Now, let's be clear on one thing right away: Not all of the incidents this book passes along are going to be appropriate to you or to the industry in which you're seeking to win a job, and a few of the stories you'll find here are included not because they offer a plan you should try to imitate, but because they're intriguing or just plain funny. (Let's face it, everyone, and especially job seekers, can use a laugh now and then!)

But this book *will* point you toward any number of inventive approaches you can use: ideas that were used by real people to get real jobs, ideas that will fit your situation and your particular needs. In these pages you will find, among the hundreds of real-life stories, a great many that are appropriate to your situation. These stories, and the advice that follows them, will help you get through to employers and state your case in a dramatic and compelling way. And only one of them has to click.

In the end, you're looking for one job—the right job, with the right employer. This book will help you get there. Of course, every job search is unique, and while a number of the ideas passed along in *303 Off-the-Wall Ways to Get a Job (That Really Worked)* can be counted on to help bring you closer to that job you want, some others won't be a good fit for you. You'll need to find out which is which before you try implementing anything outlined in the pages that follow with potential employers. That's why these early sections of the book are so important.

This section (which explores some of the fundamental issues and obstacles facing job seekers today) and the next one (which will help you match the right off-the-wall technique to your job search campaign), will show you how to use this book effectively. Once you've read both sections from start to finish, you'll be a lot closer to getting the job offer that's right for you.

So please, if you plan to use this book as part of a sustained, successful job search campaign, continue to read this section and the next one carefully, and follow all the instructions you read before you start exploring the book for ideas to use.

A sense of purpose

This book assumes that you (a) know something about the industry you want to work in, and (b) have an idea of the type of work you want to do in it. A firm sense of purpose is vitally important when dealing with prospective employers. You will get much better results by saying, "My aim is to be a training and development specialist at a Fortune 200 company in the New York City area," than you will by saying "I can do anything."

Before you start to adapt the ideas in this book, you should use the resources of your local library to develop a target employer list and to acquaint yourself with the current trends in your target industry and the specific duties of the job you have in mind. What's more, you must also use the library's resources to find out as much as possible about any specific company you hope to work for. If the library's collection of reference books, trade magazines, news articles and financial reports does not provide you with at least five to 10 pages of factual material about a company you are targeting, you should consider calling the company directly to ask for sales catalogs, employee information packets or other resources. (Some job seekers have been known to purchase a single share of stock in the target company so as to get the best, and latest, information on the company.)

If you are not sure of the industry you want to enter, the kind of organization you hope to work for or the kind of job you want to hold, consider meeting with a career counselor at your school or alma mater and asking for some help in focusing your search.

The new employment agreement

In the world of work we live in today, employers don't give guarantees. Margins are tight; competition, both foreign and domestic, is brutal; technology is advancing at a dizzying pace. If letting some employee—any employee—go will allow a company to improve the margins, become as efficient as the competition or take advantage of a new advance in design or computerization, *they will let the person go*.

This dynamic, low-commitment way of dealing with workers, because it is so much less predictable from the employment environment of a decade or more ago, strikes some as heartless. And maybe it is. But it is what we have to work with. However, the news is not all bleak. If you can *adapt* to the tight-ship, turn-on-a-dime mindset today's employers have assumed, you can actually make the current rules of the game work in your favor.

That's worth repeating. If you can adapt to the tight-ship, turn-on-a-dime mindset today's employers have assumed, you can actually make the current, seemingly heartless, rules of the employment game work to your advantage!

How? By familiarizing yourself with three of the fundamental concerns of today's employers and by being able to supply stories that address those concerns.

The first thing to remember is that ours is a time of great change. One of the main reasons lifelong careers with a single employer have pretty much gone the way of the Model T is that these days, organizations must be able to react more quickly and effectively than ever before to the competitive challenges that face them. Believe it or not, a work force made up of people who can each perform a single set of tasks quite well can actually be a handicap to a company these days. If each worker's focus is on a narrowly written job description, rather than addressing new business problems with creative solutions that may reach into previously uncharted areas, the company may not be able to react effectively to competitive challenges or market shifts. That means that employers are, as a general rule, on the lookout for workers who show the ability to adapt well to new ideas and procedures—and show a little initiative when the occasion demands.

Once you find an idea from this book that you want to use to reach a prospective employer, you will want to be sure that your ability to make sense of new surroundings, new equipment and/or new challenges are part of the employment message you incorporate.

Principle number one: When you use the ideas in this book, you must demonstrate your ability to adapt well to new ideas and procedures.

This does not mean you should tell the employer you can "do anything"! It means you should demonstrate a specific set of skills in a certain area...and a willingness to adapt those skills to *other, unexpected* problems as they arise.

On a separate sheet of paper, take a few moments now to highlight five separate occasions in your work, educational or volunteer history when you adapted well to a new setting. You can probably come up with a lot more than five examples! Think of the times you pitched in when a supervisor was ill, or mastered a new piece of computer software in short order, or performed well when given a new set of responsibilities in an area where you had little or no experience. Take the time now to jot down the details of five such experiences. Use non-work related examples if, after 10 or 15 minutes, you are still having trouble identifying such stories from your work history.

The second major principle has to do with efficiency and profit orientation. In today's economic climate, if you want to win a good job offer, you'll need to find a way to convey that you'll accomplish a little bit more than sitting at a desk, obeying the dress code and picking up a paycheck every other week. Prospective employers will be looking for performers who know that the reason they show up for work is to help the organization attain its primary goals; in the private sector, that means making money.

Principle number two: *When you use the ideas in this book, you must prove to the employer, by means of specific examples, that you are committed to helping the organization operate efficiently and that you are determined to deliver the profits and / or results he or she wants.*

Your best bet here is to prepare several *quantifiable* examples of how your work-related ideas, or the problems you've solved during the course of your job, led to savings or increased revenue for the organization you worked for. (You can also use specific figures to cite improved efficiency in a certain area.) Did you help to bring a product to market *six weeks ahead of schedule*? Did you supervise a sales staff that posted a *12 percent increase over the previous year*? Did a new idea you suggested result in *three fewer absences every year per employee*?

How well you identify such specific examples and prepare exactly what you will say to amplify them in conversations with prospective employers, will, to a large degree, determine your success on the job search front.

Most of the ideas in this book will, when used by the right applicant and in the right setting, cause an employer to sit up and take notice. To the extent that that separates you from the vast majority of candidates, who make no such efforts, you'll be ahead of the game. But what is it that you want the hiring official to sit up and take notice *of*? If you want to get the job offer, the answer had better be solid results, preferably in the form of fewer dollars spent, more dollars made or more time available to pursue profitable activity.

Take a good stretch of time now—at least 20 to 30 minutes, and perhaps as much as an hour or an hour and a half—to develop as many examples of your efficiency and profit orientation as possible. Wherever you can, appeal to independent sources: annual reports, written performance evaluations, sales reports, commission checks and so on. Use *actual figures* to express your accomplishments; if you must give estimates, be sure they're responsible and note that they are estimates.

If you get stuck, ask yourself: What problems do you regularly solve on the job? What would happen if you didn't solve them? How much would a day when you refused to do any of the things you normally do have cost your employer? Has there ever been a crisis or emergency situation that you helped to resolve? What would have happened if you had done nothing?

Take the time now to develop this list. These stories are perhaps the most important features of your job search campaign; most of the ideas that follow in this book will be useless if you cannot quantify the solutions you've delivered in the past for other employers.

The final key idea you'll be demonstrating to employers is difficult to define, but it can be roughly summarized in the phrase *market orientation*. That means knowing the value of a good sales presentation and being willing to give one when the situation demands. These days, market orientation—a sense of what the product or service in question does, who it does it for and what advantages it holds over the competition—isn't merely something for sales or marketing people to master. It's something employers want to cultivate in employees at all levels of an organization and in all functional categories.

Principle number three: When you use the ideas in this book, you must demonstrate your market orientation, even if you are not applying for a sales or marketing position.

A general knowledge of the target company's customer base, and of the details of some of its most important products or services, is essential if you plan to demonstrate your market orientation to a prospective employer. As we noted earlier, you will probably need to do a little library work in order to become sufficiently familiar with the company and its products.

Fortunately for you, that research, when combined with an appropriate idea from this book, will easily set you apart in the eyes of the prospective employer when it comes to showing your market orientation. By using innovative marketing ideas for your own job candidacy, you will have gone a long way toward convincing the employer that you understand the importance of delivering solutions in a dramatic way to customers and potential customers.

Pick one of your target companies. Take a few minutes now to list some of the ways in which the company might reach new consumers for its product or service. List at least 20 ideas—and include even outlandish ones. They may help you to develop more feasible ways the company might win new customers.

Please don't continue with this section until you've completed all three of the written exercises just described.

Those are the three main points to bear in mind as you adapt the ideas in this book. You will want to use the techniques that follow to demonstrate specifically that:

- You are adaptable and deal well with change.

- You know that efficiency and bottom-line results are essential.

- You have a good sense of the organization's products and/or services and you could, if you had to, explain them in a compelling way to a prospective customer.

Now, you may find yourself with a question as you review that list. Aren't the things you're offering to provide to the employer—the ability to manage change well, the ability to deliver results efficiently and profitably and a sense of marketing flair—things your *superiors* will be keeping their eyes out for? Aren't managers supposed to train you to take on unexpected duties? Focus on profitable activity? Worry about customers and competitive advantage? If these issues don't fall within the formal duties of the job you're after, why should you have to worry about them?

The answer: Because being your own manager, at least to some degree, is a necessity under what I call the "new employment agreement."

If you want to look—and be rejected—like everyone else, don't worry about the three points we just examined. Say it's the manager's responsibility to take care of any of those issues. If you want to get *hired*, however, you'll need to stand out from the crowd.

The job's formal duties are not the point. The employer wants to hear about your capacity to deliver results in a work environment where supervisory or managerial resources are scarce.

Let your competitors for the job you're after worry about job descriptions, formal lines of authority and other relics of yesterday's employment world. You are trying to get a job *today* and that means accepting the following terms:

These days, odds are that the employer will keep you as long as, and only as long as, you show the capacity to perform more or less independently, to handle new challenges as they arise and without panicking and to be ready to help pick up the slack for a manager or supervisor who will already be stretched too thin the first day you report to work.

For better or for worse, those are the new rules. Most of the people you will be competing with for a job won't be broadcasting their willingness to abide by them. If you use the ideas in this book to provide the prospective employer with solid proof of your ability to work under the new requirements, yours will be a successful job search. Most of the techniques that appear in the body of this book will offer you the opportunity to send the message without difficulty. A few will require some tweaking to get the point across; see the "Strategies for Success" that follow each and every story. A very small minority of the stories are so odd that you probably shouldn't try to incorporate them in your job search. They're here to providde an occasional snicker or to to help you gain new insight on the job search process.

There are rules and there are *rules*

In adapting the ideas that follow in the main part of this book, you may have to break a few of the previously accepted rules set out by writers and career counselors who were offering advice about job searching when the competition for good jobs wasn't quite as stiff, perhaps, as it is today. Here's a brief list of these rules, and some of the reasons you shouldn't feel too bad about violating them.

- Your resume should never deviate from standard dimensions, and it should be printed on a beige, white or otherwise neutral paper stock. (Your resume is an advertisement for you. Sometimes ads do strange things in order to get noticed.)

- Keep the tone of your cover letter brisk and businesslike. (And sound just like everyone else in the pile? What's wrong with a little creativity?)

- You have no business calling up the president of the company. (Any number of stories from the current collection will disprove this notion.)

- Don't do anything dramatic or out of the ordinary during the interview. (Granted, it's quite possible to make an idiot out of yourself during an interview, and no, you shouldn't continue to use a tactic that's obviously not working in a particular setting, but this book will demonstrate that there are any number of unconventional gambits you can incorporate during the face-to-face meeting with the prospective employer that will help you project an image of confidence, purpose and poise.)

- If you use a gimmick of some kind when trying to get a job, people will think you're a flake and they won't want to work with you. (Good managers know that inventiveness, creativity and persistence on the job search can be hallmarks of inventiveness, creativity and persistence on the job. Following your "gimmick" up with on-the-level examples of your best traits will impress most of the people you come across. If you comport yourself as a professional, the only people you'll alienate will be people you probably didn't want to work with anyway. And, hey, you're only looking for one job, right?)

- Don't try anything weird, because it's all been done before. (Maybe, maybe not. Some of the ideas included in this volume did show a high repeat rate—but the only likely reason for that to be the case is that they worked for more than one person! Add your own personal touches to the method in question and, if it's the right one for your situation, you probably won't regret it.)

Before you move on to the next section, here are seven brief, important points to ponder.

- As a general rule, the higher up your targeted contact in the organization, the better your chances of making one of the ideas in this book work. Believe it or not, you do not have to know the head of the company to get good results from a strategy that targets him or her.

- People like to hire people they'd like to get to know. The friendlier you are when you use one of the ideas in this book, the greater your chances for success will be.

- A little bit of nervousness when following up with decision makers is a good thing. It shows you're alive. Don't fight it. Accept it for what it is and use the resulting energy to your benefit.

- Some of the ideas that you'll read about require a generous amount of good old-fashioned, face-to-face *chutzpah*. Most, however, do not. There are many inventive ideas here that utilize creative approaches to writing resumes and cover letters, using third-party help and making the most of other methods for getting your foot in the door. Not all of the ideas in the book require you to elicit strange looks from people you've never met. You don't have to be charismatic, outgoing or even particularly creative to make the ideas in this book work for you. (On the other hand, if you have a flair for the dramatic and like to be the center of attention, you'll find quite a few ideas here that you can pursue to your benefit.)

- Once you decide on a technique that's right for your situation and provides a good potential match with the decision makers in your industry, don't contact one person at a time and wait for the results. Set up your target list and hit 20 or 30 at a time, then follow up appropriately. Worrying about an individual company's reaction to your efforts is a waste of your energy.

- Some of the stories in this book are truly outlandish; a few others describe ideas that seem pretty basic, but most job seekers probably never consider them. The general rule I've used has been this: If the story can point you in a direction you may not have considered, it is worth including.

- Congratulations once again! You've covered all the information you need to move on to the next step, matching the appropriate technique to your target employer. You're in a great position to get the very most out of this book. Give yourself another reward—a favorite candy bar, a long walk outside if the weather is nice or a positive, upbeat piece of music—before moving on to the next chapter.

No cheating! Do something nice for yourself *right now*, before proceeding to the next page.

Section

Matching up

No one will be able to use any and every idea in this book successfully. Your circumstances are unique; so were those of each of the people whose inventive employment approaches are recounted in the main chapters that follow this one. While a significant number of the ideas that follow can be adapted to virtually any field of employment, some of the techniques are more narrowly focused.

Before you decide to incorporate one of the job-search techniques that follow into your personal employment campaign, please review the following list of 10 questions closely. If, after you select an idea that seems to offer a good fit for your situation, you can answer *yes* to any *five* of the questions on the list, rest assured that you have a good chance of being able to use the technique in question successfully.

If your answer to the first question on the list is *no*, please review the previous section before continuing any further in this book.

10 questions to ask yourself before contacting a company on your list

1. Have you developed a compelling summary of the three key advantages of your candidacy (your adaptability, your bottom-line commitment and your market orientation) and are you incorporating these stories and research materials in the technique—either in the initial contact or as part of your follow-up campaign?

2. Is the target company you plan to contact small (fewer than 150 total employees) and independently owned and operated?

3. Has the idea you've selected been referenced in the "Strategies for success" section as a technique that was, in one form or another, used successfully by more than one prospective employee?

4. Are you targeting, by name, the head of the organization, rather than a human resource or personnel department representative?

5. If the method entails submitting a resume or summary of employment accomplishments, has this resume or summary been targeted to a specific position and to the needs of the target company, as determined by your library research?

6. Have you identified, as a result of your library research, a pressing competitive problem or problems facing your target organizations—and will your proposed solution to that problem be prominently highlighted to the person you will be contacting?

7. Do you have relevant professional experience in the industry in which your target company (or typical target company) operates?

8. If the technique you are considering does not target a single employer, but rather broadcasts a message to a large group of people in a short period of time, can you make your message reach at least 50 people on an average day and can you keep this method up for at least a week?

9. Have you discussed the technique you are considering with a friend or colleague who works in the industry you hope to enter and incorporated any worthwhile suggestions that he or she has to offer?

10. Is the technique you are considering highlighted in the text as possibly helpful to someone with your background or professional objectives?

If you did not answer *yes* to at least five of these questions, you should think carefully before trying to incorporate the technique in question into your job search campaign. If you did answer yes to at least five of the questions above, please bear in mind that, as a general rule, techniques targeted toward individuals will deliver the best results when they are directed toward a specifically named person at the target organization.

> *I recommend targeting a person ("John Smith") rather than a title ("Human Resources Director").*

A few words about old, conservative firms in old, conservative industries

One of the most frequently raised objections against using unusual job search techniques is that such techniques can backfire when they're applied to staid, conventional companies in staid, conventional industries. You should know, before you try anything outlined in this book, that my research indicates that this is, as a very general rule, true. The majority of the ideas passed along in the following pages probably will not be of much use to you if you're trying to gain a foothold in, say, investment banking, top-level management consulting or certain elite branches of the accounting industry.

But guess what? Most of the economic growth in this country is *not* coming about through the growth of big, prestigious firms where you have to call everyone Mr. or Ms. So-and-so, memorize an intricate organizational chart and wear a Brooks Brothers suit every day. Most of the growth—and the jobs—are to be found in smaller, more entrepreneurially-oriented companies. These are the very companies that are ideal for some of the more creative job search methods you'll be reading about, and these are the firms you should probably be targeting.

Having said that, there are *some* techniques in the pages that follow that can probably be adapted to the more traditionally conservative employment fields. So while you may decide—rightly—that you probably won't break into a Big Six accounting firm by shipping yourself to the president in a crate, there are a few other networking ideas between these covers that you may want to explore more closely.

When you get right down to it, using creative or unusual job search methods is a numbers game. The experience of researching this book leads me to believe that employing creativity to a nice big list of carefully selected target companies is, in most cases and for most applicants, potentially more rewarding than the standard boring-resume-and-cover-letter-and-follow-up-call approach. Sure, using a little inventiveness will work better at some organizations than at others, but, applied intelligently to the employers on your list, that same inventiveness will, as a general rule, work a heck of a lot better than being ignored completely by most of the people you contact.

Many of the ideas you'll be reading about will run the risk of turning off a small percentage of the decision makers you contact. And yes, you should target your job search materials to the mindset of the audience you intend to reach. But, given a minimal amount of research into the target firm's culture and some common sense on your part, what's the worst thing that can happen if you use a creative approach? The organization that doesn't like your approach won't offer you a job. That's what usually happens *anyway* when you follow the standard methods!

Messages that stand out get better responses than messages that don't. Madison Avenue has demonstrated that principle countless times, and in countless ways, over the years. Now it's time to put the idea to work for you!

Some final thoughts

Before you begin reading through the main section of this book, please take a moment to review these six important points.

- On rare occasion, you will find an idea outlined that is so outlandish that, even though it worked, it cannot be recommended for inclusion in your job search campaign. (You'll find most of these near the end of the book.) These techniques are marked with the legend "Not recommended." In other words, if you decide to conceal yourself in a large plant and burst dramatically upon the contact as he or she passes through the room, you're on your own.

- Personalize your approach. Find something distinctively yours to add to the technique, rather than appropriating everything that worked for someone else.

- Don't be afraid to combine appropriate ideas as part of your job search campaign; check each idea you plan to use against the 10-point list on pages 25 and 26.

- If you are trying to gain entry into a field in which you have no direct professional experience, keep an open mind to the idea of taking on less-than-glamorous duties in order to gain entry to the field. (You'll note many of the techniques outlined in the pages that follow use exactly this approach.)

- Sometimes, a specific technique or variation catches on with a large number of job seekers through word of mouth. This usually happens because the idea works particularly well! If the idea you are considering is cited in the "Strategies for Success" section as having been offered by multiple sources during the research for this book, that may well be an indication that the technique can be successfully adapted into a wide variety of settings.

- Time for another reward! You're now ready to get the most from this book. Take a few minutes to give yourself a high-energy treat, play a song you enjoy or otherwise treat yourself magnificently. Once you're done, you'll be ready to start in on the main chapters of the book.

Congratulations! You're ready to roll!

Section

303 off-the-wall ways... that really worked!

Does it sometimes seem that the information revolution has left you behind? Do employers think you need special training to boost your skills— but do they fall silent when it comes to outlining where that training is supposed to come from? Does your resume outline abilities that sometimes don't seem to have much relevance to today's high-tech work environments? Fear not! **Entries #1 to #16 offer techniques job seekers used to overcome "skill gaps"**—and get job offers from cutting-edge employers despite the seeming handicap of a job history that may be a few years behind the competition's.

Whether you call this phenomenon downsizing, rightsizing or just plain being laid off, it still boils down to the same thing: You've got to track down a new way to get a paycheck, and a lot of people with the same background you have are facing the same predicament. **Entries #17 to #42 offer proven strategies for success from some of today's most inventive career salvagers.** You will find innovative ideas worth reviewing whether you have recently been let go or you believe you are likely to be laid off in the near future.

Are you trying to land a position in a competitive field in which personal creativity is critical? Such industries include advertising, marketing, broadcasting and many others. Following the traditional job search advice was always a bit of a crap-shoot; nowadays, an original campaign is probably essential. **Entries #43 to #100 show some of the most inventive ways people found to gain entry to highly competitive, creative fields.**

Looking for instant employment to tide you over while you continue your search for the perfect position? **Entries #101 to #117 offer techniques for winning interest and offers from prospective employers—on the double.** Don't be surprised, though, to see that "stopgap" turn into the first step in a great new career.

All good things come to those who wait, right? **Entries #118 to #165 offer stories from people who found innovative long-term ways to win interest from key employers; this part of the book also features ideas on attention-grabbing resumes and cover letters.**

People who have to deal with subtle (or not-so-subtle) forms of discrimination have been known to come up with remarkable ways of getting hired. **In entries #166 to #182, you'll read about some of the most intriguing methods employed by people who got employers to look beyond problematic work histories, unusual backgrounds or other hurdles.** An inventive approach helped them to get the jobs they truly deserved—and can do the same for you.

Balancing a yardstick on your nose during a job interview? Constructing a miniature resume? Brushing your teeth over and over so you can network in hotel bathrooms? It's all been done. **Entries #183 to #256 feature some of the most outlandish ideas for finding employment you've ever heard—and you'll probably wish you'd thought of them yourself.** These broadly applicable ideas may well work in your own job search no matter what your work history.

Some job-search techniques took a lot of nerve to even try. These ideas may raise a few eyebrows, and they're certainly not for everyone. **If you feel like pushing the envelope, you might want, after some careful thought, to give one or more of the ideas outlined in entries #257 to #303 a try.** Then again, reviewing these methods for the sheer amazement of learning what actually got some people jobs is okay, too.

Important note: *If you try to make use of the ideas in this book before covering the basics covered in the first two sections, you may well do your job search more harm than good. Target the ideas that follow to your situations—and maximize your chances of making an employer sit up and take notice of what you have to say.*

Note, too, that many of these techniques carry both pluses and minuses. A job-search method that has shown itself effective in a particular industry may soon become familiar to hiring officials. Your best course, as always, is to add your own unique refinements to deliver a compelling message.

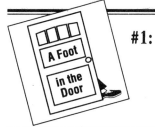

#1: Ask to help arrange interviews for your competitors.
Or:
Call me altruistic.

Nancy had been laid off from her secretarial position at one of the most prestigious charitable organizations in Atlanta. She had no relevant computer experience, and, to make matters worse, she had no college degree. Through a friend, she heard about an executive secretary position that was open at the largest museum in town. Nancy called the manager, who agreed to let her come in on a volunteer basis to screen the dozens of phone calls inquiring about the open position. Nancy dutifully scheduled interviews, directing the most qualified applicants toward the manager's office. At the end of the week, Nancy stepped into the manager's office and said something along the following lines. "Ms. Smith, I've been working in the same area you're hiring in for the last eight years, and I've personally spoken with every one of the people you've interviewed for this job. After a good deal of thought, I can say quite honestly that I can do the job better than any one of them. Now, I want to be honest with you. I don't have the computer experience you want, and I don't have a college degree. But I will make you a guarantee. If you give me this job for 90 days, on salary, I will, by the end of that time, know everything you want me to know about your computer system, and I will also convince you that my lack of a degree is no obstacle to my performing this job at a high level. If you disagree after 90 days, I'll walk away with no hard feelings." The manager hired her on the spot and never regretted it.

Strategies for success:

- A great way to go if you lack specific formal credentials for a position for which you are otherwise very well suited. (As a matter of fact, this may be among the best methods for sidestepping the "sorry-we'd-love-to-hire-you-but-you're-not-qualified" puzzle ever to come down the pike.)

- If you are trying to use this technique for a position in a for-profit business, you will probably need to do some digging and come up with a referral. Your aim will be to reach the decision maker by means of someone else's endorsement of your ability to pitch in during that dreaded period that the office is deluged with phone calls following a classified ad placement. With nonprofit groups, however, the solo "can I come in and help" approach is likely to meet with a much better response. Short staffs and volunteer help are part of the lifestyle at these organizations.

- Nancy's approach won't do you much good if your aim is to make a radical change in your career direction. Remember, you're promising to be able to perform at an exceptional level in the position during your self-assigned probationary period. That just doesn't leave you time to learn everything from scratch.

- Use the word "guarantee" prominently. Highlight your good references if you can.

- Assuming you receive the job offer, don't say, "Can I think about it?" If you get the position, it will be because you've made it clear that you're committed to working for this individual at this organization. Playing the negotiating game of using an offer from one group to elicit an offer from another is inappropriate here. Use this approach with one potential employer at a time, and only with those organizations with whom you truly wish to work. There is only one acceptable reason for not accepting an offer arising from your use of this technique: If the manager insists on making an extremely low salary offer that is clearly intended to take advantage of you, you are well advised to smile, politely decline, shake hands and walk away.

- While it may hold out remarkable promise for you if you have been denied work because of your lack of exposure to computers, Nancy's approach is only advisable if you've devoted a great deal of thought to the position, the selection of your target organization and the obstacles you face. If you commit to mastering the skills, and then don't follow through, you will in fact lose the job.

- Successful ideas based on some form of volunteer work took many forms, and were among the most popular techniques encountered during the research for this book. See #10, #58, #82, #129, #140, #154, #251 and #292.

#2: **Tape a dime to your cover letter.**
Or:
Heads I'm hired, tails you offer me a job.

Sarah's cover letter was brief and to the point. Its first line read, "I can turn on a dime to master your company's computer system." And there, at the bottom of the page, after three or four bullets highlighting Sarah's work experience and adaptability, was a shiny new dime to illustrate the point. A simple trick, yes—but it got her an interview, and a job that she supposedly lacked the qualifications to perform.

Strategies for success:

- The bullets in your cover letter should give the specifics of important problems you have solved for employers. Use precise, quantifiable terms whenever possible.

- When using visual enhancements, such as that coin in the lower corner of the letter, presentation is incredibly important. Be sure the letter to which you affix the coin is crisp, comprehensible, concise and free of typographical errors.

- Apply the square of tape with care; edges that stick up or get smudged will draw attention.

- Give compelling evidence in the letter of your ability to master new information and procedures quickly.

- If you can, supply personal testimonials that support the brief success stories you offer.

- Be ready for the prospective employer's phone call; memorize specific examples of your successes on the job, and be prepared to recount them in a fresh, compelling way.

#3: **Adapt this cool idea the next time you have to fill out a job application.**
Or:
What do you mean, she has to have computer experience?

In order to beat out the competition for a spot at a prestigious nonprofit organization, one enterprising applicant turned in a strange-looking document that looked more like a screenplay than a job application. It was, in fact, an imaginary "dialogue" between two people (let's call them *A* and *B*) whose job it was to decide the fate of the author. *A* was skeptical about the applicant's technical background; *B* kept offering witty reasons to take the person on and provided plenty of evidence from the writer's background to support the candidacy. Can you guess which character won the fictionalized argument? The "screenplay" carried the day.

Strategies for success:

- Keep the "scene" brief (one or two pages) and to the point. Be sure it mentions, by title, the opening you are hoping to fill.

- Only stage directions and dialogue between two (imaginary!) personnel officials should appear on the page.

- Offer occasional doses of humor, preferably of the confident, yet ever-so-slightly self-deprecating variety.

- Show the draft to friends to get plenty of feedback on what works and what doesn't.

- Take your time; get it right.

- Include your phone number and any other appropriate contact information. (Work this material, and any other seemingly non-conversational text, into the paragraph of "stage directions" at the top of the page.)

- When the draft looks as sharp as you can make it, go to the prospective employer's facility and ask for two copies of the application form.

- Leave the facility. With a black marker, write "See Attached" on each page of each form. (Don't fill out the forms; your "scene" replaces them.)

- Make two copies of your "scene."
- Staple a copy of your "scene" to each of the application forms.
- Mail one of the applications to the president of the company; mail the other to the person listed as the contact for the opening.
- After three days, follow up by phone as appropriate.

#4: **Stay in the car for two days waiting for your chance to meet directly with the person who can override the people who don't think your skills are right.**

Or:

Well, I'm adjusting the mirror, brushing my teeth, and changing my socks—why do you ask?

Fred, an aspiring designer who lacked the formal computer training the personnel department said he needed, did just this. When the department manager at his target company finally consented to stop on the way to the parking lot and chat about what the company's hiring picture looked like, he was impressed enough with Fred's determination to ask others in the organization about a training program on the applicant's behalf. The job was Fred's within a week.

Strategies for success:

- No, you don't have to spend 24 hours a day in the car. Once the person you want to talk to leaves the premises, you can too.
- Obviously, having a good idea of what the person looks like is a must. Your I.D. can be based on your attendance at a public talk or industry function attended by the decision maker, or by a photograph from a newspaper or trade magazine.
- A friendly reminder: Trespassing is illegal. Occupying a public parking place isn't. If you are asked to leave private property, you should do so.

#5: **Propose a lesser title for the job you want.**

Or:

What's in a name?

This is a surprisingly effective method of getting around some of the constraints of bureaucracies, especially in governmental and academic circles. One memorable organizational roadblock prevented an employee from taking on the job of "supervisor," due to the specific personal and educational requirements for anyone formally taken on in that position. The solution? The employee performed the same work under a different title—and no "supervisor" was ever hired.

Strategies for success:

- It sounds ridiculous, but such compromises are sometimes the best way to make your way through a "background mismatch."

- Be prepared to accept a lesser salary under the arrangement—but not necessarily too *much* less. Sometimes conceding very small amounts of money (i.e., just enough for you to be earning less than the next person above you on the organizational chart) will do the trick.

#6: **Persistently loiter in the department where you really want to work.**

Or:

Training? Yeah, I've been watching you for the past month.

A recent article in *The Paducah Sun* (Kentucky) relates how footwear manufacturer John Brewer got his first job selling shoes—even though he was a department-store stock boy at the time and had no formal training for the job. Apparently, Brewer spent all the time he could manage in and around the store's shoe department—"where I was not supposed to be," he told the

Sun. "One day there was a snowstorm, and I was one of the only ones there. So they took me to the boys department, fixed me up with a new outfit and had me sell shoes. I've been doing that ever since."

Strategies for success:

- Bear in mind that ignoring the duties of the job for which you were hired is a risky undertaking.

- Still, a passion for a particular area of the organization you work for can go a long way toward helping you arrange a transfer that would otherwise be denied to you because of a perceived lack of expertise in a certain area. You can learn a lot—and be ready to pitch in when an unexpected opportunity arises, as it did in Brewer's case.

- For a similar—but potentially risky—approach that does not require actually being employed at the target organization, see #66. For a story that illustrates a more low-key approach, see #123.

#7: **Read the president of the company's book cover to cover.**

Or:

May I quote you on that?

Memorize whole sections and refer to the book constantly during your interview. Maybe this *is* an example of unmitigated apple-polishing. Maybe the pronouncements of the retail king who wrote the book Alex studied so assiduously *weren't* on a par with Holy Writ. Maybe the reverent gaze that came over his face when he quoted sections from the volume *were* ever-so-slightly forced. So what? The eager-reader routine got him the job—and the spot in the company's technical training program—that he wanted, right?

Strategies for success:

- If the company at which you're interviewing doesn't happen to have a best-selling (or less-than-best-selling) author as president, call ahead and politely ask for mission statements, company handbooks, news clippings or anything else the company can supply that will give you an idea of the major ideas that guide key decision makers in the organization.

- If nothing interesting comes your way as a result of that, try your local library. (These days, the larger libraries have computerized document searches that will help you track down articles through the use of a single keyword.)

#8: Need a spot in a training program?
Or:
Anyone looking for an understudy?

Dress like the rest of the employees and show up every morning until something interesting happens. A recent Associated Press story tells how Tim Cohane, fired from his previous job, got a shot with a prestigious Wall Street firm that initially refused to take the 43-year-old on as a member of its training program. Cohane simply showed up at the company's offices day in and day out, sat in the visitor's area of the trading floor, and started talking to the company's traders. His plan: Act as though he worked at the firm, and ultimately inspire an offer. Eventually, Cohane hooked up with the right person at the firm and volunteered to enter the training program without salary, whereupon he became the oldest entrant to the training program in the firm's history. He didn't disappoint; he made lots of money for himself and his organization, and was eventually able to return to his first love: Coaching basketball. (Postscript: Some years after his stint on Wall Street, Cohane won the head coaching job at the University of Buffalo.)

Strategies for success:

- This daring approach requires persistence, the ability to observe, extraordinary people skills and a good dose of courage. It will also probably take a while.

- Be sure you dress the part.

- Warning: Trespassing is illegal. If you are asked to leave private property, you must do so.

#9:   Make a formal appeal to the office of the president of the organization when denied a job because you do not have the formal training listed as "required" in the job description.

Or:

What's a piece of paper or two between friends?

Ed, a self-taught counselor whose resume bulged with volunteer work, tried this when he was told that, although his background was right for the job he wanted at a local training center, he did not have the degree the post required. He drafted a formal letter to the president of the college protesting the decision—and got the job he wanted.

Strategies for success:

- Let's lay the cards on the table: Part of the reason this has a chance of working is that taking such an approach is essentially the same as saying, "By the way, I am the kind of applicant who is likely to consider legal action." You must back up this unstated (and at this stage it really must be unstated) message with professionalism, diligence and a strong sense of commitment to the organization. Do not come across as arrogant or overbearing. Do not mention legal options.

- Rather than handing your appeal over to administrative staff, you should probably send it through some official-looking, impossible-to-ignore channel to the top person in the organization. An overnight courier service is probably your best bet.

- If you do choose an overnight service, save yourself some money by selecting the two-day or economy rate, unless there is a looming deadline of some sort.

#10: **After being turned down because of a skill gap, ask to stay on-site for a month at no pay to observe "how the business works."**

Or:

Mind if I watch while you do that?

Cynthia got her first job at a graphic design firm this way, even though she didn't have the knowledge of the firm's computer systems that was required. She parlayed an informational interview into this "permission-to-hang-out-and-watch" arrangement, which quickly became a kind of informal internship at the firm. After a month of attentive volunteer work, she was contributing in enough important areas to negotiate an hourly wage. Within three months of her initial request, she was on salary.

Strategies for success:

- Ask to watch "how things work"—then ask permission to take on specific projects that will benefit the organization. A fair number of prospective employers won't be able to bring themselves to turn you down.

- Bear in mind that this kind of arrangement requires that you be willing to give on a continuous basis for some time without expecting anything in return. Sometimes this works out well; sometimes you will hook up with employers who like the idea of long-term slave labor. After a few weeks at the most, you should have a pretty good idea which kind of organization you're working for.

- Even a situation that does not turn into a paying position can yield important references and referrals.

- Obviously, some kind of alternate income will probably be necessary while you prove yourself. You may need to start out by "watching" your target company's operations two or three hours a day, or one or two days a week.

- Successful ideas based on some form of volunteer work took many forms and were among the most popular techniques encountered during the research for this book. See #1, #58, #82, #129, #140, #154, #251 and #292.

#11: Bring an invention to the interview.
Or:
Call me Edison.

You can bring a working prototype of an ingenious contraption you've thought up, or a photo or drawing of your idea. Whether you're holding the genuine item or a convincing representation thereof, appealing to ideas for inventions has worked in many interview settings to convince prospective employers of the creativity, ingenuity and inventiveness of the applicant in question. One non-technical graduate applying for a sales position at a computer products firm brought in the plans for a new type of portable sunshade he'd designed for joggers; although it was never produced, it demonstrated an ability to "think outside the lines." The impressed employer hired him.

Strategies for success:

- Don't exaggerate your achievements.

- If you bring a working model of the invention, be prepared to demonstrate it. Test it thoroughly before you incorporate it as part of your interview presentation.

- Practice discussing the features of your invention with a friend or family member. Encourage them to ask questions; respond to all queries directly and positively, but acknowledge areas for future development when they are pointed out to you.

- If you are concerned about patent issues or breaches of confidentiality with regard to an invention or system you have spent a good deal of time developing, discuss the matter with an attorney before outlining your ideas to others.

#12: Ask where you went wrong.

Or:

Stunned silence is sometimes your best friend.

Thanks to a downsizing campaign, Ellen lost her job of 10 years with a consumer products firm, and the job interviews she arranged in the months following were all frustrating experiences. After her fourth attempt to make her first step into a new field failed, she vowed to take a different approach during her next interview. During a meeting with an editor about a publishing position she felt was perfect for her, she asked directly what she needed to do to get the job. When the editor replied that he wasn't sure and tried to conclude the meeting, Ellen figured she had nothing to lose and went for broke. She said something along the following lines: "I'm terribly sorry, sir. I'm afraid I don't understand. I've got a strong writing background, great references and the kind of commitment you're not going to find in any other applicant you talk to for this job. I can't see any reason why your firm would not want to take on someone who is in such a great position to make an important contribution. So the only thing I can think of is that I must have done something very wrong in my presentation to you here today. I'm going to ask your help here, because I want to do anything and everything to help you take advantage of what I have to offer. If you don't mind, I'd appreciate it if you'd tell me exactly where it was that I went off track in what I outlined for you today." The stunned editor stammered that there was nothing wrong with Ellen's presentation as such, but that the formal description he'd developed for the job demanded three years of desktop publishing experience. Ellen then described the points of similarity between her old job and the publishing job—and by the end of the meeting, she had convinced the editor to take her on.

Strategies for success:

- A risky undertaking, but worth considering if you're having trouble getting employers to look past your last job title or industry specialty.

- During the speech, briefly highlight at least three parallels between what you've done in the past and what the job would require you to do.

- Great confidence—and the ability to look the interviewer in the eye without appearing to be trying to stare him or her down—are essentials.

- When you've delivered the last part of your "Where did I go wrong?" speech, quit talking and wait for a response.

- Listen carefully to the answer you get—and act on what you hear. This straight-ahead method can only work if you show a genuine interest in resolving any problem the prospective employer highlights.

#13: Call repeatedly, leaving the same simple message: Hire me and you won't be sorry.
Or:
What I lack in training, I make up for in persistence.

Ryan, who wanted a job selling communications equipment but did not have the technical background some other applicants did, took a mantra-like approach when it came to developing professional interviews in the field he wanted to enter. "You won't be sorry," he kept telling a sales manager at one target company he called repeatedly. "Give me the opportunity." After a while, it seemed like Ryan was calling in every time the sales manager sat down at his desk. The persistence paid off.

Strategies for success:

- Keep the message brief—don't give the impression you intend to make the hiring manager's life difficult.

- Instead, focus on the competitive advantage you can bring to the organization.

- A good many managers *expect* to receive multiple calls from applicants. A few will even draw out the process, refusing to interview those who call only once. Don't be discouraged. Keep your mood upbeat, and keep phoning.

- Target more than one decision maker at a time. Do not pin all your hopes on a single lead.

#14: Send a bunch of drawings.

Or:

Overcome your weak spots by blizzarding 'em with your strong suit.

A recent article in *The Detroit News* tells the story of an aspiring auto designer, Michael Santoro, who overcame his lack of formal technical training for the position he wanted by forwarding dozens of drawings of a minivan he'd been envisioning. Despite lacking "some skills peculiar to auto design," and despite his inability to construct the clay models that are a required part of the formal development of a new vehicle, Santoro emphasized his single greatest advantage: An overwhelming love of automobiles. The sketches were not textbook-perfect, but they were evidence of "an unbridled passion for cars," according to the senior Chrysler executive who took the chance and hired Santoro. The result? The Chrysler Cirrus and Dodge Stratus sedans, both huge successes for the automaker.

Strategies for success:

- Contagious enthusiasm and a genuine love of the field you want to enter are very attractive qualities. Communicating such advantages, even if it means offering dozens of examples of them over a period of time, can (and often does) result in a job offer.

- Instead of offering excuses for what *isn't* in your background, take every conceivable opportunity to focus on what *is*.

- And remember the rule followed by politicians in those televised debates: When asked a tough question that puts you in a bad light, briefly address it directly…and then answer the question for which you've prepared.

#15: Prove that you're the politest applicant of the bunch when you get rejected.
Or:
The thinking person's alternative to "Oh, yeah? Well, the same to you!"

How would you react if you'd been rejected for a position as a business etiquette trainer? If you answered "Move on to the next prospective employer," read on. Julia had met with the president of a consulting firm that specialized in training corporate professionals in the lost art of behaving in a civilized manner, and she was hoping to win a position as a coach. The president, however, who thought Julia's skill background didn't match the fast-paced office environment of the firm, notified Julia of her rejection for the job in a brusque, rather impersonal phone message on her home answering macine. Rather than let the matter come to an end there, Julia typed up a gracious thank-you note on her personal stationery and sent it immediately to the president. Guess who called back later that week with a job offer? "I figured that if she had enough poise and presence of mind to thank me so politely for *rejecting* her, I should probably think twice before passing her by," the president confessed. (Special thanks to Ann Marie Sabath of At Ease, Inc., for this contribution.)

Strategies for success:
- A written expression of thanks should be considered mandatory after *every* job interview, even those that do not result in a job offer.
- Be sure that the letter you send is neat and legible.
- If you can, mention something specific about the meeting that will help to remind the interviewer of your visit.
- Follow up every six weeks thereafter to ask again about employment opportunities.

#16: Send a strange fax message that only makes sense when your package arrives the next day.

Or:

Mastering the fax of business life.

"Big Things Are Coming Your Way," read the bizarre fax message that came churning through the company's machine. The letters were huge—the single sentence took up ten pages. There was nothing else, really: no signature, no explanation, no return phone number—only, at the top of the message, the name of the manager to whom the fax was directed. The next day, via overnight mail, came a box containing a huge set of dice—and a letter claiming responsibility for the strange fax and promising a follow-up call at a specific time the next day. When the call finally came, the strange sequence of messages began to make a little more sense to the manager. His caller wanted to discuss professional opportunities with the firm, and was eager to discuss the ways in which "taking a chance" with her would pay off. Was it because he was relieved at having finally made some kind of sense of the odd messages that he asked the sender to come in for a meeting? Or was it because he admired her inventiveness? Whatever the reason, her persistent—if sometimes baffling—efforts paid off.

Strategies for success:

- Let's say your job history is stopping employers from getting a true sense of the kinds of contributions you could make in a new field. Could your candidacy benefit from the prolonged sense of mystery engendered by this approach?

- Be ready to offer all the specifics of what you have to offer during the follow-up phone call (which you *must* make at precisely the time you promise). Your prospective employer will not be in the mood for any more elusive hints by that point.

- Warning: Ten faxed pages at a time should probably be considered the outer limit when it comes to mysterious messages to hiring officials; actually, even that may be pushing things. Small companies, in particular, probably won't appreciate having their fax line tied up for long periods of time.

- This unusually intricate, three-tiered series of messages shouldn't be stretched out for too long. Best bet: Try this approach on successive days within a single business week.
- See also #32, #97 and #143.

#17: Send a flat tire.
Or:
One way to get the employer pumped up to meet you.

After being laid off from his job with a communications software firm, Gary knew that he'd probably have to target companies outside of his local area. He also knew that prospective employers have a built-in skepticism when it comes to considering the candidacies of people who live a good distance away, even if they make it clear that they are willing to relocate. Gary decided to deliver his "I-will-come-to-you" message in a dramatic, unforgettable way. He selected three of the top firms in his industry (each in a different city), and sent the presidents of all three, by overnight courier, a flat tire. The next day, the befuddled presidents each received a hand-operated air pump, a copy of Gary's resume and a large hand-colored sign bearing the message "Please don't be deflated that I live in Illinois. I'll relocate!" One of the firms asked him in for an interview—and he got the job he was after.

Strategies for success:
- Sure, a flat tire is not terribly tough to track down. And yes, the next-day follow-up leaves an unforgettable impression. Just make sure the tires and pumps you send are all *clean*. The technique will quickly lose its appeal if the company officials you contact associate you with a greasy, dirty "gag gift," rather than an inventive, distinctive way of delivering an employment application.
- The method's effect depends on the recipient getting the air pump—and your resume and message—the *next morning* after the flat tire arrives. However you juggle schedules to get the best rates from the overnight shippers you select, be sure the pump arrives promptly on the next calendar day after the tire shows up.

- Do not send the first package (the one with the tire) for Friday delivery. You don't want a weekend to pass before the second package arrives.

- Consider contacting your prospective employer ahead of time to discreetly ask about the office schedule of your intended recipient.

- The idea can be adapted to any perceived shortcoming in your candidacy.

#18: Make 'em tell you no to your face.
Or:
Let's talk about this over dinner.

Alan, an out-of-work draftsman whose company had laid him off after nine years, had gotten tired of hearing the standard rejections he received from the companies he'd approached for work. When he got a letter from a manager he had interviewed with at a local design firm informing him that he "had a lot to offer," but wasn't "quite right for this position," he decided to call directly to get more information. "I got your letter," he said when he reached the manager, "and I appreciate your letting me know how things stand, but I'm still a little unclear on exactly why you rejected me." The manager held forth with a few minutes of vague, comforting platitudes; after a few minutes, Alan rolled the dice. "Since you don't seem to have a direct answer to what I think is a perfectly fair question, let me suggest this," he said. "How about if I take you out to dinner, my treat, and we can talk in a little more detail about what I have to offer and how I might be able to contribute to your organization." To Alan's surprise, the manager agreed—and the dinner went amazingly well. Within a month of the informal meeting, Alan had secured a job offer from the firm.

Strategies for success:

- This "can-I-take-you-out-for-dinner" gambit has a very positive resonance, and can indeed speed you toward a job offer, if you try it with a hiring official who is of the same gender you are. Such an invitation can backfire when extended to a member of the opposite sex, however, because of unintended sexual overtones. Best bet: Stick with same-sex meetings after job rejections.

- Restaurant interviews are tricky, even ones you suggest and pay for. Be extraordinarily careful about etiquette and comportment; be polite to all the people who serve you; do not consume alcohol, even if your dinner partner suggests that you do so.

- Politely and professionally make your case for employment with the company, spelling out the specific areas in which you feel you can make the contributions most quickly.

- Do not let the prospective employer pick up the tab.

Feeling Lucky?

#19: Promise never to ask for a raise.
Or:
Let's make a deal.

Believe it or not, this is how network anchor Tom Brokaw got his first job in television. After having "begged for the job" for some time, Brokaw, according to Robert Goldberg's excellent book *Anchor*, got an Omaha station to agree to employ him as a news reporter—but the management there wouldn't pay him enough to make the offer worth taking. The logjam was finally resolved when Brokaw got the figure he was after...with the understanding that that's what he would make for as long as he stayed with the station. Brokaw vowed never to ask the station's management for a salary increase, and he kept his word.

Strategies for success:

- Okay, inflation is inflation. Before you try this, you might want to consider offering to set up some arrangement whereby your raise will not exceed, say, the annual nationwide percentage increase in the cost of living. But don't dismiss the attention-getting potential of this offer when laid on the table dramatically and without elaboration.

- Many managers are reluctant to hire workers from other industries who have earned high salaries in the past. They're afraid that if they take these workers on, even at a mutually agreeable rate of pay, the yearly salary review process will become even more of a nightmare than usual.

- Offering to remove such headaches (in writing, if necessary) may well put you at a significant advantage.

#20: **When passed over, ask who got the job you were applying for; contact that person and ask if he or she has any active leads you could follow up.**

Or:

You're not using that job offer, are you?

According to an article by senior employment consultant Scott E. Davis in the *National Business Employment Weekly*, this great idea, apparently developed over time during his work with outplacement candidates, should be part of every displaced worker's book of instructions. It's a wonder no one thought of it before.

Strategies for success:

- Obviously, it's in your best interest to be enthusiastic, polite and concise during the call. (It's also common courtesy to extend your congratulations and wish the person the best of luck in the new job.)

- If the person offers any leads or guidance at all, be sure to send a written thank-you note.

- If the leads you get result in an actual *job offer*, send a small gift of thanks.

#21: **Check out *biz.jobs.offered* on the Internet.**
Or:
You won't need thumbtacks for this bulletin board.

The Internet, as you are probably aware, is a massive, global collection of computers talking to one another. One of the most popular parts of the Net is the wide assortment of Usenet newsgroups, commonly referred to as "electronic bulletin boards." Each covers a specific topic of interest to its readers and/or contributors. Among the boards of greatest interest to job hunters is one called *biz.jobs.offered* which lists scores of live job openings in both high-tech and non-technology-related fields. Veteran Net surfers say it's among the most effective employment-related forums in cyberspace, and that over the years it has paired many a downsized or reengineered worker up with many an employer. (One of the people interviewed for this book praised the board loud and long as a result of personal experience.) Worth a shot, right?

Strategies for success:
- Successful Internet-related job search stories took many forms. See #26, #35, #128, #142, #136, #151 and #252.
- For a full rundown on the ins and outs of Internet newsgroups, see John R. Levine and Carol Baroudi's excellent *The Internet for Dummies* (IDG Books, 1993).

#22: **Describe the fabulous prizes today's players will take home with them.**
Or:
Pull a Don Pardo.

What do you do when the medium in which you've spent most of your broadcasting career stops cranking out shows in your specialty? One former television game-show announcer showcased his sterling vocal technique on a special video intended not for network brass, but for corporate human resource officers who had to train their employees in new procedures. His promotional piece, in which he offered to provide a game-show environment in place of the dry-as-dust training sessions employees often expect, yielded a good many offers. The fascinating story describing the announcer's transition appeared in the *Minneapolis StarTribune*.

Strategies for success:

- Warning: Video production is expensive and time-consuming.
- For another inventive use of video in your job search campaign and some ideas on getting the best results on a tight budget, see #191.
- Guests on today's program stayed at the stylish Casa Elegante Hotel in scenic West Covina, California.

#23: Look up the names and company affiliations of the members of your alma mater's board of trustees.

Or:

You mean you didn't know you had an "in" with a dozen or so chief executives?

David Opton of Execunet passes along a story about a recently displaced executive who made the most of his connections by sending a resume and a brief cover letter to each member of his alma mater's board of trustees. The package summarized the job seekers work and educational history and asked each trustee to pass the job seeker's name along to any company in need of someone with his background. It worked!

Strategies for success:

- This brilliant idea takes advantage of the fact that many trustees of colleges and universities are highly placed figures in the corporate world. Don't you wish you'd thought of this?

- Even if you graduated some time ago, and even if you have no acquaintance with any of the trustees at your alma mater, this method is probably worth a try.

- A modest prediction: This approach will become very popular very quickly once word of the technique's success makes the rounds. Try this quick, before everyone else does!

#24: **Hang out at your favorite bar for hours on end, taking notes.**

Or:

Trust me, I'm conducting some very important field research here.

Rick got laid off from his technical writing job at a major computer manufacturer. The day he got his pink slip, he felt like downing a beer. Or two. By the time he reached number three, he'd decided, more for the fun of it than anything else, to write a feature article about his favorite local haunt, a bar and restaurant that was part of a major national chain. After a couple of days of research, he learned that the restaurant had posted a 50 percent increase in revenues compared to the same period a year earlier, thanks to an innovative series of promotions the manager had dreamed up. He wrote a detailed article about the manager's ideas and the results they'd delivered, and sent it off to an industry trade magazine—which bought it. Rick didn't get a lot of money for his efforts, but he did get a job offer. One of the magazine's readers contacted him and offered him a writing job.

Strategies for success:

- Industry trade magazines represent a great way to establish yourself as an "instant expert" in a field other than the one you've worked. A good many of them are eager to recruit the work of outside writers.

- Strong writing and research skills are a must, of course. If you decide to try to place such an article, but don't have a lot of writing experience, you should strongly consider enlisting the help of a friend or family member who is in a position to offer a helpful critique of your efforts.

- In the article, cite something of interest to the magazine's readers—a new program for incorporating feedback from consumers, for instance, or a new trend that an alert retailer has spotted.

- Even if you don't get a job offer as a direct result of placing such an article, it can be a considerable advantage when approaching prospective employers.

- For more advice on cracking the magazine market—a tactic that can help you develop credentials relatively quickly in an industry in which your background is limited—see the invaluable annual reference book, *Writer's Market* (Writer's Digest Books).

#25: Follow the maternity vacancy.
Or:
Congratulations! It's a job!

Helen heard that her old manager at the firm she'd been laid off from was pregnant, and would be talking maternity leave later that year. She immediately called and asked whether any temp work was available at the firm. As it happened, the temp work did not come through for a number of months—but when it did, it came at a fortuitous time. Her old boss had decided to stop working a few months early, and the ensuing work overload resulted in the creation of a new full-time position. Helen applied, and, as a former employee, was in a great position to make a contribution almost instantly. She got the job.

Strategies for success:

- Maternity leave is a fact of professional life these days. Part of the advantage of having a good network of contacts is hearing about the openings, temporary or otherwise, resulting from these departures.

- Keep an ear open for staff changes. Tactfully approach managers, former managers and human resource people about how you can make a contribution during the times staff will be short.

- Send flowers on the big day.

#26: **Get the company laying you off to download your resume, free of charge, to a potential audience of hundreds of thousands of potential employers.**
Or:
Hitching a ride on the employment superhighway.

When Scott Paper Company recently laid off over 500 of its workers, it set up a deal with Online Opportunities, an Eaton, Pennsylvania firm that specializes in matching up job seekers with potential employers. Online Opportunities, which was paid by Scott Paper for its efforts, distributed employee resumes via commercial online services and those parts of the Internet focusing on employment matters. A good many workers found work through the resulting leads. (The story of the innovative arrangement appeared in the *Philadelphia Business Journal*.)

Strategies for success:

- Guilt is a wonderful thing. If you're being laid off, you are probably surrounded by a number of people who feel very guilty. Making a suggestion that your company take on something like this couldn't hurt, and it might just get you some help.

- What's more, there's no crime in making the request of a company that laid you off some time ago. (You may get a referral to a resume database that will circulate your resume free of charge.)

- Need some help making your case? If appropriate, tell the firm that you have not yet developed the computer skills necessary to circulate your resume in this way.

- Successful Internet-related job search stories took many forms. See #21, #35, #128, #142, #136, #151 and #252.

#27: While a competitor is mulling over whether to accept a recently extended offer, apply to the hiring manager and offer to take the job yourself for significantly less money.

Or:

Those who snooze, lose.

It may sound sleazy, but it was the only thing Bill could think of at the time. He knew his engineering job was about to be eliminated, and he wasn't eager to relocate to another town to look for work. He also knew that the person to whom another job had recently been offered was eager to hold out for a good deal more money than was budgeted for the position, and had told the manager offering him work that he would "think about things and get back in touch next week." Bill figured he wouldn't need to do much meditating if the job were offered to him, so he contacted the manager, passed along a targeted version of his resume and offered to take the job at the pay level at which it was initially posted. The manager liked what he saw, and called the first applicant and told him the salary was non-negotiable. When this resulted in more hedging, the manager withdrew his offer and extended it to Bill, who took it.

Strategies for success:

- When the boat is sinking, you don't argue about the color of the life raft. If your competitors for a position have a less realistic view of the employment situation at your firm than you do, you may want to consider trying this.

- You must be able to demonstrate a compelling fit with the position; do not attempt this technique without developing a resume that is specifically targeted to the position in question.

#28: Follow your boss out the door—and into a new job.

Or:

Fellow travelers.

Sometimes, when you're headed for the unemployment line, your boss is on the way there as well. Jackie, an administrative assistant laid off by the building materials firm she'd worked for for three years, figured she'd make an effort to keep in touch with her old boss; he'd gotten the ax at about the same time she had. She was glad she made the effort. When he got a new job offer, he asked her to join him as his executive assistant.

Strategies for success:

- Depending on your relationship with your former boss, you will either want to send tactful, understated messages via quick phone calls and brief notes, or make a more formal alliance.

- Whatever you do, be sure to pass along any leads or opportunities that come your way that might be of interest to your former supervisor. If he or she finds a job as a result of such a lead, odds are you'll be glad you forwarded it.

#29: Offer to accept three part-time jobs when no single full-time position is open, even though it means enduring the commute from hell.

Or:

Driving the point home.

How it really worked: Annie had recently been laid off from her human resources job at a computer manufacturer, and she knew that finding a new full-time job in the same field would be quite tricky, given the economic climate in her part of the country. She contacted a state employment and training agency and made an unorthodox offer: She would take on three separate part-time positions, each in a far-flung location, and resolve a personnel bottleneck that had been bothering managers for over a year. The state employment office took her up on her offer.

Strategies for success:

- The benefits and vacation time arrangements can be tricky in such a situation. Check with the personnel office for all the details before you sign on.
- Be willing to do the jobs on a trial basis; your supervisor(s) may have justifiable concerns whether you can pull this off and still deliver top-quality work.
- Get a good car stereo. You'll be spending quite a lot of time behind the wheel.

#30: Offer to use your own apartment as office space.
Or:
Hire me and win a free branch office.

Feeling Lucky?

Suzanne had hoped, after her layoff from her marketing job with an auto maker, to return to the insurance company she had worked for some years earlier as a sales rep. When she called her old boss to ask about opening a new territory for him, though, he sounded disappointed. It turned out that he was eager to get the new business he knew Michelle could bring—but he was less than thrilled about renting new office space. He complained that there was simply nowhere to put her! That's when Suzanne offered to do the phone work from her living room two weeks out of the month. (The rest of the job would have been on the road anyway). She suggested that if she didn't deliver strong results from the new territory in 60 days, they consider the experiment a failure and part with no hard feelings. He took her up on the offer—and was delighted with the results.

Strategies for success:

- Lay out a clear objective and focus on a particular timeline for attaining it. Work-at-home jobs are hard to come by, although not as hard as they once were.

- Make an unmistakable commitment to stand by the untraditional arrangement you're proposing, perhaps in writing.

- Be prepared to cite references regarding your ability to work independently. If the references are not positive (preferably *glowingly* positive), don't expect to get the work.

#31: **Develop a personal long-range marketing plan for your "product"—yourself—and submit it to the prospective employer.**
Or:

Here's where I'm headed—want to come along?

Instead of a resume, Mark, an industrial designer who found himself out of work as a result of staff cutbacks, set up a two-page "marketing plan"—with himself as the product! The plan, which did not address the specifics of Mark's job search, was basically a sober assessment of all his attributes as a potential employee. It came complete with an overview of the competition (other job seekers), a summary of the strategic advantages Mark offered (his education and problem-solving background) and even an overview of the product's probable "lifecycle" (Mark's career goals for five, 10 and 20 years down the line.) The final series of recommendations included a suggestion that the company take him on as an employee. The plan got the green light.

Strategies for success:

- A particularly good approach to use with top-level decision makers (CEOs and the like), although you should also consider developing an abbreviated single-page version for such people. (They tend to have a natural aversion to multi-page documents.)

- Obviously, the technique has the strongest resonances with employers who are considering you for a position in a sales or marketing function.

#32: Fax to the top.
Or:
You can't tell me you're not in if I'm not on the phone in the first place.

Vicki, an out-of-work accounting professional who lost her job as the result of a merger, discovered the power of the fax machine when her "power letter" campaign resulted in direct return calls from over 50 percent of her target audience of company presidents. The letter she faxed featured a strong third-party endorsement of her abilities, a concise summary of the advantages she could offer the company and a promise to call the next day to ask about working for the company. The method resulted in two offers.

Strategies for success:

- Fax machines represent a powerful means of reaching top decision makers. Take advantage of the technology.

- Keep it to one page! The higher the position in the organization, the less like the person will be to wade through lots of text.

- State in the letter exactly when you'll be available to take calls, then keep your word.

- See, for comparison, #16, #97 and #143.

#33: **Get insized, not downsized, by making the most of the guilty-manager syndrome.**

Or:

Feeling guilty, boss? Good. Do something about it.

Shortly before his wife was to deliver their first child, Mark learned that his job at the bank he'd worked at for years was about to be eliminated. In addition to networking outside the bank, Mark made his case to his superiors: I realize my job's gone; help me find a new position in the bank. It worked. Thanks to his exemplary work record and the fact that his managers felt awful about having to let him go, Mark won a temporary spot in the bank that was good for 90 days and, shortly thereafter, a full-time position in a different department.

Strategies for success:

- Highlight your past contributions. Make it clear that you've given a lot to the company over time and that you're willing to be flexible and accept a position in a new area or with a different compensation arrangement.

- Consider the potential advantages of accepting temporary employment at the firm while you continue your job search.

- Contact other managers at other levels within the organization and explain your situation.

- Don't attack or become confrontational. Make the most of the guilt the managers feel at having to let you go by saying, "I know you must feel awful about this. Let me share an idea that might make it a little easier for both of us." Then outline a plan under which you continue to work on a temporary basis while you search for a job elsewhere in the firm.

#34: **Form an alliance with a fellow job-seeker: whoever gets a high-level job first will hire the other.**

Or:

Shake on it!

Aspiring football coaches John Robinson and John Madden struck up this bargain: Whoever became a head coach first would hire the other to a staff position. As agreed, Madden took on the brilliant Robinson as a coaching assistant when Madden was named head coach of the Oakland Raiders in 1975. Legend has it that Robin Williams was part of a group of rookie stand-up comics whose members made a similar promise, and that Williams looked out for each comic after *Mork and Mindy* established him as a star.

Strategies for success:

- This is a nice gesture of mutual solidarity, and it certainly reflects the kind of support system of which strong careers are made, but this method is best considered as an insurance policy, not a means in and of itself for getting the right job.

- That having been established, this kind of "oath" does establish a healthy competition that may serve as a significant motivating force. Who's going to be in the position to make good on the promise first?

- Obviously, this alliance only has meaning if both participants are (a) earnest and committed, and (b) very good friends for whom keeping in touch over the years is a given.

#35:   Use the cybernetwork that displaced Congressional workers used.

Or:

You don't have to lose an election to win a job offer.

Cliff Majersik's company, Employment Transition Services Group, set up a resume service for congressional staffers who found themselves out of work after the Republican congressional landslides of a while back. According to a recent story in *The Washington Post*, ETSG can circulate your resume to thousands of prospective employers, too; the service is free to job seekers. (Employers pay for the right to review electronic resumes in the company's database.) Hey, if it's good enough for the suddenly-jobless Washington elite, it's good enough for you, right? ETSG's e-mail address is *etsg@id1.com*—why not send an electronic inquiry and get all the details?

Strategies for success:

- For some advice on constructing an employer-friendly electronic resume, see #151.

- For another idea from ETSG that's working for job seekers, see #128.

- Successful Internet-related job search stories took many forms. See #21, #26, #136, #142 and #252.

#36:   Make a one-week, iron-clad guarantee.

Or:

Tell 'em you'll walk if you can't learn to rock.

Melody knew that the interviewer had doubts about her background; her skills did not exactly match the listed requirements of the position for which she was applying. So as the end of the session rolled around, she took the opportunity to address the problem directly. "Look," she said, "I know you're supposed to hire someone with two years of experience in this field, and I know I only have one. So here's what I'm going to do. I'm going to guarantee you that if you show me what you want done, it will get done *exactly* the way you want. Try me for a week. If it doesn't work out, I'll leave and you won't have to pay me a thing." She got the job—and kept it.

Strategies for success:

- Enthusiasm is the key here. (Of course, you must also be able to deliver on your promises.)

- The best way to overcome the "skill gap" problem seems to be to address the perceived shortcomings head-on.

- If there is a particular technical skill you lack, you may want to consider making your offer contingent on the employer's satisfaction with your progress toward a specific goal (such as mastering a new computer system or a particular piece of software—see #1 for a technique employing a similar method to address such an issue).

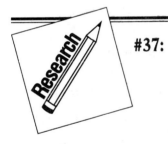

#37: Take home your company directory; before you're let go, enter the names of the company's major clients and customers onto your own computer system and base your job search campaign on the list.

Or:

I'm the guy who designed the widgets you're using right now.

Mel had just been laid off from his product design job of seven years. Almost on a whim, he decided to take home a copy of the list of the company's biggest clients. He punched every company name into his Macintosh and designed a mail campaign around the list. The first week after he left work, each firm received a resume and a query letter that promised a follow-up call. As it turned out, Mel got a request for an interview before he was able to make his first call. That very first meeting resulted in a job offer with a firm that was using a product Mel had designed.

Strategies for success:

- Although applying to your old firm's *competitors* is a pretty common reaction to a layoff, getting in touch with the people who have to make sense of what you *used to help make* is a good idea too. If you can highlight a strong proficiency in solving the problems related to a particular product, you may be in a position to cut to the head of the employment line.

- You may want to ask a salesperson or marketing department worker for help in developing your own list from scratch.

- Warning: Company client lists are proprietary information. Distributing them without authorization could get you into legal trouble. Keep the information you gather to yourself.

- Use only material that results from your own discussions with others in the organization or that appears in standard company directories issued to you by your employer. Do not pilfer lists to which you have no official access.

#38: Put together a personal portfolio of your business accomplishments with the word "SOLD" in huge red letters on the front cover.

Or:

Who says a portfolio is just for art students?

That's what one laid-off sales rep passed along instead of a resume. The leather-bound portfolio featured written highlights from his past work, letters from satisfied clients and even a photograph or two. It won him the job. (Special thanks to Mel Kinnear for passing along this contribution.)

Strategies for success:

- If you, too, are looking for sales work, try attaching one of those big red real estate signs ("SOLD") to the front cover of your portfolio.

- If you're looking for work in another field, you could do worse than to attach a sign that reads "TOP QUALITY" to the front cover.

- Practice talking your way through the portfolio before the interview. You may wish to enlist the aid of a friend or family member to play the part of the prospective employer.

#39: Formally apply to your spouse for a job.
Or:
When is a one-person home-based business a two-person home-based business?

When his wife left her corporate job to start her own designing business, Marty thought of the new undertaking as a promising, but risky, new venture. A year or so later, a downsizing campaign at the giant defense contractor where he'd worked for the last decade cost him his job. When he started assembling lists of potential employers, he tried to come up with small, entrepreneurial companies that could take advantage of his superior drafting and layout abilities. Before long, he found himself asking a question: Why shouldn't his wife's firm, which had blossomed and found a good many new clients over the past year, be on the list? He couldn't come up with any convincing reasons, so he set up and filled out a brief "application" and left it on her desk. He aced the interview and started immediately.

Strategies for success:

- Family businesses present special problems and challenges. Be sure you explore all the pros and cons carefully with your spouse or partner.

#40: Call a radio talk show and, after outlining your status as the victim of a layoff, describe your qualifications over the air.

Or:

Book me on your show—I'm breaking news!

Jerome did this after getting his layoff notice from a local aerospace firm. Because the layoff involved hundreds of workers at a company that had a major impact on the economy of the region, the producer of the show took Jerome's call and let him talk for nearly ten minutes about his experience with the company, his qualifications and his hopes for the future. Before the show ended, a job offer from a listener reached the station offices; the caller was referred directly to Jerome.

Strategies for success:

- Try this excellent idea *immediately* after you receive your layoff notice. You will, in essence, be calling the local radio talk show for the purpose of talking about your situation as though it were a news event. (Guess what? It is!)

- You are likeliest to get a positive response to this approach if your layoff is part of a large (and therefore newsworthy) company action.

- Be positive, upbeat and optimistic during the show; let the host control the general direction of the conversation, but incorporate a direct appeal to potential employers if the host does not do so for you.

- Ask that anyone seeking to get in touch with you contact the station; the producers probably won't appreciate you giving out your own number over the air. Before you end the conversation, ask to leave your number with someone at the station's offices.

- Be patient. Sometimes it takes a while on hold to make it onto one of these programs.

#41: **Go back to the place that fired you and tell them they made a big mistake.**
Or:
I'm baaaaaaaack!

A recently terminated contract worker got a headhunter friend to pass along this basic message to the firm that had let him go. The company agreed—and asked him to take on a new assignment.

Strategies for success:
- This will probably work best if you can recruit someone from the employment services industry to do the messenger work for you.
- More often than you might think, those in charge of downsizing have little or no good information to go on. What's more, they face frequent crises shortly after the departure of large numbers of their workforce. If you can provide hard information to back up your claim to be able to make an immediate contribution, you may be in a position to win some work.

#42: **Camp out on a billboard.**
Or:
Wave to the traffic and see what happens.

According to reliable reports out of New England, a displaced Boston high-tech worker rented out a billboard that featured a concise job pitch, a phone number...and the worker himself. That's right—for three weeks, the fellow sat on the ledge of the sign, waving to traffic on a nearby highway. He got multiple offers for his troubles.

Strategies for success:

- The total cost for the undertaking was reportedly in the neighborhood of $1,000. If you can handle the expense, and you're ready to brave the elements and any pesky fear-of-heights problems, you'll probably generate quite a few queries—and perhaps even some media attention.

- A working message center is a must. Your best option is probably a full-time answering service.

- Despite their significant logistical hurdles, banner- and billboard-related techniques of one kind or another appear to have delivered results for a good many job seekers. See #62, #205, #242, #253 and #256 for some variations.

#43: **Arrange to have your resume inserted in pizza boxes that will be opened at dinnertime by top people at your target company.**

Or:

I could have passed on the anchovies, but the resume looks great.

You read right—when the principals at an advertising firm accepted their customary pizzas from their customary pizza joint for their customary late-night session, they figured someone in the office must have ordered dinner for them. No one in the room could remember placing the call to the restaurant. Whoever it was must have used a company credit card, too, they figured, since the delivery person said the pizzas had already been paid for. When they opened the boxes, they found, taped to the inside of each box, a brief resume targeted specifically to their firm. How on earth could you *not* interview someone who pulled a stunt like that? Once hired at such a firm, how could you *not* be appealed to regularly spring for pizza?

Strategies for success:

- Seal the resume (or whatever written message you send along) in a transparent plastic pouch of some kind. You don't want to get mozzarella on the merchandise.

- Tape it carefully against the inner top lid; be sure to use enough tape to hold the pouch fast.

- This technique did the trick, in this case, for someone who wanted to enter the advertising field, but the pizza-and-resume trick was cited by multiple sources during the research for this book. That leads one to conclude that it has already won a good number of adherents, and that it has a decent chance of being able to deliver positive results in a wide variety of settings.

- When forced to guess about the variety of pizza your potential employer would enjoy eating, stay away from the sardine and pineapple special.

#44: Ask to scrub the toilets.
Or:
Cleaning up by cleaning up.

Ellen gave up a job she hated in a retail store when she got a job in advertising, the field she wanted to break into. The catch: She only got the job by agreeing to perform janitorial work—at low pay—in return for a promise by the head of the agency to critique her portfolio every two weeks. She was scrubbing toilets for less than a month before they offered her a staff position.

Strategies for success:

- Project confidence, poise and determination.

- Check your ego at the door. Perform the janitorial work (or whatever you suggest) as well as you possibly can.

- Tactfully remind the decision maker when it's time to offer the critique of your work. Don't be surprised if you get lost in the shuffle at first, and don't take anything personally. Calmly and professionally remind your contact of the agreement.

- At the end of each critique, ask your contact who he or she thinks you should contact about professional opportunities.

#45: **Before the game, prowl the parking lot of the Super Bowl wearing a sandwich board advertising yourself.**

Or:

The power of personal marketing...and cruising past tailgate parties.

And you thought it was tough to break into the NFL. Before a recent Super Bowl, an out-of-work marketing executive did the tried-and-true sandwich-board routine in the parking lot as people arrived for the big game. It was reported that he got a high-level job with an NFL team for his efforts! Let's face it: the sandwich-board gimmick has stuck around over the years for a good reason: It works.

Strategies for success:

- Once you've come up with a simple, concise and distinctive sign, the trick is to find the right locale. You might not think a parking lot would be an ideal spot, but the demographics for those attending this particular game were, shall we say, best described as upscale. What better way to get in front of the movers and shakers? (Then, too, there's the very real possibility of broadcast media coverage, which played a part in this story.)

- For an interesting alternative take on the same idea, see #103.

#46: **Construct an oversized matchbook trumpeting your achievements.**

Or:

Striking up the best relationship you can with the prospective employer.

Karen, in search of a position as a commercial artist, developed an unforgettable "resume" in the form of a massive matchbook. The headline promised "a good match." (Get it?) When the prospective employer opened the cover, there were 10 of Karen's strong points for the position, each set out in big letters on an individual "match." She got the job.

Strategies for success:

- A cute idea, if executed properly and with the requisite flair.
- Obviously, a "resume" like this can only pass along a limited amount of information. That can actually be an advantage, however. Your aim is to get the employer to call you up to find out more, right?
- Be sure that the strengths you outline are in fact the skills the job in question requires.
- Be sure there are no typographical errors or other potentially damaging mistakes on the resume; enlist the aid of a friend in proofreading the piece.
- Provide appropriate contact information. At the very least, your phone number must appear on the matchbook.
- Although this piece was used to win a graphic designing job, its gentle humor and visual potential make it a good candidate for adaptation to other fields as well.

#47: **Design a compelling direct-mail piece that praises you to the heavens.**
Or:
Give your job search a boost: The best mailer ever produced.

Bart was eager to find a job with a major advertising agency, but he knew the competition was tough. Instead of writing a standard resume, he designed a sample mailing piece for himself. The piece was designed to show how his writing skills could be adapted to virtually any purpose. One side of the oversized postcard featured a picture of a busy crowd scene, with the headline "A good copywriter can blend into any crowd." One the other side was a concise summary of the ways his diverse background could help an agency attract and keep clients. Bart got a number of interviews, and job offers, with this method.

Strategies for success:

- If you plan to use this idea when applying to an advertising agency, make sure you come up with a real winner. If your concept or execution comes across as anything less than stunning, your mailer will probably serve as a neon sign for potential employers: "Stay away from this one."

- Have your mailer critiqued by others in the field (not just family members or close friends).

- Be sure the piece is free of typographical errors or other fundamental problems.

- Bear in mind that stunning layout and copy can be torpedoed by shoddy printing and cheap paper.

- You're planning to mail the piece to prospective employers, so make sure the paper you select is sturdy enough to take a beating.

#48: In a Brooks Brothers box, send the head of the firm a tee-shirt with your resume printed on the front.
Or:
The medium—or the large, or the extra-large—is the message.

This one comes from the annals of the advertising industry, where it takes a lot to impress people. Apparently the principle of contrast came into play here—the garment within that swanky, uptown Brooks Brothers box was no pinstriped corporate number, but a simple tee-shirt. Then again, practicality may have played a role. Did you ever try to write a resume around a shirt that buttons down the front? Anyway, it worked. (*Getting into Advertising,* David Laskin, Random House, 1986.)

Strategies for success:

- Don't crowd the front of the shirt with information. Use as little text as possible to convey important points.

- For some interesting variations on the tee-shirt idea, which formed the basis of multiple success stories among those supplying information for this book, see #159 and #238. You will probably need to work closely with a tee-shirt printing firm to get the design just right; try to have a brief, neat and legible career summary (complete with contact information) set onto a large decal and attached. Using press-on letters probably won't look as sharp.

Feeling Lucky?

#49: **Leave three messages a day, at precisely the same times, for three weeks.**
Or:
If it's two o'clock, you must be George.

After about a week, the receptionists came to expect George's polite, confident tone on the other end of the line: "Hello, Dennis, is Mr. Smith in? Well, would you mind telling him I called?" He was so punctual that the people at the front desk joked that they could set their watches by him if they had to: ten o'clock, two o'clock and four thirty. George would always call for Mr. Smith, asking for an interview as a marketing representative. After three weeks, even Mr. Smith started asking whether George had called on schedule—and once he found himself doing that, he figured that he might as well ask the fellow in for an interview. The meeting went spectacularly and George got the job.

Strategies for success:
- Rule number one: Be nice to the people at the reception desk.
- Rule number two: Be nice to the people at the reception desk.
- Rule number three: Be nice to the people at the reception desk.
- Failure to follow rules one, two or three will result in your being instantly categorized as a pest, and pests usually don't get interviews.
- As a matter of fact, to make this technique work, you will probably have to learn the work patterns of all the people who work on the reception desk, and develop a first-name acquaintance with each of them.

- Some would argue that one of the scheduled times for the calls should be for around eight in the morning, on the theory that you might, at that hour or perhaps even earlier, be able to reach bigwigs who get to their desks before the gatekeepers show up.
- See also #109.

#50: Send the employer 11 eggs in a dozen-egg container; in your cover letter, incorporate a headline that reads, "Looking for a good egg that will fit right in?"

Or:

One great way to prove your candidacy is no yolk.

An aspiring advertising worker got a job using this intriguing, visually powerful method. (Special thanks to Chuck Strinz for this contribution.)

Strategies for success:

- Drain the eggs of their contents! Punch a small hole in the bottom of each; empty the white and yolk into the garbage.
- Pack everything with great care, using appropriate cushioning.
- You should probably attach the letter directly to the carton; a befuddled hiring manager who receives only the eggs won't have any idea what to make of the gift.
- Better yet, try attaching your message directly to the package itself, so that your letter—complete with contact information—is the label.

#51: **Print your resume on the inside of a candy bar wrapper. Send it to the advertising agency that represents that product.**

Or:

If you know that I sent my resume on the back of a 100 Grand bar, why are you asking me what kind of salary I want?

Everyone in the office had to admit that it was among the weirdest resumes anyone had ever put together, but the candy-wrapper sure did what it was supposed to do. It demonstrated creativity and strong research skills (otherwise how would the candidate have figured out that the firm represented the product?). It presented a simple, direct message—"hire me"—in a compelling way. And it stopped people dead in their tracks. No wonder it got its designer the job she was after.

Strategies for success:

- The point is to pick a product *associated with your target company* and somehow incorporate your resume into it. Sending a software company an old candy wrapper with a piece of paper glued on the back may win you points for surrealism, but a better bet would be to reconfigure one of the company's product boxes or catalogs in such a way that your background and accomplishments jump out at the reader.

- Modern laser printers and word processors are wonderful things; they'll allow you to set up text in virtually any size, shape, dimension, or angle.

- Don't be afraid to use color.

- Don't cram the (limited) text area with words! Pick two or three career highlights and make the most of them.

- See also #98.

#52: Reveal the results of a startling survey.
Or:

Four out of five dentists surveyed suggest that you offer me a job.

Ben, now a major marketing executive, got his start by circulating a provocative private questionnaire among his suburban neighbors—and eliciting some unexpected answers about sexual practices in his area. (Not surprisingly, he had to promise complete confidentiality to the survey participants!) Ben compressed the results of his interview into a compelling one-page summary and circulated it to everyone he could think of. The results? A good deal of local news coverage—and a job offer from an advertising firm in his area that was fascinated by his knowledge of an important consumer group they were trying to target.

Strategies for success:

- Responsibly developed survey results, when they point toward a surprising or alarming trend, can breathe vitality and immediacy into a personal marketing campaign. But be sure you are accurately representing the views and actions of those whom you have interviewed and do not violate any pledges of confidentiality.

- In addition to setting up your results for local employers (perhaps as an adjunct to your targeted resume), you should send a brief press release to local and national news organizations.

- Try to find out something new or exciting about your *target industry's best customers*.

- Once you've done so, send the results to the president of the organization you want to work for, and follow up appropriately by telephone.

#53: Send a short, baffling letter with no contact information.

Or:

Does anyone here read Armenian?

Foreign languages may be pushing it, but the idea here is worth considering. You develop a tantalizing, incomplete message, send it to the prospective employer, without comment, and follow up appropriately shortly thereafter. The method is known as a "teaser" in marketing circles. According to a fascinating article by Bill Corbin in the *National Business Employment Weekly*, an applicant for a marketing job used this technique—and followed up with letters that offered progressively more information about her background. It made sense, because she wanted to demonstrate how she could design a marketing campaign. The idea could be adapted to any number of job search situations.

Strategies for success:

- You might decide, for example, to send a letter bearing an image of a stop sign. (In color!)

- A week or so later, you could send the same letter, but with the words "settling for less than the best" underneath the sign.

- Finally, you could send the same letter, complete with the phrase "settling for less than the best—start talking to Jane Smith," and a copy of your resume, targeted directly to the position for which you wish to be considered.

- Applying for a marketing or advertising job? There's a good chance you're not the first person to approach the decision maker in this way. Make sure the material you send looks very sharp indeed.

#54: **Send the employer a small seedling tree, along with a note outlining your quest to "find the right place to grow."**

Or:

One way to get the idea of hiring you to take root.

This charming approach was used to get a job at an advertising agency. The tag line was inspired by the agency's own slogan, but it could certainly be adapted to other settings. (Special thanks to Chuck Strinz for this contribution.)

Strategies for success:

- Keep the note brief. Include all appropriate contact information.

- Feeling creative? Write the body of the letter in the form of watering and care instructions—while focusing on the steps the employer should take next to develop a mutually beneficial work relationship.

- As always, focus on the benefits and advantages you offer the prospective employer's organization—rather than on your own needs and objectives.

#55: **During rush hour at Grand Central Station, hand out copies of your resume to passers-by.**

Or:

If the competition is asking for spare change, who are people going to pay attention to?

An intrepid prospective employee used this method to break into the advertising agency; he was wearing a sandwich board that trumpeted his talents. The story is mentioned in David Laskin's fine book *Getting into Advertising*.

Strategies for success:

- Not for shrinking violets, perhaps, but who's not going to admire your initiative if you summon up the courage to give this a try for a day or two? Just be sure to bring plenty of copies of your handout. This is a numbers game.

- Really big, undeniably public gathering places are the likeliest spots for success. (They're also the spots least likely to produce grumpy security people.)

- Don't cause a fuss; if you are asked to leave the premises by an authority figure, do so.

#56: Blow up your resume until it's three feet tall.

Or:

The portable billboard.

Ted wanted a job as a producer at one of the top-rated television shows in the country. He researched the show for a week, targeted his resume to within an inch of its life and then had it enlarged until it looked like a low-end entry in a billboard competition. He attached a query note, taped everything into a cardboard container and sent it via express courier to the head person at the show. He received a call that week, and his subsequent interview led to a job offer.

Strategies for success:

- A nice idea—but please, please, please don't waste all that initiative by sending a "generic" vanilla resume meant to appeal to all employers. You must send one that appeals to a *particular* decision maker.

- Friendly reminder: If a typographical error on a standard resume is hazardous to your career, an error on an oversized one is nigh unto criminal. Have someone else proofread your resume carefully.

- Unless there is true overnight urgency (and there probably won't be), save yourself some money by paying for economy two-day courier service. The point is to get the package into the hands of a particular person, not to get an instant decision. The express service is for theatrical effect more than anything else.

#57: Monitor incoming call sources at your switchboard job.

Or:

You don't know me, but...

During a "stopgap" job as an operator with the phone company, Michelle often found herself connecting calls from a particular local hotel to a number in California. After a little digging, she learned that the company placing the calls was a motion-picture production company that was doing location work in the town in which Michelle worked. She went to the set, offered to help the short-handed staff out with odd jobs for $75 a week, and eventually won a full-time job at the company's California offices.

Strategies for success:

- Careful! Eavesdropping on private telephone conversations is illegal. Don't do it.

- Phone operators who place collect or person-to-person calls from one business party to another may be in a good position to know about "satellites" doing business for out-of-town superiors. If following up on such a lead, within the boundaries of the law, leads you to opportunity, congratulations. Make the most of it.

- When approaching a film production company for work on-site, be prepared to be turned down. Technical support for location work is usually arranged well in advance, although there are certainly exceptions to this. (To me the technique used by Michelle seems likeliest to result in work as an *extra*, not as a member of the crew.)

#58:   Ask to spend your vacation weeks working for free for the target company.
Or:
I wasn't doing anything then anyway.

It worked for Irna Phillips, a teacher who worked summers on a volunteer basis during the Depression for Chicago radio station WGN. Her efforts led to a writing assignment that produced "Painted Dreams," the first modern radio soap opera. Thus did Phillips parlay her vacation time into a fantastically successful radio career; she is regarded today as one of the pioneers of the daytime drama genre.

Strategies for success:

- The advantage of tying your offer to work on a volunteer basis to a specific period of time is that it puts you in the driver's seat. You have something quite valuable to offer the prospective employer: Certain specific weeks of your time on a volunteer basis. The answer will either be yes or no. If you make the offer to a number of organizations in your target industry (preferably to the top person in the firm), you will probably get an encouraging response before too very long.

- Successful ideas based on some form of volunteer work took many forms, and were among the most popular techniques encountered during the research for this book. See #1, #10, #82, #129, #140, #154, #251 and #292.

#59: **Find out the birthday of a top person at the hiring organization; send a birthday card, then follow up with a phone call.**
Or:
Now let's both make a wish!

Actually, as Mario recalls it, he had been "bugging" the top man at the production studio about a set designing job for some months—but it was the birthday card that finally helped land him the position. After finding out from an industry directory that the top banana's birthday was only a month or so away, he purchased a nice-looking card and sent it along at the proper time. (The card mentioned nothing about wanting a job.) The next time he called about the job he wanted, he got a much warmer reception—and an interview.

Strategies for success

- Nothing off-color or sexist in the card, please—and if the person you're sending it to is of the opposite sex, make a special effort to be sure you're not sending inappropriate signals.
- Don't get chintzy—pick out a card that will stand out, even if it sets you back a buck or two.
- See, for comparison, #199.

#60: **Offer to track down local sports sound bites.**
Or:
The tale of the tape.

How to break into broadcasting? Mike figured out one way. He called a medium-sized station and offered to get brief quotes from the coaches of all of the area's local high school football coaches after the weekend games—and in time for the evening news broadcasts. This was actually not that difficult to do; all the task required was an arrangement with each of the half-dozen or so coaches to give a five-minute interview after the game on Saturday by phone. The station agreed, and Mike had his first job in broadcasting.

Strategies for success:

- Negotiating pay for such work can be tricky; try to get some ideas of competitive rates by calling a similar-sized station in another community for information.

- Warning: Taping phone conversations without the other party's consent is illegal. Be sure that anyone you approach for newsgathering purposes knows that the conversations you tape are being recorded.

#61: **Offer to help the hiring official move.**
Or:
Have muscles, will network.

Mark had been getting nowhere in his efforts to break into the video production industry in Southern California...but then he heard that one of the producers he'd been applying to had signed a lease on a new apartment across town. Struck by a sudden inspiration, he called the producer up and asked whether he needed any help with the upcoming move. The grateful producer took Mark up on his offer...and, after a long, sweaty day, asked him to drop by the office to discuss a new project that had come in.

Strategies for success:

- Everybody hates to move, so if you find yourself in Mark's fortunate situation of knowing ahead of time that someone on your target list is planning to pack up, offering your time can indeed put you at an advantage. Just remember, during the project, to leave any employment issues unspoken unless you're asked directly about your career goals.

- Don't try this unless you're truly willing to help your contact negotiate a huge couch down a twisting stairwell. (But isn't your career worth that?)

- You probably won't have to do much follow-up after this extraordinary display, but if for some reason you aren't pointed in the right direction by the person you help out, make a polite phone call a week or so after the move asking about new opportunities.

#62: Hatch a publicity stunt with a local radio station.

Or:

How to raise the station's ratings and your income in one fell swoop.

In an intriguing variation on the "rent-a-billboard" approach, an out-of-work disc jockey set up a secret arrangement with a Boston radio station. He would rent a huge billboard that proclaimed his hope to find work; the station would publicize his high-profile campaign and appeal to local employers to contact him; then the *station itself* would hire him as an on-air personality. According to *The Boston Globe,* the stunt garnered a good deal of attention, especially when the "billboard man" broadcast his first show; the ruse was eventually discovered.

Strategies for success:

- Radio stations are often willing to consider unorthodox promotions; if you want to adapt this idea to your situation, contact the station manager of a station in your area and see what happens.

- You may decide to use the "publicity stunt" idea in connection with another idea in this book, and not as a means of finding work with a particular station. If so, tell the station personnel what you'll be doing (say, parading around a local subway station at rush hour wearing a sandwich board), why you're doing it (to find a job in, say, engineering) and when you'll be doing it (this Monday from 7:30 to 9 a.m.).

- Despite their significant logistical hurdles, banner- and billboard-related techniques of one kind or another appear to have delivered results for a good many job seekers. See #42, #205, #242, #253 and #256 for some variations.

#63: Fired? On your way home, apply to the former employer of the hotshot who just took over your job.

Or:

It's bigger than the both of us.

This is a common technique among anchorpersons, disc jockeys and other high-level (and frequently fired) figures in the broadcast field. A prominent New England radio personality used this approach to good effect some years ago. If you've been let go in favor of an outsider coming from another company, the idea may be worth a try.

Strategies for success:

- Accentuate the positive. Resist, at all costs, the temptation to bad-mouth your former employer or the person who took over your job.

- Act quickly!

#64: Pull an Eliza Doolittle.

Or:

By Jove, I think I've got it!

Tom was searching for a job as an on-air personality, and although his looks, resume and academic credentials all seemed pretty solid, he couldn't seem to land the offer he wanted. He mentioned his problem to a friend who suggested that the problem could be his noticeable, but not overwhelming, New York accent. After a period of intensive independent work on the problem, he shed the accent, and approached one of the stations that had rejected him earlier. He landed a weekend anchor job.

Strategies for success:

- If the job you want requires a great deal of exposure to the public (such as sales, marketing or broadcasting), you should look closely at how the way you speak shapes the perceptions of those who come in contact with you.

- Speech patterns are funny things. Some people can simply work themselves past an accent that is standing in the way of their career goals. Others may need counseling or elocution lessons.

- If you can't make significant progress in improving your speech by reading aloud, consulting speech manuals or relentlessly exercising the vowels and consonants that seem at times to twist out of shape or drop out on you entirely, you may want to consider seeing a professional speech and diction instructor.

#65: Send a plastic toy along with your resume.
Or:
The plaything's the thing!

This practice is apparently quite common among aspiring disc jockeys; they use the toy to emphasize the air name they've selected. (Someone who calls himself Jack the Knife on the air, for instance, might send a station manager a huge rubber knife.) Also included in the package is a taped sampling of the DJ's vocal work.

Strategies for success:

- It's worth a try, even if you're not trying to get a job as a DJ. The toy you select should support a major advantage of your background—or a theme of your cover letter.

- You might decide, for instance, to send a toy stethoscope along with a cover letter promising to provide "fast diagnosis of customer service problems."

- Keep it clean; don't send toys with off-color or sexist implications.

#66: **Hang out in the lobby of the theater every day until someone asks you what you're doing.**

Or:

Sure, I'm supposed to be here. Everyone has to be somewhere, right?

Beatrice, an aspiring actress, tried this at a nonprofit theater in her neighborhood. After a few days, the artistic director asked her what she was up to and Beatrice explained that she was eager to help out on anything involving the show's current season. An apprentice set-building job followed, as did an acting gig.

Strategies for success:

- It's hard to imagine this working in any other setting than a very informal nonprofit arts organization—but then again, you never know.

- If you are asked in no uncertain terms to leave the premises, do so.

- See also #6 and #123.

#67: **Pretend to be a delivery person.**

Or:

Who ordered the future Academy Award winner?

Nat was an aspiring film actor whose favorite film director was doing location shooting in town. He heard that the director had become partial to the cheesecake served up by a nearby restaurant, and would frequently order slices to eat between shots on the set. One morning he bought a slice of cheesecake and a cup of coffee, dressed up as a delivery person, and stalked onto the set, assuring security people that he had a special order for the director. He handed the order to the director, who told him, not surprisingly, "I didn't order this." "No?" asked Nat. "Then would you like to order this?" And with that, he launched into a brief audition piece. Before being led away by a pair of genial security people, Nat made sure the director had his head shot and resume. Some time later, an audition with the director led to a small part in another film.

#68:   Ask shyly whether you have permission to use a dirty word during your audition.
Or:
Which four-letter words do you mean, exactly?

Roberta, the young actress who tried this, won assurances from the director that everyone in the room was a hardened professional. She then launched gleefully into a hilarious, extended X-rated routine that would have given Andrew Dice Clay pause. When she was finished she smiled innocently at the stunned director and thanked him for granting permission. She got the part.

Strategies for success:

- A fascinating way to stand out from the crowd during an audition, but the technique depends, to a great degree, on personal chemistry. Clearly, this gambit would put some off. Use it with care.
- Any hesitation or embarrassment in delivery of the provocative monologue will probably doom your efforts.

#69:   Brag about your ability to ride a unicycle.
Or:
Big wheel, keep on turnin'.

Ellen was a recent graduate from a prestigious graduate-level acting program who was having difficulty getting parts—until she started telling producers about her ability to ride a unicycle. (She had picked up the skill when preparing for a talent show in high school.) She was more than a little surprised to find that this off-beat detail helped to set her apart during her auditions, and led to a supporting role in an absurdist piece at a major local theater. Part of Ellen's newfound appeal had to do with the desire of directors to incorporate the stunt into their productions. ("Sometimes," she jokes, "I get the feeling they'd find a way to work the unicycle into a production of *Three Sisters*.") But the unusual skill also served as an important "talking point" with those doing the casting. By listing it prominently on her resume, Ellen found a way to tell potential employers "Hey—this one's different."

Strategies for success:

- In the right setting, and with the right potential employer, highlighting an unusual skill can work wonders. Sometimes, the skill can aid your cause even if it's not directly job-related.

- Don't fake it. If you don't know how to do the stunt, you're asking for disaster if you list it on your resume.

- See also, for comparison, #229 and #183.

#70: Cast yourself in the lead.
Or:
Somehow, your face seems familiar.

Talented actress and writer Camryn Manheim, tired of focusing exclusively on supporting roles, decided to write herself a starring role. According to *People* magazine, her one-woman show *Wake Up, I'm Fat*, was one of the highlights of the 1993 off-Broadway season. The well-received production led to more prominent acting work in the film arena; Manheim was seen recently in a featured role in *The Road to Wellville*.

Strategies for success:

- Think of this as an extended audition piece based on your own improvisational work—a piece that takes, oh, three or four months, at a minimum, to develop. Creating a compelling one-person performance piece takes work, and will almost certainly require critiques from people whose opinions you trust.

- For examples of one-person plays that have won critical and commercial praise, see Manheim's *Wake Up, I'm Fat*, Eric Bogosian's *Drinking in America* and Spalding Gray's *Swimming to Cambodia*.

- Don't expect immediate results; but do expect a rewarding creative process—and a finished product that will allow you to showcase your abilities for those who might otherwise not be exposed to them.

#71: Spot an important decision maker on a cross-country flight and make your pitch after appropriating the neighboring seat.
Or:
This seat isn't taken, is it?

This was the approach used by actress Fran Drescher, who must have startled a top network executive during a long flight when she briskly claimed the empty seat next to him and introduced herself. She proceeded, for the next several hours, to explain, in a thoroughly engaging and confident manner, why the executive should design a new show around her. The result? *The Nanny*, which went on to become a hit for ABC and the breakthrough event in Drescher's career.

Strategies for success:

- If you're good with people, a lively conversationalist and capable of presenting yourself as confident without seeming overwhelming, this may be worth a try if you find yourself in a similar situation.

- Of course, a knowledge of your target industry and the imprint executives within it is absolutely essential.

- Could such networking possibilities represent a hidden benefit of flying first class? Then again, any number of top-ranking executives have drawn stares from fellow passengers in the coach (or even economy) sections. Microsoft's Bill Gates, for instance, has been known to shun the champagne and swanky food in favor of settling down in one of the cheap seats—which only makes sense when you think about it. You don't get to be a 30-year-old billionaire by *wasting* money, right?

#72:   Dress like a bum...then blow 'em away.
Or:
Who let that weirdo in here—and when can she start?

A young Barbra Streisand won over a talent-show auditioner by pretending to be a rank amateur. Having dressed quite sloppily and left her hair unwashed, she wandered into the audition room and pretended not to know that tryouts were even underway. Streisand nevertheless took advantage of the chance to sing for the auditioner, claiming that she'd "never sung in public before." The director and piano player snickered as they prepared for this "amateur" to crash and burn. They were begging her to work with them when she finished her first number.

Strategies for success:

- A nice maneuver if you can pull it off. It goes without saying, however, that anything less than brilliance will probably yield a "don't-call-us-we'll-call-you" kind of reaction.

- For another audition stunt by the inimitable Ms. Streisand, see #79.

#73:   Fling yourself from the stage during an audition.
Or:
Look out below!

Terry, an experienced film actor, knew he had delivered a top-notch audition for a big L.A. show, but as he was reaching the end of his prepared piece, he was still searching for a way to be sure the producers of the piece remembered him at the end of the day. In an instant, he decided to launch himself into the orchestra pit at the climax of speech, when his character had gone, figuratively, (and, as it turned out, literally) over the edge. He sustained only minor injury and won the role.

Strategies for success:

- Don't try this at the conclusion of a somber, slow piece unless you're eager to build a reputation as a wacko.

- Watch out for sharp objects.

#74: Insult the customers.
Or:
When confronted by temptation, yield once in a while.

Long before she broke into network television, Brett Butler held down a job as a waitress—and earned a reputation as a woman who could deliver snappy retorts along with plates of food. According to *People* magazine, when she told off a customer by informing him, "Your IQ matches your inseam," he invited her to audition at his comedy club. Thus was a career launched. Butler, of course, went on to achieve tremendous success in the situation comedy *Grace Under Fire*.

Strategies for success:

- We're talking about *good-natured* ribbing here, of the variety that makes customers laugh and keep coming back. A lot depends on *how* you say what you say. Certainly, appropriate workplace humor is a subjective thing; what one boss will appreciate as endearing, another will find horrifying. But off-color, sexist or racially insensitive humor probably won't win you points with anyone.

- Lots of aspiring actors and comedians have found creative ways to use their skills in restaurant jobs and other service-related positions; more than a few have struck up relationships with important people in the industry as a result of "chance" encounters that turned into mini-auditions.

- Bear in mind the old adage about good fortune being the intersection of preparation and opportunity, and be ready to put some pizzazz into your next exchange with a customer. It could just pay off, especially if you work in a city like New York or Los Angeles, where a great deal of hiring in the entertainment industry takes place.

- For other examples of how service-industry encounters led to important career breaks, see #81, #93, #234 and #249.

#75: Knock on every door in the building.
Or:
Anybody home?

Chet, an accomplished film and stage actor, got tired of waiting for his lackadaisical agent to line up work for him. He decided, one morning, to head for a building that housed a number of production offices, where he proceeded to knock on every casting-related door in the place, dropping off his head shot and copies of his resume. He also offered a brief spiel about his accomplishments as an actor. Most of the people he talked to thought he was nuts. A few asked if he'd come back when auditions were scheduled. One asked about his background—and gave him a job in a commercial being shot that week.

Strategies for success:
- Don't try this if you're thin-skinned.
- Leave when they ask you to leave.
- Be prepared, at a moment's notice, to showcase your talents and accomplishments.

#76: Make a two-for-one deal.
Or:
For a few dollars more...

A recent article in the *News & Observer* (Raleigh) relates how, in 1969, Don Anderson, a recent graduate of the Yale University drama school, heard a rumor about a Utah dance company in search of a manager. He and a friend went west to check out the lead. They liked the region a great deal—so much, in fact, that they made the dance group an offer it couldn't refuse: for an extra

$1,000, it could hire them both. The dance company agreed, and Anderson, who would go on to a successful career in dance and theater management, had his first real job in the arts.

Strategies for success:

- Such a deal! Of course, you may need to ask for a little more than another grand these days, but the idea is straightforward enough. You and a fellow job seeker combine leads (and, early on at least, probably combine living expenses, too) so that you can extend a slightly-modified two-for-one offer. You both enter the field you've got your eye on, and the employer gets twice as much work done for only slightly more money.

- This creative approach may require a little salesmanship, but it is likely to appeal to those who operate small, entrepreneurial oriented companies—or, as in Anderson's case, arts organizations.

- The selection of your "job partner" of course, is critical. Not only must he or she be passionately devoted to the field you want to break into, *and* committed to delivering superior results, *and* flexible enough to take part in an unconventional arrangement such as this one—your partner must also be someone you will genuinely enjoy working with. Sometimes that's hard to predict. Bear in mind, too, that one person's occasional slip-up on the job may well affect how the other person is perceived.

- A tricky maneuver, but one that might be right for your situation.

#77: Recruit a close relative to act as your "agent."

Or:

Yes, we certainly have worked together for a long time.

Legend has it that the immortal country singer Patsy Cline used this method to get her first television booking. The "agent" who called ahead and arranged for her audition was her mother.

Strategies for success:

- This has become, over the years, a popular technique for breaking into the performing arts field, although the results depend, ultimately, on a complex mixture of confidence, personal chemistry, luck and talent. This approach should probably be considered one way to decrease the long odds you face when starting out, and not as an instant guarantee of landing that big breakthrough job.

- A certain amount of rehearsal time will probably be necessary. Don't expect your partner to master the art of telephone prospecting instantly. Consider doing some role-playing exercises, in which you play the part of the decision maker, before your "agent" starts in on the calls that matter.

Feeling Lucky?

#78: Rent out Carnegie Hall.

Or:

And then I told Luciano...

In 1957, a 17-year-old pianist named Dubravka Tomsic did this—and made quite a splash in the music world. The concert was well received, turned a modest profit and helped to set the stage for a successful career based, as it turned out, in Europe, where Tomsic played over 3,000 concerts. Not long ago, she returned to Carnegie in triumphant fashion. Recalling that first concert to a reporter for *The Boston Globe*, Tomsic remembered remarking to her mother that, if they weren't able to meet all the obligations arising out of the Carnegie Hall booking, they'd simply go to jail. Fortunately, that wasn't necessary; future bookings proved the wisdom of the audacious independent recital.

Strategies for success:

- Practice, practice, practice.

#79:   Scatter things all over the theater.
Or:
What a klutz—give her the job.

A 19-year-old Barbra Streisand, auditioning for her first Broadway role, tottered uneasily onto the stage in an ungainly overcoat, spilled the contents of her handbag, scattered her sheet music across the stage, rushed to reassemble the pages, settled herself into something resembling a seated position and, finally, removed a wad of chewing gum from her mouth, sticking it under her metal chair before beginning her musical number. She then proceeded to show off the most dynamic voice to grace the American stage in a generation. After she left, the stage manager checked the bottom of the chair on which she'd been seated. There was not a speck of gum to be found. (By the way, she got the part. But you knew that.)

Strategies for success:

- "Hey—look at the weirdo who doesn't know what she's doing!" Or does she? To pull off a stunt like this, you must be able to show off a truly awesome talent after all the Keystone Kops shenanigans. Otherwise, the people you're trying to impress will think you're, well, a weirdo who doesn't know what she's doing.

- For another legendary Streisand audition, see #72.

#80:   Talk through the mail slot.
Or:
How to make a very special delivery.

Chris, an out-of-work actor, was constantly being lectured by casting agents not to barge into their offices and ask about upcoming work. "Drop your resume and headshot in the mail slot in the front door," they demanded. "We'll get in touch with you if we need you." After one too many such lectures, Chris decided to heed the instructions—and follow up in his own inimitable way. After passing the manila envelope through the slot, he got down on all fours and stuck his mouth through the mail slot. "That guy Chris is really good," he said hopefully. "He just did a show over at the Forum that got great reviews. You should talk to him." The casting people started laughing—and listening for more. Not long after that, Chris had landed work through the firm.

Strategies for success:

- Enunciate!

#81: Try out your stand-up act while you cut a talent agent's hair.

Or:

Did you hear the one about the guy who got a mohawk by mistake?

A Chicago hairstylist got a gig at a local comedy joint this way. Hey, is there anything wrong with asking what a customer does for a living? And isn't the main job to keep the customer satisfied? And isn't a laughing customer a happy customer?

Strategies for success:

- Actors and comedians are famous for finding ways to sneak their performing skills into their day jobs. The ones who *keep* their day jobs as long as they need them usually have managers who understand and accept their long-term career goals.
- You say you *don't* have a boss like that? Well, unless you're (a) supremely confident about your ability to land another day job, or (b) truly looking at the Chance of a Lifetime, you probably shouldn't go overboard with the shtick while you're working your shift.
- Off-color material? Save it for the nightclubs. (There's no need to antagonize other customers.)
- For other examples of how service-industry encounters led to important career breaks, see #74, #93, #234 and #249.

#82: Volunteer to hammer together the sets.
Or:
If you can't get in one door...build another.

The artistic director of a respected repertory theater got her start at the company when she took on set crew duties after failing to win an acting role. She got the crew assignment almost by default; her strong work ethic soon won the notice of others in the company. The would-be actor's long-term commitment to the theater group's development was evident almost immediately, and before long she was in a position to take on a full-time job with the company.

Strategies for success:

- Refusing to accept less-than-glamorous "support" positions (or not asking about them in the first place) can lengthen your job search unnecessarily. If you find the group you feel is in the best position to offer you long-term career growth, consider starting where there is a need for your help.

- Ideas based on some form of volunteer work take many forms, and were among the most popular techniques encountered during the research for this book. See #1, #10, #58, #129, #140, #154, #251 and #292.

- For another interesting parallel, see #135.

#83: Assign yourself to a story.
Or:
You don't know me, but I just got a scoop for you.

Legendary reporter Dickey Chapelle got her first byline with the Boston *Traveler* by talking her way onto a plane bearing supplies to flood victims.

After a bumpy ride, she surveyed the scene of the disaster, wrote an account of the experience and forwarded the story to the *Traveler's* editor. She recalled, in her memoirs, that she had identified herself as a student hoping to write a piece for the *Traveler*—but had a feeling that, over the roar of the engine, only the proper nouns would be audible.

Strategies for success:

- A much-praised technique among aspiring reporters, even if it is a little time-consuming. Just be sure the event you select is truly newsworthy.

- The more adventurous the means you select for gathering your facts—and the more undeniable the importance of the event you cover—the more likely you'll be to elicit the attention of readers and editors.

#84: Appeal to the I Ching.
Or:
There's more than one way to flip a coin.

Verne, a freelance writer, was looking for his next assignment. As he often did when faced with a troublesome personal or professional dilemma, he took out his battered old copy of the *Book of Changes*, the ancient Chinese oracle also known as the I Ching. After throwing three coins six times, as he had done many times before, he developed a single hexagram detailing both the past and the future. Once he read the commentaries on the lines, he came to a surprising conclusion: The next piece he developed should be about the I Ching itself! Over the next day or so, he developed an article about the ancient oracle, set it up as a proposal and included a full explanation of the hexagram that had set him on his course. The first publisher he sent it to offered him a contract.

Strategies for success:

- Whether or not you believe in oracles, using something like the I Ching to initiate new thinking patterns and help you eradicate negative emotional reactions can be a big plus on your job search.

- Motivational expert Anthony Robbins advocates a similar "distancing" technique of pattern disruption; he advises you to initiate an event that is unexpected, out of your normal routine or even bizarre in order to jolt yourself into taking a new outlook on your situation.

- Singing at the top of your lungs for a minute or so, running around the block, or, yes, even closely consulting a seemingly random pattern of words or images could all do the trick.

- Take a break. Do something unusual. Then write down whatever crosses your mind as a result. You might just find something worthwhile for you to pursue waiting for you on that sheet of paper.

- If you're interested in finding out more about the I Ching, see *The I Ching, or Book of Changes*, by Wilhelm and Baynes, Princeton University Press, 1967.

#85: Attach a small statue to your cover letter.
Or:
A monumental success will soon be yours.

Tim, a writer who got tired of waiting for months to hear from the publishers and arts organizations he was contacting, tried this with good results. The statue (in his case, a small horse) tied into the writing sample he submitted; he alluded to the "gift" discreetly in his cover letter. He got a high-profile writing assignment as a result.

Strategies for success:

- Keep it small.

- Don't send offensive or risqué material.

- Be sure the object you send relates in some compelling way to the other materials enclosed.

#86: Do a Joe Friday imitation.
Or:
Thank you, Jack Webb, wherever you are.

What follows is part of the text of a letter that won an interview and a job at a big-city newspaper. It's reproduced here with the kind permission of Michele Simos, who wrote it.

It's three a.m. in the big city. We've been watching apartment #245 near the alley at Twenty-fifth and Sixth since 10:25 this evening. We're 4-1/2 hours into the stakeout and have nothing to report. "What's that?" I ask as I withdraw my loaded gun from my holster and shake my partner. (His name's Tuesday. I'm Friday. Today's Wednesday.) But on closer inspection, we realize it's only two pigeons picking through the contents of a steel-gray dumpster. 'This surveillance stuff is for the birds,' I think to myself. Then the screen door opens—and she slips discreetly out the front door and quickly rounds the corner. We're right behind her when, mysteriously, she vanishes before our very eyes. Don't make the same mistake as Sgt. Friday. Your chance to snag an ace Managing Editor is within reach. This seasoned, creative writer, meticulous editor and results-oriented project manager would like to meet with you to discuss your paper's new magazine venture.

Strategies for success:

- A letter like this wins instant notice, especially if the position that's open is one requiring a good deal of creativity.
- Adapt the "Joe Friday" theme (or, better yet, one of your own invention) to your target position.
- Provide full contact information and a *brief* summary of your professional accomplishments after the "grabber" text.
- Your letter should not exceed one page.

#87: Get your book rejected.
Or:
While I have you on the line...

An editor at a major publishing house used this technique when trying to break into the industry; she apparently figured it would be easier to build relationships with people in her target organization if she called to inquire after the status of her book proposal rather than an employment application. It helped, of course, that the proposals she sent along were carefully assembled—and relatively well received, even though they did not result in the offer of a contract. In essence, they were extended resumes that gave her the opportunity to call the editors directly and discuss the publishing industry. One of the contacts she made in this way ended up helping her secure an interview that led to a full-time job. It took a while, but it was worth it in the end—and what was the worst thing that could have happened? A book contract might have come through!

Strategies for success:

- An interesting twist on the "how-can-I-build-up-my-contact-network" problem, but not one that you should expect to yield instant results.

- Beware: an amateurish proposal will not open any doors. Research your effort carefully; enlist the aid of professors or others with a strong writing background, and listen carefully to their assessments of your work.

- Don't pester people. Try sending your idea to a number of editors—and wait at least two weeks before following up by phone.

- For more advice on how to prepare a competitive book proposal for book publishers or magazine editors, see the annual *Writer's Market* (Writers Digest Books).

#88: Show off your eavesdropping skills.
Or:
I've got an ear for news.

Some years ago, a young woman who was eager to win a job as a reporter happened to recognize a newsman who walked into the restaurant she frequented. She took a seat at his table; after a few pleasantries, she started talking quietly about the private life of one of the restaurant's waitresses, whom she had never formally met. She described the woman's working hours, her companions after work, the interesting points of the relationship she was currently involved in and the home of the man she was seeing. The source of all the information? The budding journalist had stealthily followed the pair out of the building one night. The reporter, impressed with the display, arranged an interview for the woman with his editor; as a result, the eavesdropper won her first newspaper job.

Strategies for success:

- A straightforward, confident display of your abilities, whether asked for or not, may win you points with those who can help you win entry into the target organization. If you plan to use an approach like this, be sure to get all the details of your story down cold before you relate it.

- Respect the privacy rights of others.

- You may get the best results with this approach if you focus on gathering the details of a hard news story, rather than a restaurant romance. However, the point here is to display your diligence and inquisitiveness—not necessarily to offer a story that can be used by the publication you target. (But see #83 for an example of a more straightforward method.)

#89: Offer to do what the unions won't.
Or:
Adventures on the graveyard shift.

Sometimes, the best way to get started in a competitive field like broadcasting is to take on the work no one else wants to do. Consider the case of the New Yorker who figured out that union camera crews wouldn't film news events after midnight and before dawn...even though the news had a way of happening 24 hours a day. He'd set up his police band radio, listen for a call reporting a murder, fire, other newsworthy event, then toss his camera equipment into his car and speed over to the scene. After shooting the footage, he'd shop it around to the local news desks and network offices. Guess whose footage made it onto the national news?

Strategies for success:

- The point is not that you could do exactly the same thing; after all, union rules have been known to change over time. Whether or not you're an aspiring news photographer, the idea is to think "outside the lines" and come up with some opportunity to offer key people in your industry something valuable.

- In your field of choice, is there something that your competitors for key positions are not doing or are only doing during standard business hours? Find out what that is—and go above and beyond the call!

#90: Volunteer to help organize a charity event that will be attended by people in your target industry.

Or:

How to help two good causes at the same time.

Don, a freelance writer, used this approach to get a job offer from a large newspaper in his city. The benefit event was attended by some of the biggest names in local news; shortly after, one of the editors congratulated Don on the fine job he'd done organizing the party, Don mentioned that he'd applied for a job with the editor's paper through standard channels, but had gotten no response. A phone call for a formal interview came later that week.

Strategies for success:

- Warning: Charity and benefit events must be undertaken on their own merits. Any networking opportunities that arise indirectly are side benefits...even though they are benefits you should be aware of.

- Focus first and foremost on raising money for the organization or cause, and do a stellar job at everything related to the undertaking. Once all those pieces are in place, you can (and probably should) think about networking for employment purposes.

- Bear in mind that if a well-organized benefit can earn you brownie points with potential employers, a poorly organized one can—or one that appears to be fundamentally self-serving—damage your reputation.

#91: Write a letter with no return address.

Or:

One piece of paper, one legal-sized envelope—and a good helping of *chutzpah.*

That's the technique Dennis used to win a reporting position after he graduated from journalism school. The concise, straightforward letter featured a glowing quote from one of Dennis's professors, five concise statements of the advantages he felt he offered over any other candidates who might be for the job, a signature and a phone number. That was it—except for the P.S., which promised a call from Dennis. The editor was waiting by the phone when Dennis's call came.

Strategies for success:

- What's to reject? And anyway, even if someone wanted to issue a rejection letter, where could it go?

- Using this technique properly can help you talk directly to the people whose decisions can shape your career. Be respectful of their time.

- Don't be late—call when you say you will.

- Don't send one letter and hold your breath. Use this approach as part of a campaign that targets multiple prospective employers.

- Keep the letter short!

#92: **Write your resume in the form of a front page, complete with screaming headlines, graphics and stories about problems you've solved.**

Or:

They'll probably call you just to ask when you're sending along the comics.

This was used, as you might imagine, by someone who wanted to win a job with a newspaper. The story is mentioned in Bill Corbin's recent article in the *National Business Employment Weekly.*

Strategies for success:

- Interested in another field? You may want to adapt the idea to another written form (sending a mock "book" describing your background to a publisher, for instance).

- If you are applying for anything having to do with graphic arts or layout work, you will need to execute the design of the page with dazzling skill.

#93: **Doodle on a cocktail napkin when you meet the decision maker in a restaurant.**

Or:

Don't rest your drink on my masterpiece.

A recent story in *The Boston Globe* relates how a waitress who worked in a Harvard Square restaurant showcased her artistic talents for the producer of an animated television pilot by drawing on what was handy at the time. "She did the best cocktail-napkin drawings I'd ever seen," the producer told the *Globe.* The intrepid doodler was named to lead the team of artists developing the new cable cartoon series.

Strategies for success:

- Working at a restaurant—and less than thrilled about it? Don't bemoan your fate. Be alert, engaging and inquisitive in your contacts with customers, and be willing to show off your talents in your field of interest at the drop of a hat. Of chance encounters—and good people skills—are new careers made.

- For other examples of how service-industry encounters led to important career breaks, see #74, #81, #234 and #249.

#94: Learn to play a new instrument in two weeks.

Or:

You need a trumpeter? I'm a trumpeter.

In 1930, a musician learned that the trumpeter for a big New York bandleader had walked out on the group just a few weeks before a critical recording date. The musician, a saxophone player who had no professional experience on the trumpet, told the band leader he thought he could help out. By the time the studio date came around, he had found a trumpet, taught himself to play in just two weeks and won the job. (The story was mentioned in a recent article in *The Boston Globe*.)

Strategies for success:

- Saying "I can do that," and then following up by whatever means necessary, is a great way to get your foot in the door. (One of the people interviewed for this book described the secret for success in a given field as "never turning down work if you honestly believe you can do it and do it well.")

- Extending an existing skill, or developing an entirely new one, is probably not as difficult as you think. But commitment, perseverance and discipline will be essential components of any "crash course" that lands you the right job.

- Don't be afraid to enlist the aid of others who may be able to critique your efforts and point you in the right direction.

#95: Model your cover letter after a television advertisement.

Or:

You knew all those hours of watching Gilligan's Island would pay off someday.

"Tired of do-nothing employees who are more interested in making it out of the building by 5:01 than in helping you get results for your clients? Try new, fast-acting ME—and you'll see a difference!" That's the body text an aspiring salesperson used to present his resume to a local public relations firm. It worked!

Strategies for success:

- This approach will probably work best if you tie your "product pitch" to a key concern or fear of top management: Unproductive employees, dropping market share, advances by the competition and the like.

- Paralleling your product (you) with one of the company's products probably won't hurt your chances, either.

- Keep the tone light and humorous—and keep it short.

#96: Develop a press release about a recent company event.

Or:

News flash! I could be winning media coverage for you!

This was used by a job seeker in search of a public relations job. It's hard to think of a better, more eye-catching way to show the employer how you would perform on the job than offering a sample based on real-world events! The story is related in a recent article by Bill Corbin in the *National Business Employment Weekly*.

Strategies for success:

- This particular technique is primarily of interest to those applying for P.R. jobs—you can take the basic idea and extend it to your own field of interest.

- If you're interested in a marketing position, for instance, you could design a campaign for one of your target company's products.

#97: Mount an illustrated fax attack.

Or:

A picture may be worth a thousand cold calls.

Jack knew there was an opening that was just right for him at a local graphic design firm; he also knew the competition was fierce for the job. He found out the fax number of the decision maker, and sent strategically timed fax transmissions—each featuring only his drawings and a phone number—at various points in the week. He then called persistently until he reached his man—and won his assignment.

Strategies for success:

- "Mystery fax" transmissions are an increasingly popular contact technique, but be careful to include both the name and fax number of the person you're trying to reach. (Faxes are often misrouted and separated.)

- If you decide to withhold your name or other contact information, be sure to use some consistent graphic element that will tie all your transmissions together in the recipient's mind. Once you finally do get in touch with your contact, you can explain that you're the one who's been sending the faxes with the stars at the top and bottom (or whatever).

- Your best bet, though, is probably to include a telephone number at which you can be easily reached.

- See also #16, #32 and #143.

#98: **Send a "label" that describes you as an appealing product.**
Or:
It brightens, it whitens, it shows up for work on time.

The brightly colored label Dennis sent the software company instead of a resume read something like this: "Features: Attentive, hard-working programmer with five years of experience. Completed complex data-retrieval product development assignment with time to spare, 1991. Benefit: Knowledge of all major programming languages means reduced training time, less time debugging product. Endorsement: Cited as 'a superior, results-driven team player' in 1992 salary review." The "fine print" featured the applicant's name, address and telephone number and requested an interview. It worked!

Strategies for success:

- Don't be afraid to use vibrant, eye-catching color.
- Have friends or relatives proofread the final result carefully.
- If you can, use a verbatim quote praising you to the stars—and be sure the person who supplied it is willing to back you up during the interview process.
- Follow up as appropriate by phone.
- See also #51.

#99: **While performing another function full-time, start doing the job you want to win in your off hours.**

Or:

Boldly sketch out your future—then make it happen.

In 1977, Jeanne Boyland, who had had a lifelong interest in drawing but had no formal training, was hired as a criminal investigative assistant with the Multnomah County Sheriff's Department in Portland, Oregon. Part of her job: Interviewing the victims of violent crimes. As she told *People* magazine, "I started noticing that none of the details I'd gathered from them matched the drawing done by the police artist. I decided that trauma must affect a person's initial perceptions of a crime." On her own, she started sketching images of suspects based on a uniquely nonthreatening interview style she developed with the victims who came her way. By taking her time and starting out with questions that had nothing to do with the case at hand, Boyland was able to establish a level of personal rapport with her subjects. The technique got them to relax...and helped them provide more accurate descriptions. Although she is best known today for her identification of the suspect in the Polly Klaas kidnapping case in California, it was an amazingly accurate 1978 sketch of a gun-wielding robber known as the Waistband Bandit that persuaded her superiors in Portland to formally name Boyland to the job she had been doing on her own for some time.

Strategies for success:

- Sometimes, if you have a new idea to suggest or new viewpoint to offer, the best approach is simply to try it out and see what happens. Bear in mind, however, that neglecting your formal job duties is a major risk, especially if your supervisor is less than enthusiastic about your new initiative.

- In the end, results are what count. If you decide to mount a "preemptive strike" on the job you really want, be ready to quantify the results you achieve. You should be prepared to answer questions like: "How much money did you save the company by doing this?" (And if no one asks the question, you should take any appropriate opportunity to pose it yourself and provide the answer.)

#100: Zap alien invaders.
Or:
How to rack up 150,000 bonus points during a job interview.

At fifteen, Brian was the best on his block at destroying oncoming space monsters in Endgame, an ominous computer program featuring space viruses, loud explosions and occasional carnivorous aliens. His father suggested he contact the software company that manufactured the game (which was in the same state that Brian lived in) to show off his skills. They were impressed, and hired him as a customer service representative and new game tester. That's right: Brian got paid to play new games. Talk about a job that can hold a kid's attention!

Strategies for success:

- Think about something that is of intense interest to you. Can you contact the company that manufactures the product or provides the service directly and show off your skills?

- Don't be afraid to contact the president of the company directly, perhaps by using some of the direct-contact ideas outlined elsewhere in this book.

- For two stories that provide interesting parallels, see #114 and #201.

#101: Pour some coffee.
Or:
Mind if I pitch in?

Cassandra needed a waitressing job, and she needed it fast. She waited until the noon hour, then found a restaurant that was crowded with customers and short on staff. After being seated by a rather harried server, Cassandra stood up, walked across the room and started asking unattended customers if they wanted coffee. When she reached ones who did, she strode confidently behind the counter, took a coffee pot, cups and saucers, and started serving. It was a few moments before anyone on the staff even noticed that there was a nonemployee passing out menus, pouring coffee and wiping down empty tables. But no one complained. Finally, when Cassandra brought an order up to the cook, the manager asked her what she was doing. She explained that she had a lot of experience as a waitress, and that she'd decided to pitch in after she noticed that things seemed to be a little busy. She then confidently asked the manager whether any positions were open. He offered her a job and she accepted. Cassandra worked that evening's shift.

Strategies for success:

- A powerful technique, but you really have to know your way around a restaurant to make it work. The technique can probably be adapted without much difficulty for a position like dishwasher or bus person if you don't have significant restaurant experience, but you would definitely have to demonstrate, in an instant, that you can help to lower the chaos level rather than increase it. (As a matter of fact, Cassandra's approach could very likely be tailored to any number of service industry settings. It's an excellent way to get a job quickly, but you *must* be able to follow through on your strong first impression.)

- Don't try this if your aim is to secure a skilled managerial or executive position, or in any setting in which the public is not welcome on-site.

- Say something along the lines of, "It looked busy and I thought, given my background, I could help out."

- Never say, "How do I do this?" or any variation thereof. If you can't help make life easier for the restaurant staff, don't pitch in in that area. (If someone offers instructions, of course, that's an entirely different matter.)

- Executed with spirit and confidence, this method can be quite startlingly effective and can save you a lot of time. (This may be an important factor if you're looking for a "stopgap" job to tide you over while you continue a job search in a different field.) If this technique doesn't work at one place, don't be afraid to try it again somewhere else. Knowing what you're doing is essential, however. *Don't* try this if you have the slightest hesitation about making an instant positive contribution.

#102: Have a friend crash a company party, corner the director of human resources, and say, "Has Jim got an interview or not?"

Or:

One way to shorten the "yes-we're-reviewing-your-resume" period.

Jim, the retiring sort, was a little nervous about the idea, but his friend was quite enthusiastic. Shortly after his representative slid into the party and made her straightforward query, Jim got a call for the interview that led to his job offer.

Strategies for success:

- A nice alternative for those who are a little uneasy about high-profile "stunts."
- Be sure your friend understands that he or she is to be persistent on your behalf, but is not to use abusive, threatening or otherwise inappropriate language.

#103: Make a public spectacle of yourself by carrying a sign that proclaims you to be the "unemployee of the month."

Or:

You are your own ad.

In his excellent book *Guerilla P.R.*, Michael Levine tells the story of an out-of-work accountant in Los Angeles who, "tired of discouraging head-hunters and go-nowhere want-ads...strapped a sandwich board over his body and hit the streets of Beverly Hills. Emblazoned on his homemade billboard were the words 'Unemployed of the Month.'" By passing out his resume to interested parties, he landed a good job in a matter of days.

Strategies for success:

- High in *chutzpah,* low in risk, but you have to be willing to put in the shoe leather time.

- Your results will, in large measure, be dictated by "location, location, location."

- Part of the effect depends on the curiosity of passers-by about what, exactly, the sign *means.* If you've got a strong work record and a good explanation for your status, this technique can deliver results in short order.

- See also #45.

#104: Network while you park cars.
Or:
Keys to success.

Joe had a night job as a valet at a prestigious night spot. His generally gregarious manner made for easy, upbeat banter with the customers who entered the establishment. One evening, he struck up a pleasant conversation with an important real estate executive; Joe casually mentioned that he had always wanted to enter the field. Along with the keys to his car, the real estate executive gave Joe his business card and asked him to call for an interview. Within a month, Joe had won an entry-level position at the firm.

Strategies for success:

- Easy does it. If your current position affords you a large measure of exposure to the public, you can adapt this technique...as long as you don't come across as too aggressive.

- The best approach is to be optimistic, pleasant and genuinely interested in each customer you serve. If you appear to focus exclusively on "big fish" you'll run the risk of alienating your current employer.

- Don't exaggerate your background or your level of interest in a particular field.

- For an intriguing story that outlines an inventive way to make sure you're remembered by those whose cars you've parked, see #115.

#105: Wash out animal transport cages.
Or:
Scrub-a-dub-dub.

Offering to take on such "undesirable" jobs as scrubbing out dog cages is what got Brad, an eager new college graduate, his first job in the airline industry in record time. Brad also loaded cargo and mail bags before applying for, and winning, a customer-service job at the airline.

Strategies for success:

- Taking on less-than-popular jobs is a classic entry maneuver. Contact a key person, demonstrate your commitment to the company and the industry and show a good attitude. Repeat the process as necessary and you'll get your shot.

- Having offered to take on the least glamorous assignments, remember that you have no right to grumble. Do the job well without complaining.

- After an appropriate time, return to the person who hired you and ask politely (but pointedly) about further opportunities in the organization.

#106: Watch the foreman for three days.
Or:
The indirect approach...followed by the direct approach.

The managers at the construction company at which Jack wanted to work weren't hiring—or so they thought. When he showed up at the work site at the break of dawn with the other workers, and calmly watched the foreman from behind the chain-link fence, people simply assumed he was waiting to pick up someone who would be leaving early that day. But Jack kept his vigil up all morning, through lunch and on into quitting time. He repeated the waiting game all the next day, and the following day as well. Finally the foreman, who was getting a little tired of being stared at, left the job site, walked over to the other side of the fence and challenged Jack. "What are you doing snooping around here?" he demanded. "I'm not snooping," Jack replied. "I'm waiting to see how long it takes you to figure it out." "Figure what out?" demanded the foreman. "That you're getting screwed. So far, it's three days, and I'm curious to see how much longer it's going to take for you to wise up." "How do you figure I'm getting screwed?" the foreman asked. "Half the people here aren't doing anything when you turn your back," Jack replied. "I can out-frame any three guys here, and I'll carry my own wood while I do it. If you give me one day to prove it to you, you won't regret it." The foreman asked Jack to come back the next morning. At the end of the day, he took Jack on full-time—and fired three of the men who'd been working for him earlier in the week.

Strategies for success:

- A daring maneuver, but a dramatic one that can yield impressive results if you follow through on your promise. Be sure you are in a position to do so before you issue a challenge.

- Do not identify employees you consider to be taking advantage of the employer, even if you are pressed to do so by the prospective employer. Simply reiterate your confidence in your own abilities.

#107: When a telemarketer calls, demand to speak to the manager; turn the call into an on-the-spot job interview.

Or:

Just great, thanks—how are you doing this evening?

Brian, a freelance writer, was between assignments and in need of some part-time work. He hadn't considered returning to telemarketing (a field in which he'd done quite well a decade or so earlier) until he received a call from a firm that wanted him to consider buying aluminum siding for his home. Instead of issuing a polite "no thanks," he said he'd consider seeing a representative if he could speak to the sales rep's manager. A few moments later, when the manager came on the line, Brian outlined his past accomplishments, mentioned the kinds of hours he was looking for and asked if he could come by for an interview. The manager was impressed—and asked to see him immediately.

Strategies for success:

- Talk about setting yourself apart from the competition. The sheer audacity of this will certainly gain a high degree of initial interest from any self-respecting sales manager.

- The technique can be adapted to any number of selling environments.

- It should go without saying, of course, that your phone technique must be quite strong if you hope to pull this off.

#108: Quick—watch Spanish-language soap operas all day for a week.
Or:
Sure, I'm bilingual.

The software development company Angela worked for was about to go bankrupt. She decided to polish off her high school Spanish skills by checking out a cassette tape from the library—and tuning in the Spanish-language channel on her local cable system. A week later, with the basics of the language relatively secure again, she applied for a job as a customer service representative at a computer manufacturer. During the interview, she highlighted her ability to provide solutions for the firm's Spanish-speaking customers—and got the job offer. Continuous practice with the tapes (and regular viewings of the Spanish-language station's soap operas) helped her deliver the results she'd promised.

Strategies for success:

- Many employers are in dire need of workers with good Spanish. Demographic pressures are forcing them to hire quickly. If you can find a company where your other job skills may be a good match at some point down the road, you may find it easiest to get in the door by dusting off those old high school or college language textbooks.

- This approach is not recommended if you've never developed any facility with foreign languages. However, if you showed promise in another Romance language during your school years, you may want to try the crash-course in Spanish idea and see what happens.

- Don't go it alone. In addition to keeping up with the latest developments on your favorite soap opera, find a friend to practice with. You should feel quite secure in your language skills before you apply.

- Other languages in demand often include French and Vietnamese. Demand can vary radically by region.

#109: Call your list of prospective employers at 6:30 a.m.

Or:

Here comes the sun...

Anna wanted to work for a very specific type of firm—a nonprofit community arts organization within 75 miles of the city she lived in—but she was having trouble getting through to the decision makers who could help her win an entry-level job at the organizations she'd targeted. So she assembled her list of potential employers and began calling the numbers at the crack of dawn, on the theory that the only people who would be around before standard office hours would be the directors of the organizations. As you might expect, the majority of her calls went unanswered. But when someone did pick up the line, her theory proved resoundingly correct! (The same principle worked, she found, when she called after seven in the evening.) After a week or so, she'd reached nearly a dozen top-level decision makers, about half of whom were fascinated by her initiative and eager to talk to her about employment possibilities. She won a modest entry-level job offer (is there any other kind in the arts world?) and was on the job within a month of the day she'd begun her early-morning call routine.

Strategies for success:

- These days, Anna's inventive approach is likely to work in a hurry only at smaller organizations that don't have voice-mail systems.
- It can, however, be adapted to larger entities. A few of the job seekers interviewed for this book opined that calling between 11:30 a.m. and 1:30 p.m. is a great way to catch sandwich-munching workaholics at their desks, free for an hour or so of their gatekeepers.
- You may also wish to experiment with the idea of leaving creative messages on a company's voice mail system.
- See also #49 and #285.

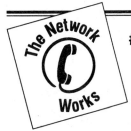

#110: Find out what an instructor is doing over the summer and get an instant recommendation to work at the same place.

Or:

The semester was so great, we really ought to work together.

Karen's high-school English teacher had a summer position as a restaurant manager; when Karen asked for a recommendation, her instructor was happy to provide it. Karen's summer job turned into a full-time management job within the restaurant, which encourages its summer employees (many of whom are teachers) to refer qualified applicants.

Strategies for success:

- Many high school and college students never think of networking with their own instructors about employment opportunities, but a good many teachers hold down jobs during the summer at companies that are eager to recruit promising new employees.
- This technique is ideally suited to finding a good summer job in short order, but the possibility for long-term employment through this method is also worth exploring.

- The instructor you approach should be one who knows your work well and will speak highly of you. Do not approach an instructor with whom you would be uncomfortable working; you may well be reporting to this person!

#111: List your CB handle on your resume.
Or:
Big Bad Wolf, when can you start?

How it really worked: More than one trucker, sources attest, has received a job offer over the airwaves by circulating a nickname in this way. Apparently, this method can speed up the interview process quite a bit.

Strategies for success:

- The idea is of interest primarily to people in the trucking industry.

- If you try it, be sure you know the customs and language of the medium. People who aren't familiar with CB terminology, but chatter away on the radio anyway, are easily recognized as rookies—and avoided.

#112: Show up at the crack of dawn and pitch in without being asked.
Or:
I'm with what's-his-name.

Charlie, 17, was in need of a summer job—and just a little bit jealous that Tom, his high school buddy, had picked up some work at a local dairy. On a dare from Tom, he simply showed up at the dairy at the crack of dawn one morning and started in helping out with the task at hand: Pitching bales of hay into a truck. About an hour into the job, the dairy owner walked over and asked him what he was doing. "I'm with Tom," Charlie answered. "With

Tom, huh?" the owner mused. "Am I supposed to pay you like I do Tom?" he asked Charlie. "Yes, sir," said Charlie. "Okay, then," said the owner, who smiled, nodded and walked away.

Strategies for success:

- Admittedly, this takes a good deal of courage, a willingness to be thrown off the site if things don't work out and the ability to impress the employer with your abilities almost immediately. If those prerequisites are in place, you may want to give something like this a try.

- Friendly reminder: If you are asked to leave someone's private property, you should do so. If you don't, you'll risk some unpleasant legal episodes.

#113: Bring a clip-on bow-tie.
Or:
You've got customers waiting, so why are we wasting time talking?

One enterprising waiter, who knew what it took to get work in a hurry, would always dress in black slacks, black shoes and a white dress shirt for his meetings with restaurant managers. After describing his background, the employers would usually ask him about his schedule. That's when he'd whip out the bow-tie he kept in his pocket, snap it on and inform the prospective employer that he could start immediately. The story appears in Lishka DeVoss's excellent book, *How to Be a Professional Waiter (or Waitress)*.

Strategies for success:

- A direct, dramatic approach that's likely to earn big points with prospective employers in the restaurant field.

- If you don't have restaurant experience, you can use the same technique in applying for busperson work, as a prelude to waiter or waitress employment.

#114: Go to the auto dealership from which you bought a car you love and demand a sales job.

Or:

How to turn a love affair with a car into a paying gig.

Passion makes a difference: An out-of-work musician, in love with the foreign car he'd recently purchased, decided to return to the dealership from which he'd bought it. He asked to see the sales manager and, appealing to his love for the vehicle he'd driven out of the showroom, drove himself back in again as a salesperson. Management didn't regret the decision; the new guy immediately made salesperson of the month. The story appeared recently in *The Boston Globe.*

Strategies for success:

- Part of the reason this worked was that the applicant had an abiding passion for the car he'd bought at the dealership—and it showed. Maybe you feel the same way about your car; then again, maybe your passion is for some other product or service. Appealing to the company behind the thing you love as a happy, enthusiastic and *knowledgeable* customer can put you at the head of the employment line.

- Research the company and its products!

- For some more interesting consumer-turned-employee stories, see #100 and #201.

#115: Leave a flower—and your card—in someone's car.
Or:
An air of confidence.

A freelance auto detailer, Vince found that the best way to win new assignments was to leave a single rose on the dashboard of a car he had just brought to a shimmering finish. Next to the rose was his business card. He got dozens of referrals through this method.

Strategies for success:

- An intriguing method that could probably be adapted successfully by anyone who handles others' cars. If you work (or can find work!) in a strategically situated parking lot, you may be able to reach top decision makers in your industry by appropriating Vince's technique.

- Leave a flower and a brief summary of your qualifications on the dashboard—but beware. You should undertake your campaign discreetly, preferably when you're working on your own. Supervisors may well frown on such activities.

- Red roses symbolize love, and you're not interested in personal issues here. Pick another color. (If you're planning a large-scale campaign, the economics of the floral industry may dictate the selection of, say, carnations.)

- See also #104.

#116: Walk into the kitchen of every restaurant in the area, offering to demonstrate a particularly tricky recipe.
Or:
Trust me, it'll be delicious.

This did the trick for a chef who found himself stranded in a foreign country, nearly broke and facing an impressive language barrier. Further evidence that confidence is the universal language of job seekers. The story appeared recently in *The Boston Globe.*

Strategies for success:

• If it burns, you can always call it "blackened cheesecake."

#117: Be the first in line—even if it means bringing a sleeping bag the night before.
Or:
Visions of job offers dance in your head.

This made quite an impression on the hiring officials at the hotel where Alice, an applicant for a front-desk job, camped out. If it were *your* call, wouldn't you try to find a way to say yes to someone who showed that kind of initiative?

Strategies for success:

• This is an excellent way to stand out from the crowd when a new local employer is opening its doors. The trick, of course, is learning when the doors will open for hiring purposes—intelligence you may be able to gather by calling the management directly.

• Bring a good book, a warm set of clothes and plenty of snacks.

• Plead your case earnestly and with hopeful, fawnlike eyes to any law enforcement or security officials who question your presence.

#118: Cut a puzzle piece-shaped hole in your resume.
Or:
Something's missing here.

Prepare your resume so you can cut a hole through the center without eliminating any text. After you cut the hole in the resume, reproduce the outline of the same shape on your cover letter—filled in with solid black. Don't cover any text—put the text around it. The administrative applicant who used this led off her cover letter with a clever line about fitting in perfectly in the organization. The story appeared in a fascinating Bill Corbin article in the *National Business Employment Weekly.*

Strategies for success:

- A cute idea that will certainly get your application noticed. As with all such visually inventive ideas, you must follow through and give specific examples proving your ability to contribute to the organization.

- Be prepared to summarize your background and the ways you could make a contribution for the target organization at a moment's notice. This approach is likely to lead to a phone call inquiring after your candidacy. You must be ready to make the most of it.

- Multiple variations on the "puzzle-piece" technique arose during the research for this book. See also #137 and #148.

#119: "Apply" while you're in high school, then follow up appropriately years later.
Or:
Remember me?

A recent article in *The Milwaukee Journal Sentinel* describes the determined career path of Ed Welburn, the first black auto designer ever hired at

General Motors. While still a teenager, Welburn wrote GM, asking what specific steps he should take to become a designer at the company. The answer he got back outlined the education he'd need; years later, having following the advice he got, he applied for the job...and got it. Do you think that early letter sent any messages to those doing the hiring about Welburn's level of commitment to the job?

Strategies for success:

- No, you don't have to be a teenager to make something like this pay off. Why not contact your top-of-the-list target company directly now and ask exactly what additional skills or training would be required for you to win the position you're after?

- Keep your query brief and to the point, preferably no longer than a single page. *Do not* submit a resume. (Your letter will probably be "filed" with all the other applications if you do.)

- The heart of your letter should be a 20- to 30-word summary of your background.

- Conclude with a direct question to a specific person (for example, the president of the firm): "What additional training or skills would I need to develop in order to become a (blank) at your firm—and how would you suggest I go about doing this?"

- Keep a copy of the letter you send and the reply you receive.

- If you decide to follow the advice you get, make your letter and the response you received part of your formal application. (Ideally, you should apply to the person to whom you originally wrote the letter.)

#120: In your cover letter, acknowledge that the person wading through the pile of resumes probably needs an aspirin.
Or:
Let me open that bottle for you.

"You must have a headache going through these mountains of resumes. It sounds as if you're in need of the kind of quick relief only a seasoned problem-solver can provide." So began Mel's cover letter to a pharmaceutical company! Not surprisingly, it won the interest of the person whose job it was to sort through the dozens of resumes resulting from an ad in the Sunday paper. The company hired him. (Special thanks to Mel Kinnear for this contribution.)

Strategies for success:

- Don't go overboard. Keep the cover letter brief.
- Note how Mel tied the "hook" (pain relief thanks to superior employee performance) into the company's specialty (pharmaceuticals). Cute, huh?
- The "you-must-have-a-headache" line might work in any number of industries, but it's particularly appropriate here because it's directly targeted to the employer.
- Can you develop a similarly compelling line that highlights your target employer's product or service?

#121: **Include a box of cereal along with your resume.**

Or:

Pat, please schedule this one for an interview on Thursday...and ask her to bring a half gallon of milk, a bowl and a spoon.

This idea was used with good effect by someone who wanted to win a job in the broadcasting field, but the general concept can be adapted to other industries. In this case, the applicant used the brand name of the cereal to emphasize a strong suit of his candidacy.

Strategies for success:

- As long as you use the trick to support an important message for the prospective employer, this may be worth a try. The cereal you select should probably highlight, in a humorous way, a major advantage that your background provides over those of competing candidates. Alternatively, you might decide to use the brand of cereal to reinforce a theme you establish in your cover letter.

- You might decide, for instance, to send a small box of Rice Krispies along with a cover letter applying for a job as a sound engineer, along with a promise that, if the employer hires you, the cereal represents the only snaps, crackles and pops he'll hear.

- Keep it clean; don't send letters with off-color or sexist implications.

#122: Use your cover letter to describe, briefly, your life philosophy.

Or:

Make a big point, you'll be running the joint.

The letter Mel used to win a high-level sales job wasted no time in passing along its message: "My goal in life is to help people enjoy themselves and fulfill unmet needs—and to have some fun and turn a profit for myself and my company at the same time. I have 12 years of experience in sales; I'm in the business of helping people solve problems. When can we get together?" (Special thanks to Mel Kinnear for passing along this contribution.)

Strategies for success:

- Be sure the note is legible and neat.
- Do not exceed one page in length.
- Do not ramble! Keep the message concise and focused on core values of interest in a business setting.
- Do not bring up religious issues.
- Follow up as appropriate by phone.

#123: During regular visits to the workplace of your prospective employer, good-naturedly order the decision maker to hire you.

Or:

Smile, issue simple instructions, smile, issue simple instructions, smile, issue simple instructions, etcetera.

A recent article in *The Boston Globe* describes how Boston disc jockey Dale Dorman used the power of sustained, purposeful loitering to get a job at a promising new outfit, WXKS-FM (now a powerhouse station in the region). "I used to come over and visit and hang out, and kept saying, 'Just hire me,'" Dorman told *The Boston Globe*. After a while, the general manager apparently got tired of the routine—and decided to break it by hiring Dorman to fill a temporary gap in the station schedule. He stuck around for the next decade and a half.

Strategies for success:

- Dorman was a known entity in the Boston market, and thus had relatively easy access to key people at the station. For some intriguing variations, see #6 and #66.

#124: Send a distinctive purple resume with a bold black border.

Or:

Born to be wild.

It was a striking two-toned number, in a matching light purple envelope, the resume that Joe sent along for the editorial assistant position he wanted. In so doing, he ignored the advice passed along by countless job-search guides, which implore their readers to select white, cream, beige, or similarly sedate colors for resumes. But the version that Joe sent along to a local publisher was the one did the trick. He believes this had something to do with his decision to target the resume as closely as he could to the requirements of the particular position he was after, but he feels the color selection probably helped, too. Purple is hard to miss, after all. Message: every little bit helps.

Strategies for success:

- Day-glo or screaming yellow, no. Intriguing pastel, yes. Your aim is to stand out from the crowd without coming across as unprofessional.

- Ready for a surprise? A recent Chicago *Tribune* article (July 3, 1994) cited a study by Bill Potter, vice president of A Better Resume Service; Potter tracked over 10,000 resumes and found that the textbook white or beige resumes, praised for years for their ability to project professionalism, actually put the average job seeker at a statistical *disadvantage*. Resumes that used color intelligently, without hurting the eyes of hiring managers, were less likely to be ignored. (The exception: traditionally conservative fields of employment like banking and medicine, where resumes printed on neutrally colored paper performed best.)

- Warning: An eye-catching resume that features solid, specific information of direct interest to the particular employer reading it, will probably get results for you—but an eye-catching resume filled to the brim with generalities and unsupported claims won't.

- Once the hiring manager has stopped to read your resume you must provide immediate and compelling evidence of your ability to contribute to *that particular company in a particular position*. The more specifically you address the prospective employer's concerns, the better off you'll be.

- Beware of exotic typefaces, and of using more than one face on your resume. You don't want to confuse the computer scanners that are becoming an increasingly common element of the employment process these days. See #151 for more details.

#125: **Enclose a page of baseball trivia with your summary of professional achievements.**

Or:

Next year in Fenway.

The chatty, engaging page of trivia was the writing sample enclosed by a canny applicant who knew that the person who would review his package was, like him, a huge baseball fan. The inventive approach resulted in a freelance assignment.

Strategies for success:

- Research is the key here. Whether it's through an article in an industry trade magazine, a chance remark by a receptionist or a question you pose to someone who used to work at the target company, you need to find out what gets the person you're addressing excited.

- If the decision maker's passion turns out to be golf, send along something golf-related. If she happens to be a needlework aficionado, send something related to that interest.

- Good research on your decision maker can make all the difference!

#126: **In your cover letter, politely request that the prospective employer not throw your materials away.**

Or:

Emily Post to the rescue.

"Please don't throw this letter away," the headline Alice's cover letter read. "It's here to help you." The body text briefly described her personal philosophy—which had to do with helping other people attain their goals in a professional setting—and tactfully suggested that her commitment to this idea would make her a better employee than the other applicants in the stack. A targeted resume accompanied the letter. This brief, confident appeal did the trick.

Strategies for success:
- Keep it short!
- Make your case quietly and with confidence, then let a resume focused specifically on the needs of the employer for *this position* do the rest of the talking.
- Follow up appropriately by phone. It's a good bet you'll be remembered.

#127: Ask to meet with the president so you can interview him or her for a hot story.
Or:
Yes, that's right; I want to interview you, so I can submit the interview to you, so you can interview me.

Kate founded her own newsletter and circulated it privately among friends and professional associates. She then contacted top people at her target companies and asked for a meeting—not to *be* interviewed, but to interview *them* for her newsletter. Some of the sessions that resulted were in-person discussions, others were conducted over the phone. During the course of each interview, Kate displayed her knowledge of her target industry...and of each of the companies she profiled. She made a point, of course, of passing along copies of her newsletter to all those she met with, and within a month or two she got a job offer from one of her interview participants.

Strategies for success:
- For this to work, you must follow three important rules.
- Rule one: Deliver a quality product. Your newsletter must look sharp, must deal with breaking trends and developments of interest to professionals in your industry and must be well written.

- Rule two: Never ask for a job. You're trying to distinguish yourself from the rest of the crowd by appealing to the decision maker (typically, the head of the target company) as if he or she were a *newsmaker,* not a potential employer.

- Rule three: Be patient.

- See also, for comparison, #141.

#128: Post a color picture of your smiling face on the Internet.

Or:

Flash your pearly whites in cyberspace.

Washington-based Employment Transition Services Group offers a high-profile way to get your resume onto the World Wide Web—and the firm has made plenty of job seekers happy in the process. Using ETSG's Web Resume 2000 site, you can post your resume, complete with a color photo of you at your most charming, for thousands of employers to review. You can also integrate key phrases from your background into the Web's hypertext search-and-retrieve system, so that anyone prowling the Web in search of the phrase "IBM," say, or "graphic design," will, if you've highlighted those phrases, summon up your little electronic billboard. Worth an e-mail query? Sure it is. Zap off a letter to ETSG at *etsg@id1.com* and get all the details.

Strategies for success:

- For advice on preparing an electronic resume, see #151.

- Successful Internet-related job search stories took many forms. See #21, #26, #35, #136, #142, #151 and #252.

- Say "cheese"!

#129: Take over a public-school library.
Or:
Sure I'm authorized; I'm a parent.

Anne invented a volunteer library position at the school her daughter was attending—and turned it into a full-time position. It only took a month, but then, given the zeal with which she attacked the library's dusty, disorganized stacks, it would have been surprising if school officials *hadn't* given her a job.

Strategies for success:

- Parents may have an "automatic in" when it comes to being assigned (or simply starting in on) such volunteer assignments.

- Bear in mind that school budgets are sometimes stretched fairly thin. If you are targeting your volunteer efforts toward a specific position you want to be offered, you'll probably want to make a few inquiries about the school district's finances.

- Private schools may be more likely to turn powerhouse volunteer workers into staff members.

- Ideas based on some form of volunteer work took many forms, and were among the most popular techniques encountered during the research for this book. See #1, #10, #58, #82, #140, #154, #251 and #292.

#130: Feature the logos of the companies for which you've worked along the left-hand margin of your resume.

Or:

If people think in pictures, why are resumes always crowded with words?

This inventive approach comes courtesy of David Opton at Execunet. The visually arresting technique was an instant success for the consultant who used it to re-enter the corporate world. Each logo served to introduce a brief summary of the work he'd done for the company in question.

Strategies for success:

- This is a powerful idea even if the logos of the firms you've been associated with are not widely recognized. Let's face it: Most resumes are so visually boring that it doesn't take much to stand out!

- Don't exaggerate your work record by including high-profile companies to whom you had only a vague connection! Stick with firms you've helped to achieve tangible results.

- Ask the companies you plan to highlight to supply brochures, company reports or other materials bearing the graphics you need.

- Or check in at your local library for books, articles or financial reports related to the company. Photocopy the logos on the library's copying equipment. (If you have access to some of the more sophisticated software and computer equipment out there, you may be able to scan the images directly onto your resume's main document file.)

- Be sure the various logos are reproduced at similar sizes, and that they support, but do not overwhelm, your text.

#131: Write a fiery letter to the editor.
Or:
To whom it may concern...

In 1885, in response to a fatuous column entitled "What Girls Are Good For" that held forth on the proper sphere of the members of the female sex, an irate reader of the *Pittsburgh Dispatch* set down a long, indignant letter and mailed it off to the paper. The managing editor was impressed enough with the author's impassioned sentiments (if not her style, which was a little rough) to ask her in for an interview. The young woman, Elizabeth Cochrane, won a reporting job with the *Dispatch*—and became famous as the daredevil and crusading social-issues reporter Nellie Bly.

Strategies for success:

- Although Cochrane's letter did the trick in short order, this should probably be pursued as an ongoing component of a balanced campaign that features other strategies.

- With persistent effort and a good writing style, you may be able to gain notice through the letters section or the "guest column" space featured by many papers. (But note that, in general, shorter letters are more likely to be published in the "To the Editor" section than longer ones.)

- E-mail alert: These days, many mid-sized and larger papers feature an electronic mail address that speeds up the submission process somewhat.

- Do it to keep up your writing practice and because you feel strongly about the issues you are writing about. If you are determined to use this forum as a platform for impressing editors, be prepared to keep it up for a long period of time and to make the letters you send immediately recognizable as your own.

- Published work of any kind can help you impress prospective employers, so the technique may be worth considering as part of a campaign to break into an industry other than journalism.

#132: Set up your resume in the form of a pyramid.

Or:

How to get big attention with little type.

One job-searching executive was determined to get his resume to look a little different from the run-of-the-mill document. He got the results—and the interest—he wanted by stacking his professional accomplishments in a "text pyramid," with the longest line of text at the bottom, and the shortest (only a few words) at the top! Contact information, educational background, and other supporting material was included at the bottom of the sheet in a standard paragraph.

Strategies for success:

- This one takes a little tinkering, of course, since the brief top line must relay a knockout piece of "grabber" information likely to encourage the prospective employer to read on.

- Bear in mind that the resumes that get the best results are the ones that *directly* address the concerns of a particular employer and/or *specifically* summarize parallels between your background and the requirements of the position. Even a cool piece of graphic setup, such as the "skill pyramid" described here, will be relegated to the circular file if it does not deliver a compelling case for your candidacy for *this job at this employer*.

- Be prepared for a phone call. Your unorthodox resume may result in a "better-check-this-out" screening call from the employer. Make the most of this opportunity to make your case directly to the prospective employer; memorize and be ready to recite a number of compelling anecdotes illustrating contributions you made at a previous job.

#133: Submit a college paper describing a new profit center in the target company's industry.
Or:
Profits, anyone?

A recent article in the *Boston Business Journal* describes how Kenneth Leibler, formerly the youngest president of the American Stock Exchange, and eventually the president and CEO of Boston's Liberty Financial Companies, once wrote a college paper on an underexamined market topic: options. The research project won him his first job. "It gave me visibility," Leibler told the *Journal*. "It was an unusual opportunity for someone in their 20s to be an expert on something." By way of explanation, options allow investors the right to buy or sell a security at a certain future date and price. Options, in other words, allow bets on a stock commodity's or index's price movements; they can serve as hedges against undesirable price swings. Back in 1971, when Leibler was a senior in college, options deals were over-the-counter affairs, agreements between individual buyers and sellers. In his paper, Leibler examined the notion that options, like stocks, could be traded on a public exchange. (The idea had been circulating elsewhere in the securities industry at around the same time.) Thanks to the superior work in his paper, Leibler got a job offer from the former Abraham & Co. and was assigned to launch an options department within the conservative securities firm. A career was underway.

Strategies for success:

- Choosing a topic of undeniable competitive interest to a prospective employer as a research topic is a great way to enhance your marketability. The topic you choose will, of course, depend on your knowledge of current industry trends. Because professors are often behind the curve on the latest developments in your target industry, you will do yourself a favor if you follow industry trade magazines closely.

- Don't be afraid to enroll in or audit a community college course for the express purpose of developing such a research project.

- Looking to make a splash? Send the paper directly to the head of your target company, then follow up by phone.
- For an interesting variation, in which the target company itself is the topic of a research paper, see #141.

#134: Send a page of rave reviews.
Or:
Two thumbs up!

The colorful flyer that Trina enclosed with her resume featured endorsements from former employers, colleagues and clients. She'd laid out the page as though it were a movie advertisement, highlighting key words from the quotes and using a headline that described her as "A Real Blockbuster!" She credits the piece for winning her an offer in the public relations field.

Strategies for success:
- If you can work with your quote sources to develop the right quotes, you may be able to get them to provide endorsements that use show-biz terminology.
- Do not fabricate endorsements.
- Presentation counts: Use a good desktop publishing or top-level word processing program to assemble the flyer.

#135: Offer to sweep up the joint.
Or:
Brushes with greatness.

One western publishing magnate reportedly broke into the newspaper business as a teenager by taking on janitorial work at a small rural paper. Writing and reporting for the publication only came later.

Strategies for success:

- Starting on the ground floor (so to speak) has a pretty good track record for those eager to gain entry to a particular organization and learn all they can. You may want to consider such an approach even if you don't fall into the "earnest young rookie" category.

#136: Find a travel-related reason to surf the Internet—and build your contact base.
Or:
On the move.

James was surfing the Internet for a reason—he was planning a summer trip to the Orient and he wanted to get information on the best ways to get along on a tight budget during his trip. As it happened, however, he was also in the job market, and was eager to set up some kind of employment upon his return to the U.S. in the fall. After asking for advice on hotels and restaurants that wouldn't clean out his savings he, having struck up acquaintances with his fellow travelers, briefly mentioned his professional background and ambitions. By the time he left for Japan in June, he had arranged the job he needed in September.

Strategies for success:

- The hundreds upon hundreds of special-interest bulletin boards on the Internet provide a remarkable opportunity for networking—as long as you play by the rules and learn the protocols of the various boards before you start chatting aimlessly.

- You will get the best results from the boards if you take a day or two to read some of the postings left by long-time participants. That way, you can get an idea of the kinds of issues discussed—and the kinds of problems usually solved in the group you're examining.

- This technique, which requires you to gain entry into the group by posting a valid, on-topic query, will allow you to develop a good many private e-mail relationships with group members. It's a good way to build up contacts, and if you pick the right bulletin board, it can point you toward particular segments of the professional community you're trying to enter.

- Successful Internet-related job search stories took many forms. See #21, #26, #35, #128, #142, #151 and #252.

- For a full rundown on the ins and outs of Internet newsgroups, see John R. Levine and Carol Baroudi's excellent *The Internet for Dummies* (IDG Books, 1993).

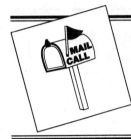

#137: Cut up your resume as though it were a jigsaw puzzle.
Or:
Putting it all together.

A job-seeking design professional took this innovative approach. There's no reason the idea couldn't be adapted to other fields, however. The story is recounted in Bill Corbin's recent article in the *National Business Employment Weekly.*

Strategies for success:

- Feeling brave? Send the puzzle in a box, unassembled, with a label identifying it as your resume. (But don't make the puzzle too complicated! Four to six pieces will suffice.)

- Mount the pieces on stiff cardboard. Be sure they are easy to assemble.

- Your cover letter should offer your contact information and some brief tie-in to the gimmick, along the lines of "Here's an applicant who puts it all together!"

- Be ready for a telephone call from the person to whom you send this. Having piqued the prospective employer's interest, you must be able to capitalize on that interest by briefly relaying success stories and some specific ways you can make a contribution to the target organization.

- Be sure you send all the pieces!

- Multiple variations on the "puzzle-piece" technique arose during the research for this book, which may mean that it is worth reviewing closely. See also #118 and #148.

#138: During a stint as a cab driver, tell every fare you pick up that you're interested in breaking into your target industry.
Or:

I know this is where you wanted to be let off, but let's circle around the park once more while I tell you what I did on my last job.

Trent, who was working part-time for a local taxi company, used this technique to break into the financial services industry; one of his fares was intrigued about his background and asked to see a paper Trent had written on credit issues. A freelance assignment with the fare's organization, a top company in its field, followed.

Strategies for success:

- To put this approach into overdrive, be sure you take full advantage of any trade gatherings or industry conventions connected to your target industry. A day of driving to and from a convention center could put you face-to-face with more decision makers than you'll know what to do with.

- Best bet: Use this approach in concert with the "resume-on-a-business-card" idea. See #186.

- For a parallel story, see #207.

#139: Submit a detailed written outline of your job search battle plan as part of your employment application.

Or:

Now, imagine what I might do with a project you assign.

John Caple's book, *Finding the Hat that Fits* (Plume, 1993) tells the story of a job seeker named Jamie who created a customized personal business plan for himself that he submitted to top-level people in real estate, his target industry. The plan included a personal mission statement, a series of strategies for obtaining key goals (each bolstered by specific references to important experiences and educational attainments in Jamie's background) and a final summary of the approach he planned to use to reach his goal of excelling at commercial real estate sales: "Contact Real Estate Leaders." This part of the plan gave a brief overview of the *very job search campaign it represented.* Jamie sent over 100 of the plans to key people in the real estate industries. He was called to nearly two dozen interviews, and finally got the right position.

Strategies for success:

- Bear in mind that company presidents and other top-level people like to meet with people who know what they want. By incorporating a plan like Jamie's you can make that principle work for you.

- The plan you send along can (and probably should) take up five or six pages—but it must be well organized, free of typographical errors and written in a concise, compelling fashion. Enlist the help of a friend or family member; have him or her review the plan closely before you send it to anyone on your list.

- Don't be afraid to send the plan to the top person in the organization—and to follow up by telephone.

#140: Volunteer to take some abuse.
Or:
Mission—Impossible.

Lynne, a teacher who wanted to win a job with a nationally known reha-bilitation center, decided to get a foot in the door the hard way—by taking on the toughest assignment she could find at no pay. The head of the school had no instructor to handle a group of students with behavioral problems, and no budget to pay anyone to handle them, either. Lynne took on part-time teaching duties with this exceptionally difficult group for a full semester and didn't receive a penny for her efforts. As anyone who has worked with emo-tionally disturbed kids can attest, the job of teaching them is among the most difficult on the books. Instructors are routinely insulted, threatened, ignored and even, on occasion, attacked! But Lynne did a marvelous job, and after the semester ended, the head of the school promised there would be a full-time position waiting for her at the beginning of the next fiscal year. He kept his word.

Strategies for success:

- Know what you're getting into. Taking on an exceptionally difficult assignment is a great way to get in the door, but it's also a great way to mount a high-profile disaster.

- Before accepting anything approaching the difficulty of the assign-ment Lynne took on, you should probably sit down with two or three experienced professionals in the field and get their advice on how best to approach the task.

- During the assignment, appeal to your "mentors" from time to time for advice on how best to get past the hurdles you face.

- Ideas based on some form of volunteer work took many forms, and were among the most popular techniques encountered during the research for this book. See #1, #10, #58, #82, #129, #154, #251 and #292.

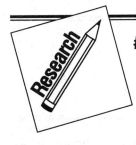

#141: Do your senior research project on the company you'd like to work for, then submit the paper as part of your application after graduation.
Or:
You don't want me to flunk out, do you?

Dianne chose to focus on a fast-growing chemical company for her big senior project for two reasons. The first was that it fit her instructor's requirements for the course. The second was that she wanted a job at the firm. The paper provided an excellent excuse to contact key people at the firm, and when she submitted the 50-page profile as part of her employment application, she impressed everyone. She got a job offer with the firm only a month after graduation.

Strategies for success:

- You say you're not in school? Don't let that stop you from using this inventive, impressive technique. Enroll in a local community college course—or audit one at no cost—and find a way to focus your classroom efforts on a research project relating to your target company.
- Don't be afraid to start at the top. Call the president's office and ask for permission to interview him or her for the project. You may be pleasantly surprised with the response.
- See also #127.

#142: Check out the weirder Internet boards.
Or:
Adventures on the fringes of cyberspace.

Some of the most rewarding friendships established on the information superhighway begin with notes posted on the truly outlandish newsgroups. These include *alt.bizarre* (strangeness for its own sake), *alt.barney.die.die.die* (for those less than enamored of the Purple One) *alt.buddha.short.fat.guy* (Buddhist news and views) *alt.sex* (take a guess) and *alt.paranormal* (UFOs, crop circles, out-of-body experiences and the like). An online job search campaign that incorporates a true full-court press will incorporate occasional visits to these unusual sites—and benefit from a quick, convenient and fascinating way to expand a contact network. One woman in England got her first on-screen film job as a result of a contact she made through a correspondence that developed on *alt.bizarre*—and no, it didn't involve doing anything lewd. The shoot involved filling in the gaps in an incomplete sequence of an already existing film, the kind of work that's probably more difficult to track down than other acting jobs.

Strategies for success:

- There are literally hundreds of interest groups, with contributors from all over the world. Take your pick of five or six that seem genuinely interesting to you—and then see who you can meet.

- Avoid rookie mistakes. Read the postings on the boards for a while before posting something yourself. (Some residents of cyberspace tend to be rather harsh to obvious newcomers.)

- Each note will usually feature the writer's personal e-mail address; if you prefer, you can respond privately. On non-employment-related newsgroups, you may wish to hold off outlining your employment aspirations until you've exchanged a few notes and developed a good rapport.

- Consider posting to boards with a local angle, or asking for correspondence from those in your area.

- This is a good *supplemental* contact-builder. Beware of spending too much valuable time (or money!) discussing aliens or Brady Bunch trivia in the name of your job search.

- Successful Internet-related job search stories took many forms. See #21, #26, #35, #128, #136, #151 and #252.

- For a full rundown on the ins and outs of Internet newsgroups, see John R. Levine and Carol Baroudi's excellent *The Internet for Dummies* (IDG Books, 1993).

#143: Fax an idea for a radically different approach on a current company project.
Or:
Care for a little free advice?

Carl tried this after hearing from a friend about a series of seminars being planned by a consulting group—a firm Carl wanted to work with. He felt the seminars were targeted to the wrong audience, so he set up a brief letter to the president of the firm that said so and asked for the opportunity to work with the company. The week after he faxed the letter, the president of the company called and asked to meet with him. He got an employment offer shortly thereafter.

Strategies for success:

- Don't try this unless you know what you're talking about! A strong background in the industry, as well as good knowledge about exactly what your target employer is up to, is essential.

- For other inventive ideas on ways to make that great business communication equalizer, the fax machine, work for you, see #16, #32 and #97.

- For a parallel idea in which you save the advice for a face-to-face interview, see #286.

#144: Try a nervy cover letter.
Or:
A lesson in the power of confidence.

Eileen's cover letter got right to the point: "I am the only person you need for this opening. I don't care how many other letters are in the stack. Call me at (number) and I'll give you the details." What's not to like? She had targeted her resume directly to the position for which she was applying. When she got the call, the prospective employer told her, "After that letter, I just had to meet you in person." Not long afterwards, she got the job she was after. (Special thanks to counselor Tony Dias for this contribution.)

Strategies for success:

- Sure, this letter is a persuasive piece of personal salesmanship, and you'd definitely have to be pretty jaded not to be even a *little* curious about who'd be behind such a letter. But winning an interview with this gambit will depend on superior phone technique.

#145: Schedule a company representative for a "career day" at the school at which you teach—then use the contact yourself.
Or:
Listen, while you're here...

Betty was getting a little restless with her job as a teacher and was eager for new challenges. She'd invited a company representative from a major telecommunications firm to speak to her seventh-graders about opportunities in the high-tech field; after he'd visited her classroom, made his presentation, and answered some questions from the students, she made a point of talking with him. The fellow was impressed with Betty's college background and supplied her with the names of some people in the company to contact about a marketing position. Some time later, she got a lead that eventually resulted in an interview with the company—and a job.

Strategies for success:

- Teachers—including those who handle teaching duties on a volunteer basis for local community groups—are in an excellent position to schedule these types of meetings. The beauty of this approach is that you attain "insider" status almost immediately.

- Be sure that the meeting you schedule is one that will fit into your curriculum and benefit your students.

- Schedule enough free time for you to talk with the company representative after the presentation.

#146: Submit your resume in a specially-constructed envelope.

Or:

Does this package seem strangely familiar to you?

Jack figured, correctly, that his competition for the new customer-service manager position at the biggest hotel in town would be intense. He decided to jazz his application up a bit—by building, from scratch, a customized envelope from the hotel's new four-color brochure! He placed a neatly typed label on the packet and sent it off addressed to the hiring manager, whose name he learned through some enterprising phone research. Whose resume and cover letter do you think rose to the top of the pile?

Strategies for success:

- Here's a perfect example of how a very little bit of initiative (obtaining the brochure from the hotel) and research (calling to find out the name of the hiring manager) can pay off big-time.

- Be sure your finished envelope looks neat and clean; if you're not particularly adept at folding paper in such a way as to yield sharp, clean edges on all sides, enlist the aid of a friend or family member.

#147: Figure out who owes your family money.

Or:

How nice have we been to you?

Paul, an out-of-work carpenter, decided the best way to get a good lead on a new job was to appeal to good, old-fashioned guilt—subtly, of course. A business associate of his father's had taken out a big loan a year or so back, and had had some difficulty repaying it. Paul's father had agreed to extend the terms. When Paul heard that the man who owned his father money was thinking of remodeling his home, he called up and asked to submit a bid. Paul never mentioned his father's kindness in drawing out the terms on the loan. He didn't have to. He submitted a competitive bid, supplied a sheet of sterling references and got the job in short order.

Strategies for success:

- Subtle appeals such as this can work out well—if you are confident of your ability to perform the best possible job and can demonstrate as much.

- Do not come off as heavy-handed or judgmental when you apply for a position. Simply ask for the chance to make the best contribution you can.

- Even if your family doesn't routinely hand out large loans, you or one of your relatives have probably extended a helping hand to any number of people over the years. Are any of those people in a position to benefit from what you have to offer?

#148: Send a huge jigsaw puzzle piece.
Or:
How the heck do I file this?

Michael sent a big jigsaw puzzle piece along with the following letter: "Regarding: Your opening for an account executive. With five years of experience in the field and a proven record of delivering results, I'll fit on your team as perfectly as a piece in a jigsaw puzzle. Call me at (number)." The call came and Michael was ready for it. He got the interview and the job.

Strategies for success:

- This snazzy little cover letter was used in concert with a resume. You can also send it on its own if you prepare properly for the telephone call it may elicit.

- Memorize five key contributions you made on your last (or a recent) job. These contributions should be in story form, and they should focus on ways you saved your employer time or made your employer money. Wherever possible, use specific time references and specific dollar amounts.

- Make sure you are ready to provide these stories at a moment's notice. If your letter results in a call, you'll have about 15 seconds to turn that intrigued paper-shuffler into someone who just *has* to meet you in person.

- Multiple variations on the "puzzle-piece" technique arose during the research for this book, which may mean that it is worth reviewing closely. See also #118 and #137.

#149: Join a community theater group.
Or:
How to succeed in business by really connecting.

Max was eager to find a job that would take advantage of his writing skills, but he was new in town and had no professional connections to speak of. He decided to audition for a local community theater production of *The Winter's Tale*. The large cast afforded him plenty of new acquaintances—and, as it happened, one of the cast members was himself interviewing for a position as an editor at a local publishing firm. Max shared his background and his aspirations with his fellow performer, and hoped for the best. The play went well...and some months after the show closed, Max got a call from his editor friend asking if he could come in to talk about a new research position that had recently opened up.

Strategies for success:

- New in town? Getting cast in a local theater production, which often does *not* require great acting skill, may be one of the best ways to make contacts, professional or otherwise.

- This method takes time, and doesn't always result in *direct* referrals, but it is an excellent means of getting the word out about your accomplishments and career goals.

- Have fun first; network second.

#150: Ask what's open at the unemployment office.
Or:
What do you mean, you want to work here?

Paul got tired of the numbing routine he went through every week when picking up his unemployment check. He would inevitably be asked, "Are you looking for work?" He would always answer "Yes." Then would come the question: "Where?" One week, he answered this by saying, "Here. What kind of employees are you looking for?" As it happened, the office was looking for someone with good Spanish skills to work with applicants whose English was not good. Paul's six years of high school and college Spanish finally paid off—he started a little over a month later.

Strategies for Success:
• File this under "It couldn't hurt to try."

#151: Write your resume in computer-speak.
Or:
Standing out in cyberspace.

New data-retrieval methods are quickly rendering everything you ever learned about how to write a resume obsolete. These days, more and more employers are filing resumes, not in file cabinets, but in massive computer databases. When they want to fill a particular position, they don't go back to the hard copy, and they don't give two hoots about the format you select. They search for particular words, and every resume that contains those words pops up for review. A recent *New York Newsday* article profiled a job seeker who filed a resume with a national resume database and listed particular keywords he knew would stand a good chance of attracting the kind of employer he wanted to meet. (In his case, the keywords were "office products," "packaging," "product development" and "Spanish.") Sure enough, his leaner, more computer-friendly resume yielded an interview, and then a job offer.

Strategies for success:

- Many of the new resume databases have specific functional specialties. You may want to try to hook up with one that caters specifically to your work background. Check with a career counselor or a local library for the latest details in this rapidly changing area of employment networking.

- Commercial on-line services, such as Prodigy and America On-Line, may be able to point you toward a resume database that is right for you—but before you commit yourself to subscribing to the service, see if you can take a test drive on someone else's system. You'll save time, cash and frustration.

- To get the most out of the new resume banks, customize the resumes you submit to them, and remember that potential employers will be looking for specific, quantifiable skills.

- Develop four to six keywords, then elaborate on each. Be sure to include foreign language skills and particular computer software skills. Don't beat around the bush: name names. ("Fluent in three Romance languages" or "Proficient on all major spreadsheet systems" won't elicit queries from prospective employers searching through the database. "Spanish" and "Lotus 1-2-3" will.)

- Keep it brief. All resumes, and electronic resumes in particular, should elicit a desire on the part of the employer to find out more by contacting you directly. Leave a few tantalizing questions unanswered, and you'll get a better response.

- Pick a straightforward, non-ornamental typeface (such as Courier or Times Roman) for the resume you submit to the database. Such typefaces are easier for text scanners to read.

- For more information on database-friendly resumes, and for information on how to file your resume with a firm that services your industry, check in with your trade association or professional group—or visit your local library and ask about electronic resume systems. (Most will not charge you a fee to file your resume—be wary of any organization that does.)

- Note that successful Internet-related job search stories took many forms. See #21, #26, #35, #128, #136, #142 and #252.

#152: Start a newsletter and distribute it to the 100 most influential people in your industry.

Or:

You don't know it, but you subscribe to this.

A personal computer is a powerful thing. Carol, a graphic designer who had recently lost her job, harnessed her system's potential by entering the names of the major movers and shakers of the publishing industry into her contact management software. She then fired up her Pagemaker program and developed a biweekly letter that featured the latest ideas on developing good relationships with book retailers, whom she interviewed for the letter's feature articles. She then sent the newsletter, which happened to showcase her superior layout abilities, to the bigwigs on her list. Within three months, she had a job offer from one of her letter's recipients.

Strategies for success:

- Focus on a topic of intense interest to your audience.
- Be sure the newsletter looks sharp, not amateurish. Get a friend to proofread it and critique it.
- You may wish to request interviews from important people at your target organization for profiles in your newsletter. This is a great way to build your contact list.
- Duplication and postage fees can be hefty. Is there a high-quality copier you can borrow? Are there any firms to which you can deliver your newsletter by dropping it off at the front desk, in a large envelope marked "Personal" and addressed to the contact?

#153: Attach a balloon to your application.
Or:
Up, up, and away!

Melanie wanted an entry-level designing position at a hot new sports-clothing designer in her town, but she knew the competition was fierce. Instead of the standard cover-letter-and-resume-via-regular-mail approach, she sent a brief, tantalizing one-paragraph memo that cited a few key achievements, attached it with a piece of ribbon to a big red helium-filled balloon, then boxed everything up and sent it, via UPS, to the president of the company. She got a call the next day asking her to come in for an interview, and eventually landed the job she was after.

Strategies for success:
- A shameless attention-getting device, yes, but it can be effective if the message you choose to accent is a compelling one.
- Consider using a positive quote from a former supervisor as the heart of your letter. Be sure the sentiments expressed are genuine, and that the person you quote will back them up.
- Keep the letter brief!
- Include all appropriate contact information.
- You may wish to close with an aggressive follow-up promise: "I will call your office on Tuesday the 5th at 9 a.m. to discuss this opportunity further."

#154: Quietly "apply" for a job that doesn't exist.
Or:
You know what you need around here?

Leslie was looking for work on the Air Force base in Misawa, Japan where her husband was stationed. ("We really had no choice," she points out. "It was the only place anyone spoke English.") Her specialty was photography—but she was told there was no instruction position open in that area at the base arts center. Leslie started spending all the time she could at the center, getting to know the teachers and staff. Initially, she never mentioned her desire to work at the center—but she did spend a good deal of time at the potter's wheel, working on her own pottery projects. Leslie knew that the center, which was short of staff, did not have a pottery instructor—and that others were interested in pursuing pottery classes. Before long, she was talking to one of the senior staff about the new position of pottery instructor. She got an offer for the job shortly thereafter, and her responsibilities increased steadily. Eventually, she got the photography instructor position she wanted...and then worked her way up to the position of director of the center!

Strategies for success:

- This just might work when you're interested in finding a part-time position—although, as Leslie's experience indicates, you will certainly be in a position to move up to full-time work after you accept an offer.

- It's hard to imagine this laid-back approach winning much notice in any other environment than community or nonprofit organizations. But in those types of groups, Leslie's approach could be quite effective. Leslie's method neatly sidesteps the concerns of the small but vocal number of nonprofit managers weary of people offering to do "volunteer work" that is in fact an opportunity to audition for a salaried position. (Some nonprofit people feel this tactic is a violation of the sense of "mission" that should guide their organizations; others are happy to get help in any form, regardless of motive.) By developing an entirely new area of activity, and then letting the powers that be suggest that she take on a new position, Leslie avoided perception problems, which can be deadly in small groups such as this.

- Use Leslie's approach when there's a specific organization with which you have a good match, and when you have some time to spare.

- Say something along the lines of, "I've always loved pottery." (Or whatever your area of interest is.) In Leslie's case, she made a point of highlighting her interest in a variety of fields, including watercolor, stained glass, pottery and, of course, her chief interest, photography.

- Subtlety is the key here—if the organization is understaffed, it's probably because funds are short. Outright prospecting will likely be a turnoff. The aim is to become an insider first...and let the job offer follow as the result of a new area you develop.

- Ideas based on some form of volunteer work take many forms and were among the most popular techniques encountered during the research for this book. See #1, #10, #58, #82, #129, #140, #251 and #292.

#155: Write a Post-it Note that's only one sentence long.
Or:
The personal touch.

How it really worked: The "letter" that accompanied Mary Ellen's resume was actually a handwritten yellow adhesive note that read simply, "I am the right person for this job, and I can prove it to you; call me at (number)." It worked.

Strategies for success:

- Human resource people are always complaining about vague, over-long cover letters. Make their life easier—and your job search shorter—by addressing their concerns.

- If your handwriting is less than attractive consider asking a friend or family member to help out.

- To the best of your ability, target the resume directly to *this particular position*, not to a general "ideal job in the industry." (The yellow note is basically a dare to the prospective employer: "Prove me wrong." You must be able to support your claim instantly in a persuasive way.)

#156: Write your resume in the form of a press release.

Or:

For immediate release—I'm magnificent!

How it really worked: Lauren had recently lost her job as publicity director for a major recording organization. Instead of following the textbook advice on preparing her resume, she arranged hers as though it were the type of release she would write for a new artist she was promoting. The single-sheet summary was complete with a "For immediate release" heading, initial "grabber" paragraph, contact information in standard press-release format, and even the legend "–end–" at the bottom of the page. Throughout the release, Lauren spoke of herself in the third person. The unusual resume generated multiple interviews and, eventually, a job offer at a firm she'd wanted to work with for years.

Strategies for success:

- Obviously, this exact technique will work best if you are applying for a job where the ability to compose captivating copy is at a premium. But the underlying idea can be adapted into virtually any field.

- Is there a written format that key decision makers in your target industry see or develop every day? Your model could be a recipe, a table of contents, a listing of ingredients, a traffic citation or even a formal invitation to interview you.

- Find the right format for your target audience, then customize your resume to the industry by showing how well you can combine the unfamiliar (your ability to help the employer) with the familiar (the written format you choose to use as a model).

#157: Send a tennis shoe.
Or:
The sole candidate for the job.

Stephen won an interview, and a job offer, with a major sporting-goods manufacturer by sending the head of personnel a single large shoe (the target company's brand, of course), accompanied by a concise letter of application that began, "Now that I've got a foot in the door..."

Strategies for success:

- Cute, huh? Actually, this is one of the more popular off-the-beaten-track approaches out there. It must work, because a whole lot of people seem to be using it. If there is any danger here, it's probably that a good many company presidents and human resource people have already encountered it. Still, when these things catch on, it's for a reason.

- For an interesting variation, see #185.

- Given this stunt's popularity, you should probably consider adding your own personal twist if you use this technique to apply for a job. For example, if your specialty is computer programming, you might set up a letter that reads, "Now that I've got my foot in the door, let me hop in for an interview. That way, you can meet a programmer who will really put the pedal to the floor to help you develop superior software products."

#158: Join a religious group for the express purpose of job networking.
Or:
Sure, I'm a big fan of Reverend Moon's.

Mel, an ad copywriter whose firm had recently shut down, tried this and was amazed at the network of opportunities that opened up for him as a result. The group he joined (about which he had read a few intriguing articles, and which turned out to be a good match for him) proved invaluable not only in terms of his connections for job interviews, but also with returning a much-needed sense of calm and control to his work life that had been missing in previous jobs.

Strategies for success:

- Best bet: Focus on initiating or strengthening connections with the group to which you already belong—or to which you feel a strong calling.

- It is illegal for an employer to ask you about your religious status or preferences during an interview, so steer clear of such issues at that time. Raising the issue at any time during the company's formal employment consideration process will probably set up more obstacles for you than it would remove. (A competent manager will realize that discussion of religious issues during the interview is highly inappropriate and, legally, quite risky.)

- Use your "shadow network" of religious affiliation, whether it is a new network or an old one, to point you toward new opportunities; then let your qualifications and enthusiasm carry the day.

#159: Wear a tee-shirt that has a huge picture of an eye, and then the words "am an accountant"—or whatever the job you're looking for is—and your phone number.
Or:

The shirt on your back.

Tim tried this hard-to-miss variation on the tee-shirt-as-employment-advertisement technique (see #238) and wore the shirt everywhere he could think of: rock concerts, jogging expeditions, library excursions. Before long he was receiving phone inquiries about his services; one of them led to a full-time position. (Special thanks to counselor Tony Dias for this contribution.)

Strategies for success:

- For best results, be sure there's someone to answer the phone for you at all times! You should strongly consider hiring an answering service if you try this technique.
- At the very least, you should set up a quality answering machine, with a straightforward, businesslike greeting, and leave it on at all times.
- T-shirt-related techniques were cited by multiple sources during the research for this book. This approach, and the variations on it, seem to have caught on among creative job seekers. They may be worth particularly close review. See #48 and #238.
- Do not wear the shirt to formal job interviews.

#160: Breaker, breaker: Canvas for a job by chatting on your CB radio.
Or:
Smokey's behind the billboard near Exit 17—and by the way, do you know who's hiring?

How it really worked: This is apparently a very common means of contacting prospective employers among truckers, many of whom list their CB handles on their resumes. Although jobs in other fields aren't usually Topic A on these airwaves, you never know what's going to come up. CB radio, like the Internet, represents a way to expand your base of contacts while actually having fun, and thus is worth a look every once in a while, if only as a break from the routine. Monitor your time closely, though.

Strategies for success:

- If you're unfamiliar with the language and etiquette common to CB channels, listen for a while before you dive into a discussion. You don't want to earn a bad reputation right off the bat by saying something stupid. The same basic idea applies to relationships you develop through electronic chat rooms and bulletin boards, which are the cyberspace equivalent of CB radios.

- Make friends first, ask about jobs second. (Unless you're a trucker, in which case you're in a great position to conduct an employment interview, and maybe even get a job offer, right over the radio.)

#161: Give 'em the silent treatment.
Or:
How to apply for a job without applying for a job.

Jennifer was ready to move on from her position as director of development at a local hospital, but she was uneasy about leaving the position before she had secured another job offer. She decided to take advantage of a joint media event protesting state funding cutbacks that she had recently scheduled with a local cancer research foundation. In the process of setting up that demonstration, she was able to develop a relationship with the head of the foundation, a woman who was, as it turned out, on the lookout for new and talented staff members. Jennifer dropped a few subtle but well-designed hints that she was getting a little restless with her current employer, but she never said she was in the job market. As the media event concluded, Jennifer took a moment to say a special good-bye to the president of the foundation. "It's been a really wonderful experience working with your group," she told her, smiling and looking her straight in the eye. "I hope our paths cross again." Not long afterward, the head of the foundation called with a job offer.

Strategies for success:

- Subtlety is important here. The aim is to get the prospective employer to make the first move.

- The project you initiate is, for all practical purposes, an audition for a job with the target organization, but it must succeed completely on it own terms, as well. Don't arrange an event that will be anything other than mutually beneficial to both organizations.

- Having developed a relationship with the top person at your target organization, follow up as appropriate via telephone or mail.

- Remember, strong careers are built on mutual fan clubs. Demonstrate what you can do—but, wherever you can, show a genuine admiration for the goals and methods of the person with whom you're working.

#162: Ask to redesign the organization's marketing materials—at no cost.

Or:

Let me bring you business... Let me make you smile...

According to a recent article in *The Boston Globe*, college basketball coach John Calipari took his first job running the University of Kansas' summer basketball camp at no salary—and more than doubled the camp's enrollment in two years. He did it by asking to be allowed to redesign the camp's humdrum brochure. Once he received the okay to take a new approach, he arranged for a key camp sponsorship by an athletic-shoe firm, and completely revamped the graphic approach. The new brochure was a big success—and Calipari's record quickly won him a job offer as recruiting coordinator at another school.

Strategies for success:

- Word tends to spread quickly about miracle workers. This story is one of many examples in this book of a reliable principle employed by any number of determined job searchers: If you deliver results, the job will come.

- It's nice to have enough financial security to take on a job for free, but sometimes, if you set your mind to it, you can overcome even the lack of salary. (Calipari, for example, served food in the cafeteria for the summer at the Kansas job: "That was the only way I didn't starve," he explains.)

#163: Fold, spindle and mutilate your application and cover letter.
Or:
Try to ignore me this time.

Reed, an applicant for an artistic endowment, had been turned down two years running. The third time, he took the application form and crumpled and uncrumpled it a dozen or so times. Then he spilled coffee on the form. Then he burned the edges of the sheet with matches, at which point he scrawled "see letter" across the front of the form. Using the same marker, he wrote the words "Gimme an endowment" in rough handwriting, and then his name and address. Finally, he subjected the cover letter to the same wrinkle, burn, and stain approach he'd used with the application, and sent the whole mess along to the address listed on the application form. He won the endowment.

Strategies for success:

- It worked for Reed, in part because he was already familiar to the panel reviewing his "application."

- It may seem outrageous to think of using this technique as part of a professional job search, but keep an open mind for a moment. Suppose there's a similar person or group of people who are likewise familiar with you.

- Suppose there's a company you've wanted to work with for some time, and suppose you've tried everything (well, nearly everything) to get an interview, and nothing has worked. Suppose further that the decision makers at the firm are well aware of your repeated efforts to secure employment, but have apparently decided that the match just isn't right. Suppose, to put it bluntly, that there's nothing to lose. (Apparently, that was Reed's situation.)

- Adapting the "slash-and-burn" approach outlined above, using your resume and a cover letter bearing the words, "I'll go through hell and back for you—call me at (your number)"—and a stained, torched, mangled pair of documents could elicit, perhaps, a long-overdue smile from the people considering your fitness for the organization. That smile could possibly lead to a phone call.

#164: Get your resume onto the back of a wine bottle label.

Or:

Heard it through the grapevine that you needed someone like me.

How it really worked: According to a recent article in *Newsweek*, a French wine firm recently made common cause with out-of-work college graduates by reproducing selected resumes on the backs of its bottles. The campaign resulted in some great P.R. for the firm—and some much-needed job offers for the graduates.

Strategies for success:

- Setting up a similar arrangement with a local consumer products firm may seem farfetched to you...but it's worth a shot, right? Who's to say that there's not a company in your area willing to develop good community relations, garner some positive P.R. and help out local job seekers in the process? (Anyway, how different is the resume-on-a-wine-bottle technique from the common practice of highlighting photos of missing children on milk cartons?)

- Such a maneuver is likeliest to succeed when a *group* of displaced or laid off workers approaches the media relations people in a major firm.

- Remember that the "carrot" for the company is positive coverage by the local media. If you find a company willing to help you and your fellow job seekers out, be sure to make yourself available to reporters if called upon to do so.

#165: Submit the first draft of your resume, corrected, and with editing marks in place.

Or:

Mistakes—I've made a few, and here they are, marked for attention...

An applicant for a copy editing job thought this one up. Hard to miss, wouldn't you agree? The story appears in a recent Bill Corbin article in the *National Business Employment Weekly.*

Strategies for success:

- Not recommended for nonediting positions. You'll probably just confuse the prospective employer.

- You won't be doing your candidacy any favors if your edits do not correct all the errors on the page. Just to be on the safe side, show the piece to someone else before you send it off.

- If you don't have nice, neat handwriting, you probably shouldn't try this.

- Use a red or blue pencil for that authentic look.

#166. When questioned about your age, report a remarkable coincidence.

Or:

You say you need me to be how old?

A recent article in the *Connecticut Post* tells how Ronald Shaw, a former standup comedian who eventually became president and chief executive officer of Pilot Pen Corp. of America, got his start at Pilot as a retail sales representative. He interviewed for the job at the tender age of 22. "The man who interviewed me said he wanted to hire me, but couldn't," Shaw told the reporter, "because he was told to hire someone who was between the ages of 24 and 30. I told him I was 24. I guess he liked that gutsiness." Shaw concludes the story by acknowledging that he now doesn't suggest such misrepresentation.

Strategies for success:

- The point is not that you should lie about your age, but that you should be on the lookout for any and every opportunity to prove your commitment to getting the job done—regardless of any obstacles perceived by the interviewer.

- For another instance of on-the-spot creativity, see #25.

#167: Enlist the aid of an employment agency that specializes in placing disabled workers—or start one yourself!

Or:

Where there's a will, there's a way.

Though they're not exactly *common,* such agencies are out there; one, Kidder Resources in Rochester Hills, Michigan, helped an electrical engineer (who was blind) to land a job after his own three-year search turned up nothing. Kidder Resources was profiled in a recent article in *The Detroit News.*

Strategies for success:

- If you can't locate such an agency in your area, start your own! Kidder Resources was launched when the proprietor got tired of hearing about how her son, born with Down's syndrome, would face a lifetime of low-paying, menial jobs.

#168: Find someone to sign on as your legal guardian.
Or:
Age requirement? What age requirement was that?

Legendary jazz musician Stan Getz had an offer to tour with Jack Teagarden's band. There was one problem. Getz was only 16 years old, and the truant officer had problems with letting the youngster adopt a musician's lifestyle, no matter how promising his fellow players insisted he was. Getz finally got to tour with the band—and start a legendary career—when Teagarden was set down as his formal legal guardian.

Strategies for success:

- Always check with a qualified attorney before making any final decision regarding legal guardianship.

- Bear in mind that child-labor laws require strict attention to such issues as education and daily workplace scheduling. These laws also vary by state.

- While on the road, stay away from the Blue Plate Specials and don't be afraid to experiment with a bossa nova beat.

#169: Use free voice mail services to camouflage the fact that you're currently without a permanent residence.
Or:
Have your people call my people.

Across the country, several suppliers of phone services and cellular phone equipment have helped local homeless people find jobs in this way. The company serves as a transfer station, fielding incoming messages from prospective employers who require applicants to furnish phone numbers. If you find yourself on the hunt for a job, but without a number to refer people to, consider this approach. Get in touch with your local phone company, social services organization or state job matching service.

Strategies for success:

- You may have the best luck arranging for a free forwarding service if you can get an employment counselor to make the initial contacts for you.
- If you're already facing major employment hurdles, it's risky to leave "creative" messages on a voice-mail system that will be used by prospective employers. Save your ingenuity for face-to-face contacts. Keep it professional.
- Check the system daily and return all calls promptly.

#170: Offer to take only half a job for starters.
Or:
We half to talk, boss.

Irene, eager to break into the male-dominated construction industry in the mid-1970s, had worked in an administrative position at a local demolition company for a year and a half; she was eager to get the opportunity to work in an on-site capacity. Her boss was uneasy about the idea of her taking over an on-site position—until Irene suggested that she split the job in half, performing her administrative work two and a half days a week and working with the job foreman the rest of the time on demolition jobs. He agreed. Irene delivered superior results; by the end of the year, she was working full-time in the field she wanted to enter.

Strategies for success:

- Such an approach may be helpful if you face deep-rooted skepticism about your ability to perform the job you're after. Make the offer in a confident, direct way, and specify a starting date you think could work for both you and the employer.
- Be sure to attend to all the duties assigned to you, whether in your target job or the one you currently hold.

• If the employer agrees, try to establish a specific date by which the outcome of your request for full-time status in the area you wish to work will be decided.

#171: Apply where your previous position (Dumpster Contents Reclamation Specialist) puts you at an advantage.
Or:
Business is really picking up!

Sometimes, if people want to make the transition out of despair and into empowerment, they need to take advantage of their current survival skills—and find a potential employer who's willing to let them put those skills to work in a positive way. A recent article in *The Baltimore Sun* profiles the founders of A&G Cleaning, Anita Dunham and Grace Blackstone, who built a business around the idea of hiring the homeless. Their idea was simple: take the picking-through-the-dumpster skill and channel it into the picking-up-the-local-stadium-after-the-game skill. Often approached by disadvantaged people from local shelters, Anita and Grace train them to march in perfect time up and down the stairs of sporting venues, collecting trash. A&G workers deliver sparkling, trash-free stadiums in record time—and, in the process, make their way back into the world of work. "Even people who live on the street are programmed," Blackstone told a reporter. "It takes strategy to be a bum. It takes strategy to survive. They know where to go when it's cold to stay warm. They know what time to get their food from the soup kitchen. You find out what their programming was before. Then you can use that to help them feel more comfortable working with a new program. We have taken some young boys who have lived on the street who haven't had any kind of education, were on drugs, and...now they are positive and trying to do better." These two inspired community-based entrepreneurs won a market niche by transcending stereotypes, challenging their employees and offering decent pay for honest, efficient work. What's more, they consider it a success when their hires leave for more promising employment.

Strategies for success:

- If someone you know is facing severe job obstacles such as homelessness, drug addiction or the lack of an education, check with your local social services office. Find out whether there are praiseworthy outfits in your area like A&G Cleaning, companies that are willing to train and employ disadvantaged members of the community.

#172: Set up a 24-hour hotline.

Or:

Call 1-800-NO PROBLEM. Operators are standing by.

One career counselor interviewed for this book told how she was only able to convince a restaurant manager to hire Brian (who was mentally retarded) because she herself promised to answer any question and resolve any problem, personally, at any time it might come up on the job. Considering that the young man was applying for a midnight-to-dawn shift, this promise was not one to be extended lightly! But extend it she did. She gave the restaurant manager her home and office phone numbers and told him to feel free to phone her at any time of the day or night. After a few (relatively pleasant!) post-midnight calls, she was able to help the manager integrate Brian into the restaurant's operation with little difficulty. He was soon working successfully on his own.

Strategies for success:

- Sometimes, hiring managers need to know there's someone they can appeal to if things get difficult. If you or someone you know opts for this approach, be sure the number(s) you give out really will be answered by someone who cares, and who has a commitment to resolve any questions or concerns the employer may have.

#173: Make the Washington bureaucracy work for you for a change.
Or:
Who's really got the vision problem?

Experienced truck driver Tom Breth, virtually blind in one eye, learned to his surprise that he had been driving illegally for a good chunk of his career. His interstate trucking license was suspended when his vision-impaired status became known during an audit of a company that had assigned him a route. One protracted legal wrangle and a whole lot of personal lobbying later, Breth won a waiver from officials at the Federal Highway Administration (FHWA). He was once again free to drive lucrative interstate freight routes. (By the way, FHWA statistics indicated that drivers in Breth's category actually have a *safer* driving record than fully sighted drivers.) For more on Breth's case, see the article by Jill Hodges in the February 11, 1995 *Minneapolis StarTribune*.

Strategies for success:

- This is a good story to keep in mind if you face regulatory or administrative hurdles from a government agency. As many other stories in this book illustrate, persistence is often everything; Breth got his waiver through a full-court press on the federal regulatory establishment. He attained his goal even though he had missed a deadline for drivers in his category to apply for waivers during a special regulatory study period.

- For more guidance on dealing with the often bewildering Federal regulatory establishment, call your Congressional representative. If they take too much time to answer a question or promise to get back to you without doing so, call again, explain that you are a constituent, get the name of the person who is supposed to handle your question and refuse to hang up until you are allowed to speak directly with that person.

#174: Offer to report on the high-school sports scene from a teenager's perspective.
Or:

Extra! Extra! A whole bunch of your readers think just like me!

That's how Paul, a 16-year-old, got his first job at a local paper. The editor he spoke to was fascinated by the possibility of bringing new readers to his sports section by recruiting someone *from* that audience group. Paul's work on his high school paper served as evidence of his strong writing ability.

Strategies for success:

- Is there some group you represent that editors want to reach? Is there some experience you've had that gives you the ability to speak convincingly to others in a similar situation? If so, consider writing from that perspective and submitting your samples to the editor of a local newspaper.

- Do yourself a favor: Have a friend critique the pieces you write before you submit them.

- Follow up as appropriate by phone.

- Be prepared to make a few calls; you may have to approach a number of people.

- The stronger the local angle, the greater the likelihood of your work being published.

- The "real life" angle—when executed in a powerful, persuasive way—is a source of unending interest to readers and, by extension, editors. Are you a "real-life" victim of a layoff? Entrepreneur? Crusader for a cause? Mid-life career changer? Lots of other people are, too, and editors like to reach large groups of people. Pick a group whose interests (and preoccupations) you share, and present yourself as a representative of that group.

- For more on approaching editors, see the invaluable annual reference book, *Writer's Market* (Writer's Digest Books).

#175: Age or background problems? Offer to give up your salary.
Or:
A low-risk proposition for the boss.

A recent article in the *Central New York Business Journal* tells how travel cruise executive Bob Falcone got his first job in the insurance agency. At the tender age of 18, he inquired after an opening outlined in a blind ad for a local insurance company. Asked in for an interview, he lied about his age, claiming to be 21. When the offer came through, Falcone's conscience apparently got the better of him; he admitted that he was only 18. As Falcone related the story to the *Journal,* "I told them that if they were ready to hire me, I would work for commission only. Lo and behold, the first night out I sold three policies and made $180. Soon I was leading the office."

Strategies for success:

- This can be an excellent technique for sales openings, even if you don't have any qualifications-related problems. But the gambit requires confidence, drive and a certain engagingly optimistic quality that's hard to define precisely.

- Don't try it if you don't think you can attain the performance levels necessary to meet your personal quota.

- For an interesting variation based on a promise to attain a certain performance level by a particular point in time, see #1.

- If you wish to review an inventive—but not recommended—approach to dealing with a "background problems" issue similar to the "How old are you?" dilemma, see #258.

Feeling
Lucky?

#176: Apply with a job coach.
Or:
Two by two.

A special needs counselor, whose job is to help find employment for her hearing-impaired students, says this is one of the most reliable ways to place developmentally disabled applicants in mainstream employment. The prospective employee is accompanied at the interview—and, eventually, on the job—by a coach. One such job coach, fluent in sign language, accompanied Nancy, a deaf applicant for a job at a hardware store. He helped to translate the manager's questions, relayed Nancy's responses and even passed on a few stories about past job coaching assignments that helped to put the manager at ease. "He was very skeptical about the whole undertaking," the counselor recalls. "There's no way we would have been able to place her there without that coach, and even then it was only on a trial basis." When Nancy started work, her coach passed along a few basic signing and communication skills to the other workers, helped to make the training period a breeze and, best of all, soon proved himself to be absolutely unnecessary. "Nancy turned out to be one of the best workers that place ever had," the counselor recalls. "She got a good-sized raise only two weeks after she started, and the manager decided before too long that the job coach didn't have to stick around." Nancy was on her own—after a little help from some friends.

Strategies for success:
- Talk with a local social service agency or vocational education counselor to find out more about job coaches.
- Let the hiring official know ahead of time that a coach will be accompanying the applicant to the interview. The interview will go more smoothly.

#177: Reading problems? Quietly ask to take an oral exam.
Or:
The tale of the intrepid subway driver.

According to a recent story in *The Boston Globe*, George Metsger, an applicant for a Boston subway driver position, asked for and received permission to take the test for the job orally. He had to; he couldn't read. He passed, and performed the job with no problems for six years, but was reassigned when his superiors found out about his inability to read words longer than four or five letters.

Strategies for success:

• Oral exams may be worth asking about even if your problem is not with reading, but with written tests in general. Many people perform poorly on written exams, but score better when the test is offered in oral form. Some prospective employers may respond sensitively to such requests.

#178: Appeal to the time you once spent as a local gang member as your strongest qualification for the job.
Or:
I speak the language.

After two stints in prison, a former member of the X-Men, a notorious Boston street gang, finally straightened out his priorities in life. When he talked to a local social service center about working as a counselor for troubled area teens, he highlighted his sobriety, his commitment to staying on the straight and narrow and (perhaps most important of all) his ability to speak confidently and credibly to the people with whom he'd be working in delivering the center's anti-drug message. Now he's helping the kids in his old neighborhood to make life choices that will help them succeed in the long term.

Strategies for success:

- This story is another reminder that any experience can be turned to your advantage when it comes to finding the right job. If you've been handed a tough break or two, or made some poor life choices, you may actually have a significant competitive advantage. Once you've learned from the experiences, gotten back on your feet and developed the ability to deliver a message to those who face the same hurdles you did, your background—coupled with an unfailing positive attitude—may be exactly what someone is looking for.

- Attitude is everything! If you let the prospective employer know that you have something unique to offer, you won't have to worry about camouflaging your background. You can appeal to it as your strongest point.

- Such an approach is not limited to job searches for public-sector or nonprofit human service positions. These days, innumerable employers face a workplace productivity crisis as a result of employee drug and alcohol abuse. A good many of these employers are willing to consider hiring human resources people with "real-world experience" who are clean, sober and free of negative past influences, and who know how to help their employees overcome substance abuse or other problems as a result of first-hand experience.

- For another example of someone who turned problems with the law into employability, see #180 and #222.

#179: Find an "angel" who will help you make a money-back guarantee.
Or:
If I screw up, I'll pay you back all the salary I've earned so far.

In Hollywood in 1917, script clerk Anne Bauchens broke into film editing by taking on a studio disaster. A director had shot a film but had abandoned the project, leaving tens of thousands of feet of film unassembled. The project was a shambles, and the studio's investment was in grave danger. Bauchens, who had a strong background in what would now be known as continuity work, won the assignment—despite the misgivings of the studio executives about letting a woman work on the project. Bauchens and another director made an arrangement under which the studio would be reimbursed for the salary she was paid if it did not like the finished result. The director personally guaranteed the rebate.

Strategies for success:

- The guarantee will have the greatest impact if you either enlist the help of an ally within the organization (as Bauchens did) or set it down in writing for the prospective employer.
- Better still, consider doing both!
- Clearly, this is not a maneuver you should consider if you have any doubts whatsoever about your ability to deliver the promised results.

#180: Trying to overcome the stigma of past drug problems? Apply for a position at the rehab center that helped you get clean.
Or:
You know who the real me is.

It worked for Ted, whose substance abuse problems led to a number of self-destructive life choices...and some time in prison. After his release, however, he undertook a year and a half of hard work in a transitional program and regained control of his life. When employers proved to be wary of his criminal record, Ted appealed directly to the director of the center that had helped him kick his drug habit. The director heard him out—and offered him a counseling position.

Strategies for success:

- This strategy has been used with success by a great many in the recovery movement. Just be sure that you're in a position to follow through on the commitments you make, as a bad employment experience in this setting can have disastrous emotional and career implications.

- Are you sure you can make a real contribution in such an environment? If not, think twice before accepting even a well-intentioned offer.

- If you wish, for the sake of thoroughness, to review a particularly inventive—but not recommended—approach to dealing with a "background problems" issue similar to the "Have you ever been incarcerated?" dilemma, see #258.

#181: Appeal to the Supreme Court.
Or:
Making a Federal case out of it.

A dock worker at a freight company mounted a court challenge that reached all the way to the U.S. Supreme Court in an effort to win back the job from which he had, he felt, been unjustly let go. It worked. The worker, who admitted lying to his employer and the National Labor Relations Board in an attempt to avoid being discharged, was able to demonstrate to the high court's satisfaction that the true reason for his dismissal was his work on behalf of the union to which he belonged—and not his alleged chronic tardiness. When asked by a supervisor about the reason for a late arrival, the dock worker had told his employer that his car had broken down on the day in question. It hadn't—but that mattered less to the Supreme Court than the company's actions, which were found to constitute illegal attempts to rid the company of an employee engaged in lawful union-related activities. Such issues overshadowed any "collateral" questions of perjury, the court held. The company was ordered to reinstate the worker. (The story appeared in a recent article in *Traffic World.*)

Strategies for success:

- Employees who engage in union-related activities may be able to take advantage of special protection under current law if it can be proven that actions taken against them by their employers, such as dismissals, are reprisals for legitimate organizing work.

- Considering legal action against an employer for what you feel to be wrongful dismissal? Talk with a qualified attorney first.

- Make it easy on yourself. Don't lie to your employer in the first place.

- See also #192 and #290.

#182: Grow a mustache.
Or:
Bristle with enthusiasm.

An applicant for a bank position, turned down for lack of experience, tried this. When he reapplied to the same place a month or so later with the same resume, he got a job offer.

Strategies for success:

- This approach may not result in much in the way of positive results when adapted by women on the job hunt. (Do write the author if you find otherwise.)

#183: Balance a yardstick on your nose.
Or:
Wait till you see what I can do with a pocket calculator.

Myra listed her ability to do this on her job application under her special skills; she was seeking work with one of the largest software development firms in the country. She reports that, during the interview, one of the managers brought in a yardstick and handed it to her. She passed the test with flying colors and got the job.

Strategies for success:

- Don't laugh. The name of the game is standing out from the competition, right?
- Be prepared to demonstrate any unusual skill, job-related or otherwise, during the interview if you highlighted it on your resume. If you think there's the slightest chance you may freeze up as a result of nerves, either practice the stunt until you can do it in your sleep or don't brag about it in the first place.
- See, for comparison, #69 and #229.

#184: Brush your teeth repeatedly.

Or:

This candidate, when incorporated in a conscientious program of dental hygiene, is recommended by the American Dental Association.

When a 24-year-old congressional aide by the name of Lyndon Johnson wanted to get himself established in Washington, DC, he had his eye on the Little Congress, an organization of House staffers. Johnson seems to have sensed that he'd need to develop a huge network of contacts in short order if he hoped to rise in that organization. Accordingly, he made his base of operations at the Dodge Hotel, where he and a great many other House aides were staying. More specifically, Johnson set up shop in one of the *bathrooms* at the Dodge. His first night in the capital, Johnson took four consecutive showers—and introduced himself to other congressional staffers who happened to be in the bathroom at the same time. The next morning, he brushed his teeth repeatedly at 10-minute intervals—and introduced himself to other congressional staffers who happened to be in the bathroom at the same time. You get the idea. Within 24 hours he had met virtually every guest in the building. Not long afterwards, he was elected the youngest speaker of the Little Congress in history.

Strategies for success:

- Strange as it may sound, the bathrooms of prominent hotels are excellent networking venues. Johnson's technique could be profitably adapted to, among other venues, hotels occupied by executives attending trade conventions.

- Confident social interaction skills are obviously a plus here. If you are ill at ease in such settings to begin with, this may not be the method for you. If, on the other hand, you're a "people person," this technique may be worth trying.

- Be prepared to summarize your accomplishments and objectives concisely.

- Note your conversational partner's name, company affiliation and title; keep a small notebook in your back pocket and jot the information down at the first opportunity.
- Follow up as appropriate, either by phone or with a visit to the executive's booth (if the setting is a trade show).
- For another memorable Johnson maneuver, see #288.

#185: Leave a mystery package at the front desk.
Or:
Special delivery!

Mary Anne won an interview and a job with a pharmaceutical firm by delivering a good-sized box to the front desk, addressed to the president's office. Inside the box was another box. Inside *that* box was another box. Inside *that* box was a small shoebox. Inside the shoebox was a carefully wrapped newspaper. Inside the carefully wrapped newspaper was a single baby shoe. Tucked inside the single baby shoe were two sheets of paper, folded into a tube. When unwrapped, the two sheets turned out to be a letter from Mary Anne that began, "Now that I've got my foot in the door..." and a copy of her resume.

Strategies for success:

- Sure, it's cute as a button, but the sad truth is that this basic idea is actually on the verge of being overused. For a variation that incorporates the target company's product as the prop, rather than the "awww"-eliciting baby shoe, see #157.
- Part of the "package" should be your own demeanor as you drop off the big box at the front desk. Eventually, whoever gets to the bottom of things is going to call the receptionist and ask, "Hey, who dropped off that big package?" You want them to answer, "This really nice person who'd make a great employee," not "Some weirdo who looked really nervous."

#186: Put a summary of your resume on the back of a business card, then hand it out to everyone you meet.
Or:
Who says a resume has to look like a resume?

Eric tried this "mini-resume" approach at the urging of his career counselor. It worked with surprising speed, generating interviews and an offer in under a month. There are a number of likely reasons for this, including the card's portability and ease of storage in a wallet or pocket. Those who don't toss the card out probably won't file it with other resumes "waiting to be reviewed"—it would be instantly lost in a standard filing system. (Special thanks to counselor Tony Dias for this contribution.)

Strategies for success:

- Don't cram the card with information—list two or three career highlights and your contact information.

- Since the "mini-resume" must be distributed to many people, you probably shouldn't specify a career objective on the card. Such an objective gives people an excuse to toss the card if a similar job is not open at the moment.

- Give the card to *everyone* you meet or come in contact with. Wide distribution of a simple message is the key. Did you ever hear the story of the salesman who beat his quota by tossing his business cards from the window of a moving bus? You don't have to do that, of course, but you get the general idea.

#187: Refuse to leave the building.
Or:
Who's waiting out whom?

Mark must have checked his schedule 10 times: Tuesday, 1 p.m., interview at Farris Industries. Here he was in the reception area of the firm, and here it was, quarter past three, and there was still no acknowledgment of his existence from anyone in the company. He'd showed up 15 minutes early, and he'd left his name with the receptionist—in fact, he'd done so several times—but he'd gotten no response whatsoever from the man he was supposed to meet. Nor, for that matter, had anyone else come out to let him know what the problem was. Mark figured he had a choice: Stay and take this kind of abuse or head out and keep looking for work at a company that knew how to treat people with something resembling common professional courtesy. Although he found himself wondering how on earth the place treated its *hires* if it was so inconsiderate toward those interviewing, he found the idea of leaving less than appealing. Maybe there was a crisis that he didn't know about— something so serious that there had not been a moment to spare. Maybe he and his contact had miscommunicated somehow about the meeting time. Maybe he was simply being tested. What would you have done? Stuck around for another two hours or hit the road?

Strategies for success:

- If you picked "hit the road," you certainly had good reason. In this case, however, the right answer was, wait around until the contact finally steps into the reception area.

- As it turned out, Mark was being tested. The interviewer knew that the person to whom Mark would report if he landed the job could be difficult to work with at times. As a means of testing the patience and poise of *all* the applicants for this position, the interviewer tried to simulate one stressful condition (working with a short-tempered boss) by substituting another one (waiting for four hours). Mark's calm reaction to an absurd delay won him the job offer he wanted.

- If you find yourself in this situation, or in anything vaguely resembling it, you will only aid your candidacy by sticking around and showing unfailing good humor when your time finally does roll around.

- Even if you do conclude that the organization in question has a lousy way of dealing with people, why jeopardize the potential for a good referral by blowing your top or stalking out in a huff?

#188: Set up a prepared series of flip charts during the interview.
Or:
Win from the start with a bold color chart.

When Mark scheduled an interview with an A-list company in his field of choice, he spent days preparing for the meeting. Still, he was a little worried that he would forget key points or lose track of his personal story when summarizing his qualifications. His solution? He secured a large flip-chart and designed a detailed presentation in answer to the questions he knew he would be likely to encounter. Early in the interview, when he was asked a question that led into his prepared material, he said, "That's an excellent question; let me show you how I would respond to that." He took a moment to unzip his portfolio, set up his easel and set out upon a five-minute summary of the materials he had prepared. Needless to say, the interviewer was mightily impressed both with Mark's thoroughness and his ability to prepare. The job offer followed quickly.

Strategies for success:

- After taking the time to develop your presentation, you may be tempted to launch right into your spiel without any meaningful preparation. This may lose you some points with the interviewer. During the interview, try to manage things so that the flip-chart comes out as a result of the *interviewer's expression of interest.* In other words, you probably shouldn't open your portfolio until you're invited to do so, or at least receive some kind of informed assent from the interviewer.

- Warning: A typographical error or other obvious mistake on a prepared presentation can be fatal to your candidacy. Have another person check your work carefully before you head for the interview.

- Don't be afraid to use color to enliven your visual presentation.

- Practice your "pitch" carefully. Do not get lost in the charts; maintain appropriate eye contact with the interviewer.

- Remember, your best bet is to design your presentation around the answers you would give to such timeless interview questions as: "Tell me about yourself," or "What most interests you about working with our company?" When those questions or anything vaguely approximating them come up, you can explain that you've spent some time preparing some visual aids that would help you respond more fully. Ask if the interviewer would care to see them. He or she will most probably say yes.

- Do not monopolize the interview session. Your presentation should be a brief chance to shine, not an extended lecture.

#189: Take out an ad on the side of a bus.
Or:
Rapid transit offers rapid results.

How it really worked: A New Englander eager to get into marketing plastered his photo and an abbreviated resume onto local transit vehicles. It paid off.

Strategies for success:

- Cramming too much copy into too little space is a common mistake made by the beginning ad designer. Don't let it happen to you.

- Choose a large, legible typeface.

- You don't have to include a photograph of yourself, but your ad should incorporate some strong visual element.

- It should go without saying that typographical errors or other basic problems with your ad can be catastrophic. Have the copy and layout checked closely by another person.

- Include a phone number that is available 24 hours a day. (Your best bet is probably an answering service.)

- For a parallel story, see #215.

#190: Apply for a vacant position immediately following the death of an employee who held the job you want.
Or:
Making the obituary method work for you.

Mark, who was in search of work as a foreman in a tight employment market, got word of a nasty incident at a local job site. One of the workers had brutally beaten the foreman following a personal dispute between the two. The foreman's wounds were severe, and he was rushed to a hospital, where he died a little later. Mark quickly made his way to the site and applied for the job. He got the job offer as a result of tight deadlines.

Strategies for success:

* The danger, of course, is that you may be perceived as ghoulish. Nevertheless, in any number of competitive fields, vacancies do occur as a result of people passing on. A sensitive inquiry in this situation may well yield results. Sources of information could include the obituary section of your local newspaper, the rumor mill or industry trade publications.

* Be tactful, polite and straightforward; make every effort to avoid coming across as crass or overly ambitious.

* Approach the supervisor of the person who passed on, not his or her subordinates.

* Do not press for an immediate response to your query for employment. Although Mark's experience on the construction site led to a quick offer, many other settings (including most professional workplaces) will require a good deal of time before a final decision on filling the vacancy is made.

#191: Send a video.
Or:
Lights, camera, action!

The pair of freelance writers who used this method to get a lucrative writing assignment passed along footage from a national news magazine about a story they'd worked on that received considerable national media attention. If you're not in a position to send along a copy of your recent interview with Peter Jennings, but you still want to take advantage of this intriguing approach, bear the following pieces of advice in mind.

Strategies for success:

- Video production is a time-consuming, expensive process. Sending along a home video has a significant disadvantage: If the footage looks amateurish, *you* may be perceived as amateurish! And why risk that?

- On the other hand, renting out a studio and hiring a technical crew isn't financially feasible for most of us. You may be tempted to "split the difference" and hire a local videographer to do a little impromptu, back-porch shooting for your brief promotional piece. Ask to see finished samples of the videographer's work first—and don't cave in to any suggestions that you include baby pictures, yearbook outtakes or wacky cutups better suited for a wedding reception. You're trying to get a job, not win a spot on *America's Funniest Home Videos*!

- Best bet: Keep the message brief, focus on a single theme and let whatever humor you use take the form of understated charm rather than anything vaguely related to slapstick. One interesting approach might be to adapt David Letterman's popular "Top Ten" list format, and offer, in reverse order, ten compelling (and, perhaps, ever-so-slightly self-deprecating) reasons you should have a face-to-face meeting with the decision maker.

- Don't ramble! Before you send the tape along, review it closely and ask yourself, "If I didn't know me, and had the opportunity to shut this off and do something else, would I watch it all the way through?" If your answer (or, even better, the answer of a trusted friend) is no, start again.

- See also #22.

#192: Take the money—and reapply.
Or:
Has the message gotten through yet?

A checker at a West Coast grocery chain wanted to be admitted to the store's management training program. Her superiors told her not to set her heart on the idea. One manager informed the checker that the men in the store would not work for any woman—let alone a woman of color. Of such remarks are lawsuits made; the checker and a number of other frustrated women employees initiated a class-action suit against the chain and won, citing a disturbing pattern of racist and sexist practices among store managers. The chain ended up paying hefty cash awards to those whom it had discriminated against. Most of those who won the awards left the chain, but the young checker, who apparently felt she still had a point to make, re-applied to the training program...and was accepted.

Strategies for success:
- Before undertaking any legal action against a current or prospective employer, discuss the case thoroughly with a good attorney.
- Expect a few chilly looks from senior management (and even fellow employees) if you mount a legal challenge against your company.
- Warning: Legal battles are costly, time-consuming and, in the final analysis, not a heck of a lot of fun. Still, there are some points that can only be made in court.
- See also #181 and #290.

#193: Tell the employer you refuse to allow him to make the mistake of not hiring you.
Or:
That word you just used—"no"—what exactly does that mean?

Glenn had applied for entry to a management training position at an extremely selective Los Angeles financial services firm. He went through a rigorous recruiting process that included psychological testing, aptitude testing and a battery of one-on-one and group interview sessions. When he was finally rejected, he was told that there was nothing tangibly wrong with his background or academic history—he simply lacked that elusive quality known as "a good fit" with the company. Glenn's response was immediate, if a little unconventional. He immediately demanded a personal interview with the head of the firm. Told that this would be impossible, he elicited the help of a headhunter he knew did a good deal of business with the firm. A week or so after having been rejected, Glenn had his interview with the top man at the firm. He got right to the point. "Your firm has made a terrible, terrible mistake," he told the president. "You've put yourself at a severe competitive disadvantage by not taking me on, and *I simply won't let you make an error of this magnitude.*" A hush fell over the walnut-paneled office, and it lasted for a good long time. It was finally broken when the president admitted he was impressed not only with Glenn's record, but also with his persistence. He held out his hand and congratulated the firm's newest employee.

Strategies for success:
- Glenn's "I-have-to-have-an-appointment-with-the-president" gambit represents perhaps the single classiest twist on the much-adapted category of persistence maneuverings, in which one basically refuses to go away until hired. Executed with tact, confidence and a good measure of deep concern for the future of the company in question, it can pay off.
- Be careful to steer clear of arrogance if you are attempting this with a CEO. The trick is to position yourself as persistent because of a profound concern for the position of the firm.

- Avoid saying "You must," "I insist," or any other such formulations with the head honchos of firms (and, especially, with the head honchos of *big, prestigious* firms). Stick with the daring, but essentially altruistic, "I won't let you make a mistake like this." Then, no matter how much you may be tempted to rattle on, sit back and stop talking. The ball is in the prospective employer's court.

- This is, of course, a risky technique, but if you execute it well, the only bad thing that can happen is that you'll get a polite, but firm, "No thanks, now get out of here." (Executed *poorly*, that is to say with a spiteful, go-ahead-and-call-security tone, it can land you in a world of trouble.)

#194: When your spouse gets a job offer, have him or her start inquiring after the possibility of your being employed at the same company.

Or:

Networking starts at home.

It started as an offhand thing; Bill "happened" to mention to the president of the company that had just hired him that his wife had an advanced degree in engineering. The president, in search of good engineering talent, wanted to know more, and Bill was glad to oblige by suggesting that the president talk to his wife directly. Before long, husband and wife were co-workers.

Strategies for success:

- This approach—which must be used with subtlety and discretion— is likeliest to yield good results at comparatively small, entrepreneurial organizations. In such results-first, politics-second settings, potentially challenging conflict-of-interest issues can probably be managed most successfully.

- Working at the same organization as your spouse presents a unique set of hazards. Before you formally accept such an arrangement, be sure all concerned have examined the potential problems closely and are willing to work in good faith to resolve any workplace or relationship dilemmas that may arise.

- If the offer is extended, consider asking for a trial period under which you, your spouse and the employer can get a sense of the pros and cons of such an employment arrangement.

#195: Recite a mantra.
Or:
Try this instead of "hummanuh, hummanuh, hummanuh."

In a classic case of enthusiasm winning out over style, a flustered applicant for a high-tech job kept repeating "I can do the job, I can do the job" every time he came up short on an interview response—which was pretty frequently. The interviewer later said that anyone who could sit through such an ordeal would probably give a little extra effort to the position. She was right.

Strategies for success:
- Most of the time, interviewers are on the lookout for poise and a sense of direction as much as they are for specific elements in your employment background. If you are uncertain about your ability to perform well at the interview, you may want to consider a "safe phrase" that highlights your determination to deliver results in a certain area.

- There is something to be said for doing your level best to answer the specific questions you're asked during the interview, though. Prospective employees who fail to do so are one of the most common peeves of interviewers.

#196: Send a cassette tape for the decision maker to listen to in the car on the way to or from work.
Or:
If you've got time to drive, you've got time to think about calling me in for an interview.

Eileen, a freelancer, swears by this technique, in which a "verbal resume," targeted directly to the prospective employer's needs is passed along for review. The trick is to get it directly to the person you want to reach (she suggests the head of the company). Best bet: an overnight courier service.

Strategies for success:

- Research, research, research. If you can make a convincing case for your ability to make contributions *in key areas of importance to your decision maker,* you may get good results. If you ramble on aimlessly about nothing in particular, you'll get switched off in a hurry.

- With the tape, include only a *brief* note suggesting that the decision maker listen to the tape in the car, as well as your contact information.

- Record in a place where background noise will be minimal or, better still, nonexistent.

- Be sure the first 30 seconds of your tape contains a "grabber" of some kind. If the tape does not incorporate a striking claim, promise or endorsement right off the bat, it will probably fail to hold the listener's interest.

- Keep the tone upbeat, professional and direct. Do not indulge in any inappropriate familiarity or chitchat.

#197: Highlight your karaoke skills.
Or:
Young lady, anyone who actually understands the lyrics to "Staying Alive" is our kind of candidate.

Maria, a lip-synch aficionado, did this when interviewing for a bartending job at a particularly upbeat, let-it-all-hang out chain of restaurants. It fit in with the general tone of the place, and since she got the job she's been known to let loose with a few numbers on Saturday nights during the customer karaoke competitions.

Strategies for success:
- Stay away from Billy Ray Cyrus unless you're willing to teach people how to line dance.

#198: Psych out the competition.
Or:
This company's not big enough for the both of us.

Alicia developed a fascinating way of gaining the upper hand before job interviews. While waiting in the lobby with another applicant, she would smile engagingly when her competitor was summoned to meet the hiring manager and say, ever so quietly, "It's really too bad you're going to lose out to me today." She didn't have to try it very often. Her shell-shocked competitors fell by the wayside, leaving the way open for her.

Strategies for success:
- Okay, it's mean. But it just might work, right?
- The best way to pull this off is to deliver the line (or your adaptation of it) very sweetly indeed. Avoid coming off as meanspirited.

• If the competitor reports your remark to the interviewer, and you find yourself questioned about it, simply say, "Ms. Smith, I told her that I didn't think she was going to get the job because I firmly believe that I'm the very best candidate for this position. Let me give you an example of the work that I've done that leads me to that conclusion..." Then supply an example of your strongest performance. The psych-out-the-competition move is not without risk, of course, but when executed with confidence (as opposed to vindictiveness), it beats fading into the scenery.

#199: Send the president of the firm a holiday greeting that happens to include your resume.

Or:

One way not to let acquaintance be forgot.

An article in the *National Business Employment Weekly* by Sinara Stull O'Connell and Raymond R. Cech tells the story of Joan Brown, a legal assistant in search of work in New York City during the holiday season. When she spotted a classified ad placed by a Manhattan firm in search of a legal assistant to the corporation's chief counsel, she did some research. The ad didn't mention the counsel's name, so Joan called the firm directly and asked for it. She then ignored the ad's instructions for contacting the company and sent a "Happy New Year" card (and her resume) directly to the man for whom she wished to work, who was impressed not only by her inventive approach, but also by the fact that she'd gotten the spelling of his unusual name right. She got her job offer less than a week later.

Strategies for success:

• You say you're looking for work and it doesn't happen to be December? Tempting as it may be to send your contact a "Happy Arbor Day" card, it probably won't have quite the same impact. (Birthdays, however, are another matter. See #59 for some ideas.)

- It is far better to send a card celebrating the New Year, or the holiday season in general, than a religious holiday of any kind.

- Follow Joan's example. Call ahead and get the person's name right!

#200: Show off your fish-cleaning abilities.
Or:
They always told me it would take guts to break in.

A top-level chef got his first job in a prestigious restaurant by making it known he was more than willing to don the rubber gloves, sit down next to a bucket and eviscerate the day's catch. The money wasn't great. His determination to work where great food was prepared, however, was. The moral: Let them know you'll do the grunt work because you love the business, and you'll come out all right.

Strategies for success:

- Demonstrate a passion for the particular business area you have chosen—then make it clear you will do anything necessary to make a contribution.

#201: Show off your yo-yo skills.
Or:
Yes, but can you loop the loop?

That's how Michael Caffrey got his job with the Duncan Toys Co. of Columbus, Ohio. Caffrey, who competed in his teens at the popular yo-yo contests of years past, knows more than 200 tricks; he impressed the brass at Duncan enough that they hired him to fill a sales position. Caffrey eventually became Duncan's national sales manager. Caffrey's story appeared in a recent *The Indianapolis Star* article.

Strategies for success:

- File this one under "Do what you love and the rest will take care of itself." Okay, okay, maybe you're not a yo-yo fiend—but what is your obsession?

- Consider contacting the company that is responsible for the product or service you can't get enough of. Customers who know the merchandise inside and out often make great employees.

- For two stories that provide interesting parallels, see #100 and #114.

Feeling Lucky?

#202: Stalk out before the interview.
Or:
I didn't want this job anyway.

In an article in *USA Today,* writer David Craig recounts how Wall Street legend Seth Glickenhaus won his first Wall Street job trading bonds in 1934. Glickenhaus had agreed to meet with Herbert Salomon, one of the founding brothers of the prestigious Salomon Bros. firm, but because he had recently won a spot at Columbia Law School, he was not planning to accept any offer that Salomon might extend. When he was told that Salomon would be unable to make the meeting for some time, Glickenhaus headed out the door. Salomon, however, stopped him at the elevator. "I told him I had grave misgivings. The ethical sense of (Wall Street) is corrupt," Glickenhaus recalled in an interview with the newspaper. Salomon apparently liked Glickenhaus's outlook and felt he had something to offer the firm: he offered him a job then and there. Glickenhaus agreed to try the job for three months, but warned that if Wall Street didn't agree with him, he'd have no qualms about entering law school. As it turned out, Glickenhaus stuck around for four years.

Strategies for success:

- Leaving in a huff is not exactly recommended practice; nor is questioning the ethics of the target industry as a whole. (Then again, Glickenhaus's sentiments were apparently genuine, which says something about standing behind your core values as a means of scoring points with the employer.)

- When faced with a delay, you are probably better advised to follow the advice in #187.
- Unless you're feeling quite lucky, you probably shouldn't count on this tactic.

#203: Tactfully, but steadily, increase the pressure every day.
Or:
Guess who?

Legendary author Napoleon Hill, during his public speeches, often told the story of how he targeted a particular company he wanted to work for. He sent a query letter that outlined his skills and asked about full-time employment. When it was rejected, he sent the letter once a week. When that didn't work, he took to hand-delivering the same letter once a day. By the end of the process, he claimed, he was sending a telegram to the president of the firm every hour on the hour. He got the job.

Strategies for success:

- The "accelerated message" plan is fine in theory—but you must be careful. Your application must be presented in such a way that it cannot possibly be interpreted as threatening.
- By adopting this method, you are in essence claiming, not that it would be a "good idea" for the company to take you on, but that you represent a *perfect match* for the firm. It is incumbent on you, then, to research the company thoroughly and provide ample proof of your claim to be able to help achieve its objective.
- It should go without saying that it is a waste of your time and the employer's to attempt this technique with a company that you are not sure you want to work for.
- Maintain unfailing politeness.

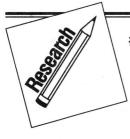

#204: Memorize every abbreviation on the New York Stock Exchange.

Or:

Pretty impressive, huh? Now, what was your name again?

A memory-improvement course offered the story of one of its graduates who managed this stunt and got a top-level job offer with a brokerage firm as a result. Apparently the hiring manager with whom the candidate was meeting refused to believe that such a feat was possible and demanded proof when the candidate made his claim. Sure enough, the intrepid applicant had mastered the entire list of obscure abbreviations and was able to offer them for any company the manager rattled off. You may be skeptical about your ability to pull off such a trick, but rest assured that such feats are, given a day or two of effort, not at all difficult once the basic principles are mastered.

Strategies for success:

- All memory is based on association; by studying a few simple methods for improving your association techniques, you can pull off an eye-popping demonstration just like the one described here.

- Obviously, you would want to adapt the memory feat to your own field of interest, and feature it prominently on your resume or in conversation with prospective employers.

- Although training in the development of enhanced memory techniques is beyond the scope of this book, you should strongly consider reviewing the methods available and adapting some form of this basic "show-off" technique to your job search campaign. It takes comparatively little time, and it has a remarkable (and welcome) tendency to leave interviewers gasping for breath and asking when you can start.

- For more information, see Kevin Trudeau's *Mega Memory* series of cassette tapes (Nightingale Conant/Soundworks, 1993), which were used by the featured applicant.

#205: Rent a billboard.
Or:
Do you know sign language?

A recent article in the *National Business Employment Weekly* tells the story of a new college graduate who was eager to break into the marketing field. Wallach reports that the fellow was doing battle with his resume when he happened to notice a nearby downtown billboard—waiting for an ad to occupy it. Only a week after posting his resume on the sign, he got five offers.

Strategies for success:

- Be sure the type is legible from ground level. This will probably mean limiting the amount of copy you use.

- Provide a phone number where you can be reached easily or have a message passed along. Your best bet: Hire an answering service for the period the ad runs.

- A typographical error can undercut a dramatic (and expensive!) appeal. Be sure to have a friend or family member review all copy carefully.

- Despite their significant logistical hurdles, banner- and billboard-related techniques of one kind or another appear to have delivered results for a good many job seekers. See #42, #62, #242, #253 and #256 for some variations.

#206: Take advantage of a managerial feud.
Or:
You only think you just fired me.

Kathy, a kitchen worker at a popular New England restaurant, had a bit of a falling-out with one of the owners of the chain. After a long night and some tense words, the boss told her she was fired. She contacted the owner's partner, who was, at that time, not on the best of terms with the man who'd done the firing. Kathy described the exchange and asked for a new job in a different restaurant in the chain. She got it.

Strategies for success:

- What is there to lose if you've already been fired? If you find yourself in a position to benefit from unresolved tension between higher-ups, a tactful meeting along these lines may get you another offer. Just be aware of the complicated political issues that may arise from such a situation and do your best to get an assignment that will not leave you vulnerable to recrimination.

- Present your case honestly, professionally and with no self-pity. Avoid the temptation to say cruel or inaccurate things about your previous supervisor.

#207: Tell a friend who's a cab driver that you're looking for a job; check with him regularly.

Or:

Just think of it as a placement office on wheels.

Ellen's talkative brother-in-law drove a cab; she gave him copies of her resume and asked him to pass it along to anyone in her target industry (broadcasting) with whom he happened to strike up a conversation. Within a week or two, the engaging driver had circulated her job history to three local television executives; one of them called her in for an interview for an editing job. She got it.

Strategies for success:

- This works best, obviously, if you're related to the driver. If you're not, and you take cabs fairly regularly, you might want to consider asking specifically for a particular driver's call number in order to build up the relationship.

- Only engaging, nonthreatening, outgoing drivers are likely to help your job search campaign.

- For an intriguing variation, in which you drive the cab yourself, see #138.

#208: Give the Boy Scout salute.
Or:
Thrifty, brave, reverent... and hired.

Eric was facing some stiff competition for a bartending position at an upscale restaurant—until he happened to mention his past history as a Boy Scout. It turned out the hiring manager had also been a Scout. The two spent 15 minutes swapping camp stories, which brought the interview to a pleasant, upbeat ending. As he left, he offered the traditional Scout salute. The next day Eric got a call informing him that he had won the job.

Strategies for success:

- Although any number of books on resume and interview preparation may advise otherwise, discreetly highlighting potential commonalties with prospective hiring managers can pay off.

- Your best bet: Focus on popular group or institutional involvement (scouting, public television volunteer work, online services or local charity drives, for instance) rather than more secluded or solitary pursuits (chess clubs, art projects or personal exercise routines).

#209: Interview by computer.
Or:
I'm not sure what you mean by "people skills," Hal.

According to the Greensboro *News & Record*, a North Carolina shoe store has set up an automated telephone interviewing system, in which applicants punch buttons on their touch-tone phones in response to prerecorded queries.

Those who succeed in conveying their suitability for an opening are granted a face-to-face meeting with a real, live human being.

Strategies for success:

- Don't bother trying to key in those long stories about how you increased sales or reduced down time. The computer won't want to hear it.
- The good news: You can conduct your initial job interview in a bathrobe.
- The bad news: All that work on projecting the right image through good body language won't do you any good with a digitized interviewer.

#210: Incorporate a detailed analysis of the company's soon-to-be-launched product as part of your application package.
Or:
Put in the research time—and you'll be first in line.

An enterprising sales applicant looking for a job with a communications firm used this with great success. She figured she'd have to sell the product anyway when she got the job, so she went out and interviewed people in the target group and summarized her findings about the product's market potential for the hiring manager. It worked.

Strategies for success:

- Clearly a research-intensive undertaking, but a great way to make an indelible first impression. Think twice before you unceremoniously slam a project that's been in the pipeline for seven or eight years, though.
- Give specifics on your interviews with potential consumers: names, towns, ages and so on. Quote them verbatim.
- Submit your report in an attractive format. Don't be afraid to use color.

#211: Prove that you're an Aquarius.
Or:
Wow, man. You're hired.

How it really worked: During the '60s, an aspiring young playwright by the name of John Guare was looking for a theater to produce his first play. He spoke to Joe Cino, proprietor of the avant-garde Caffe Cino theater. Cino had his doubts. "I'm only doing plays by Aquarians," he announced. Guare, as luck would have it, was in fact an Aquarius. Cino, dubious in the face of the lucky coincidence, demanded to see Guare's driver's license. When the date proved the young writer's claim, he had won his first production. Guare went on to write such landmark pieces as *The House of Blue Leaves* and *Six Degrees of Separation.* The story appeared in *The Boston Globe* on December 11, 1993.

Strategies for success:

- Let's face it. It was the '60s. There are probably laws against this sort of thing now. But keep your driver's license handy just in case.

#212: Sing.
Or:
Let's see, our next request is— "Get a Job."

Stanislav Kotyza, a Rye, New York contractor, elicited a curious glance or two (and, as it turned out, plenty of new business) by singing arias at the top of his lungs as he fixed the ceilings in an office building one night. According to a story in the *Westchester County Business Journal*, Kotyza, proprietor of Figaro Construction, is a classically trained singer as well as a talented craftsman. He pursues both of his passions at once, leading to visits from inquisitive passers-by. The "singing builder" won sufficient business through positive word of mouth in his area to make advertising unnecessary.

#213: Wait tables where you know decision makers eat lunch; outline your qualifications before you outline the day's specials.
Or:

And along with the wine list, you'll find a copy of my resume.

Judy got a job as a waitress in a district of the city that served as home base to a good many law firms. After telling her patrons about the specials of the day, she mentioned her status as a recent law school graduate and touched on her desire to work with a corporate law firm. Her initiative paid off; a senior partner at a local firm asked to interview her and eventually offered her a job.

Strategies for success:

- Unless you have a very understanding boss, you will need to be discreet as you discuss your professional objectives with customers.
- Keep a pad of paper handy to record names and phone numbers of people you meet.
- Collect business cards whenever you can and be prepared to offer your own in return.
- Follow up appropriately by phone or mail.

#214: Dress to match, precisely, the decor of the prospective employer's office.
Or:

What do you mean, they've just painted the office day-glo orange?

"So what should I know about the place?" Ginny asked her friend Frank, who had gotten her an interview for a secretarial position at a local architecture firm. The answer she got surprised her. The man she would be interviewing with had just had his office redecorated, and had been overheard asking employees to choose clothing that complemented the new interior, which was done up in beige and pink. The next day, at the interview, Ginny dressed in those two colors, and made a point of mentioning that her wardrobe included plenty of beige and pink outfits. This was an ever-so-slight exaggeration, perhaps, but it was for a good cause. She got the job offer that day, and then headed to her favorite clothing store to stock up on garments beige and pink.

Strategies for success:

- Warning: In most professional interview settings, men don't have anywhere near the latitude women do when it comes to color selection of clothing and accessories.

- Prudence demands the cautious—but nevertheless pertinent—observation that a man interviewing for the same job, clad in a beige shirt with pink tie, pink jacket and pink slacks, might not have impressed the interviewer in quite the same way.

#215: Take out ads on the interiors of city subway cars.

Or:

Just watch out for that painted-on mustache problem.

An enterprising accountant ponied up the money for this one. The ad pictured a smiling picture of the fellow, a brief description of his background and a number to call. He only had to run the ad for a month.

Strategies for success:

- Be absolutely sure the ad is free from typographical errors or other basic mistakes.

- Provide a number that you can be reached at, or that can accept messages, 24 hours a day. (Best bet: an answering service.)

- Keep the ad text brief; don't try to cram too much information into the small space at your disposal.
- Have your heart set on sending a bigger message? See #189.

#216: Confidently tell the interviewer you'd like to change something about the interview room's surroundings.
Or:
And while you're at it, take another look at that tie of yours, will you?

When Karen sat down to interview at the management consulting firm that eventually hired her, she noticed that the light from the window behind the interviewer's was shining in her eyes. Without hesitation, she said, "Would you mind drawing those blinds, please?" She eventually learned from the interviewer that that simple question had put her over the top for a very competitive position. The company was eager to find someone who could work well in challenging situations, someone who wouldn't be afraid to stand his or her ground with a number of difficult co-workers in the department. The sunlight-in-the-eyes problem Karen faced was not a deliberate effort on the part of the employer to test her mettle, but her response to it did serve to distinguish her from a number of other candidates with similar backgrounds.

Strategies for success:

- Warning: There's a fine line between establishing a clear sense of personal space and mouthing off like an abrasive jerk. Avoid the latter option at all costs.
- If you do decide to use an approach such as this to identify yourself as an applicant with clear standards and a strong sense of purpose, be sure to do so in a polite, professional manner.
- For another story that illustrates the potential advantages of letting the employer know you're willing to stand your ground, see #269.

#217: During a temporary assignment, ignore the job description.
Or:

I wasn't hired to make you more money? Are you sure?

A major food service company hired Ken to run the company's booth at an industry trade fair. Ken not only fulfilled the basic duties of the job he'd been assigned—monitoring traffic, handing out preprinted brochures and the like—but he also set up a series of flashy promotions that drew huge crowds to the booth. In addition, he took on a number of janitorial tasks when the assigned help failed to show up. "He worked 14-hour days and just did whatever it took to get the job done," the president recalled. It was the best trade show in the company's history. Ken received a job offer to manage a chain of restaurants shortly thereafter.

Strategies for success:

- Any number of warnings about getting things approved beforehand are likely to be sent your way if you try something like this, but the fact is that people in authority like to find self-directed workers who, like them, are driven to accomplish things.

- Take some time to strategize. Map out exactly what you plan to do ahead of time. Consider the temporary assignment your audition for a big role in a Broadway play. Know what you'll be performing.

- Be sure that all the essential duties you were originally hired to perform are attended to. (If necessary, show up well ahead of time—say, 6 a.m.—to see that they are completed properly.)

- Avoid problems with authorization and set things into motion with lightning speed so that results are the first thing people notice.

- Do not take on anything you can't complete to a high level of quality.

- You may get a standing ovation; then again, you may get some flack from bewildered managers. After you leave, you can insure yourself to some degree by sending a one-page summary of what you accomplished during the assignment to the head of the organization, and then following up by phone to ask for a job.

#218: Send your resume in a gift-wrapped box.
Or:
Just try to ignore this.

Nancy, a recent college graduate, used this to win a job at a bank that was looking for management trainees. Talk about standing out from the crowd!

Strategies for success:

- A brief cover letter with a big headline making reference to "how much you have to give," or some such clever line, is probably in order if you try this. Be sure to include all appropriate contact information.

- You will probably want to deliver the package in person to the decision maker's assistant or executive assistant. Do so with an air of confidence and poise.

- Be prepared to cite compelling success stories and outline the ways you can contribute to the organization. You may well receive a phone call from the prospective employer and you should be ready to make the most of the opportunity.

- The box should be big and/or splashy enough to inspire curiosity about its contents.

- This technique was cited by multiple sources during the research for this book.

#219: When asked to prepare a short presentation on a topic of your choice, use the opportunity to outline how a job seeker should contact employers.

Or:

How I managed to get this interview with you.

Ellen had contacted DataLibe, a local software company regarding a position selling and training clients on their electronic library products. For the interview, she was to prepare a 10-minute presentation for the manager of the office, on any topic she chose. She decided to do a how-to session on getting a job interview with DataLibe. Ellen reproduced the ad the company had placed in the local paper; she even broke the ad down into essential components, and explained how to design a cover letter and resume to present oneself as the ideal candidate for the position. The interviewer was delighted, and shortly afterward offered Ellen the job.

Strategies for success:

- "Self-referential" presentations during the interview can be a major asset to your job search campaign, but they must reinforce the key skills you offer. In Ellen's case, the key skill was the ability to deliver a visually interesting presentation that offered concise analyses of a variety of information sources.

- Let the humor of such a presentation support your message ("I am the best qualified applicant for this job") without overwhelming it.

- Maintain appropriate eye contact; don't get lost in your graphs and copies. If you are uncomfortable delivering such information to an individual or group, this will be obvious immediately. If necessary, practice your "pitch" with friends or relatives.

#220: **Bring along your sample drawings in a handsome handcarved container.**
Or:
Packaging does make a difference.

In her fine book *Interviewing*, Arlene S. Hirsch tells the story of an architect who showed off his woodworking skills by bringing along a striking handcarved box to his job interview; it contained his sample drawings. After he'd won the job, the architect learned that the lovely, intricately detailed box was the factor that had been most responsible for setting him apart from his competitors for the job.

Strategies for success:

- Props leave an impression! You don't have to use exactly the same method as the woodworking architect, but you *should* find some physical object (perhaps of your own making) that helps the interviewer distinguish you from the other 10 or 12 people he or she will probably be speaking with about the job.

- Possible alternatives include: A hand-embroidered cover for your portfolio; a customized leather folder for your resume and related job materials; or a uniquely personalized business card or career summary that features cartoons.

- Unless you're applying for a job in the graphic arts field, most of your competitors will not be supplying much in the way of visual stimulus. Use that to your advantage!

#221: Book yourself on a local radio show as an expert in your field.

Or:

Talk, talk, talk.

How it really worked: Over the course of a year and a half, Mel had done a great deal of volunteer work in the arts, all as part of his search for a theater management position. He jokingly mentioned to his wife that he ought to market himself as an expert in the field of working for free. His wife assured him that it was a wonderful idea—and suggested that Mel contact some of the local radio talk shows in town with an eye toward booking himself as a guest. As it happened, voluntarism was a hot topic at the time Mel made his calls, and he found himself booked relatively quickly for several shows. As a result of a connection he made on his third appearance, he arranged an interview with the artistic director of a local theater—and won a job in the development office.

Strategies for success:

- Good phone technique is an absolute must here. Producers must feel confident in your ability to project a confident, interesting and comparatively unflappable verbal persona, and they will decide within a few seconds of talking to you on the phone whether or not you fit the bill.

- Pick your own specialty. It should be something with which you've had a great deal of experience, something you're passionate about. It does not necessarily have to be related to what you're currently doing for a living.

- Develop a general script outline so that you will be familiar with the points you want to cover with producers, but do not follow this outline slavishly. A "canned" delivery will serve as a neon sign for radio people: "Stay away from this guest."

- Practice your calls to producers thoroughly before you make a single call. If you can, enlist the aid of a friend or relative.

- Consider taping a sample exchange with your partner; listen to the results and critique them honestly.

- Often, you will be booked with other guests on a program; consider approaching these people for employment.

- This technique was cited by multiple sources during the research for this book.

#222: Cop a plea.
Or:
A single sentence can change many lives.

In his book *Awaken the Giant Within*, Anthony Robbins tells the story of an ex-con-turned-private investigator named Dwayne Chapman who had fallen seriously behind on his child-support payments. Rather than demand money he knew Chapman didn't have, the judge offered him an alternative to jail—a new line of work that would help him meet his obligations. A rapist who had attacked many women was on the loose in the area, and Chapman accepted the assignment of tracking him down. Police had searched for the rapist for over a year, but Chapman arrested him only days after receiving the task. Chapman, realizing he had a knack for this sort of thing, began focusing on his new specialty: working closely with law enforcement officials in the risky business of tracking down escaped criminals. According to Robbins, this remarkable change in focus resulted in an unbelievable success rate of about *one arrest every day*.

Strategies for success:

- Sometimes opportunity turns up in the most unlikely places. Keep an open mind and be ready to look at even unwelcome developments as possibilities for you to find a new avenue in which to apply your abilities.

- For another example of someone who turned around a seemingly dismal employment situation, see #230.

#223 During the interview, drop quarters into a trash can.
Or:
Roll out the barrel...

A recent article by Brad McBucklin in the *National Business Employment Weekly* related how a West Coast mechanical engineer by the name of Laszlo Balogh won over an interviewer. Balogh brought a generous supply of quarters to the interview; any time a question was put to him, Balogh would reach into his pocket, extract a coin and drop it into a nearby wastebasket before answering. After a while, the puzzled interviewer asked for an explanation of the unusual ritual. Balogh replied that he was illustrating how much money the company had lost so far by sitting him down and asking questions rather than hiring him and putting him to work immediately. He got the job.

Strategies for success:

- If you can back up the strong talk with a record of equally tangible results, this approach could well do the trick. Just remember not to deliver that 50-megaton punch line with any trace of arrogance or impatience.
- Whatever you do, don't spoil the effect by scouring the bottom of the trash can for change at the end of the session!

#224: Enter a contest.
Or:
You never know if you don't try.

A recent piece in *Yankee* magazine offered readers the chance to run—and, for that matter, own—a 188-year-old country inn in Center Lovell, Maine. The rules? Write a brief essay about why you should operate the place—and pony up a $100 entrance fee. Competition was fierce. The winners of the contest, Janice and Richard Cox, used their essay to highlight their background in the hospitality field (she was a restaurant manager, he was a chef). According to an article in *The Boston Globe*, the new career path the couple embarked on as a result of winning the contest has, at times, had its challenging moments—but it appears to agree with them.

Strategies for success:

- This is basically a toss of the dice, of course, but if you enter something along these lines, be sure to address the likely concerns of those who will be judging the competition. (The Coxes, a hard-working team with a strong background in the guest-pleasing field, seem to have gone out of their way to demonstrate a capacity for keeping up with the many physical demands of the job, including ongoing maintenance of the antique structure.)

- For an interesting parallel directed at computer hackers, see #268.

#225: Make your live video debut.

Or:

Don't be too surprised if you find yourself on the cover of TV Guide after you try this.

Using technology arranged by Management Recruiters International, a search firm with franchises across the country, job applicants are overcoming distance barriers via live broadcast hookups to speak with employers about current openings. The companies pay for the hookup, which is often followed by an in-person meeting.

Strategies for success:

- You may want to commandeer a friend with a video camera for a "dry run" rehearsal session that you can review before you set out on a video interview.

- Although the following tics or habits are not going to do you much good during a person-to-person interview, they're potentially catastrophic when you're under the penetrating gaze of a video camera. Watch out for:

- Blinking too much.
- Glancing all over the room.
- Fidgeting in your seat.
- Talking nonstop.
- That last item is of particular importance; you don't want to give curt, information-free responses to questions, but you should remember that there is a partner at the other end of the conversation. It's easy to forget the natural rhythms of two-way interchange while you're staring at the little red light.
- Check your local phone directory for more information about Management Recruiters International franchises in your area.

#226: Send the prospective employer a favorite industry-related book you think he or she might enjoy.
Or:
Throw the book at 'em.

The book Allan sent was accompanied by a very short letter indicating that he hoped to speak with the decision maker soon about a customer-service-related opening. He got a call the next week, was interviewed over the phone, and eventually won a job offer.

Strategies for success:
- The book you send will, of course, say a lot about you. If it is directly related to the position or industry in question, and if it contains information of interest to the decision maker, you will have gone a long way toward standing out from the completion.
- Do not send a book you have not read.
- Do not send a book that has already received a great deal of exposure in the media.
- Keep the letter brief. Mention that you got a lot out of the book, and think that the employer may, too.

- Follow up as appropriate by phone.
- This technique was cited by multiple sources during the research for this book.

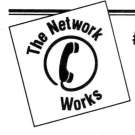

#227: Attend the annual meeting of your target company. Walk up to complete strangers, summarize your background and ask for a job.
Or:

How do you do, Mr. Importante? Glad you could make it.

Where else, Sylvia figured, would you be more likely to run into a significant number of company bigwigs? Armed with multiple copies of her resume, a clean, pressed suit and a smile, she sat through the long, dreary meeting for the express purpose of introducing herself to anyone and everyone she could during coffee breaks and post-meeting social time. It paid off.

Strategies for success:

- Dress sharp!
- Develop a brief (very brief!) summary of your professional aims and accomplishments; practice it until it comes naturally.
- Prepare yourself to recite it to everyone in sight at any conceivable opportunity during your target company's annual meeting.
- Jump right into the pool. Stick out your hand, smile, and say your name. Get the other person's name, repeat it, say "Nice to meet you," and deliver your summary.
- Ask who you should talk to.
- Repeat the process.

#228: Hang out at the message center at an industry gathering.

Or:

What a coincidence!

Having purchased a visitor's pass, Myra simply stationed herself at the message board of a major industry trade organization's annual meeting and waited for bigwigs to swing by. When they did, she briefly introduced herself and concisely stated her career goals and background. When she spotted someone who had interviewed her a few months earlier for a position she did not get, she quickly stepped over to reintroduce herself. As it happened, there was a new spot open in the same department she'd visited earlier. Thanks to the "chance" encounter, Myra got an interview—and a job offer—from a company that had turned her down.

Strategies for success:

- Not for the faint of heart. Be willing to hear a lot of "no's" before you hear a "yes." The advantage to this approach, of course, is that you'll hear them over the course of a day or two, rather than weeks or months.

- If you can, try to supplement the "loiterer" technique with pre-arranged meetings during the conference or trade show.

- If you prefer, simply drop by the booths or stands of companies on your target employer list.

- Keep careful notes on all the people you meet. Follow up by phone or by mail after the show. Even a show that does not yield an immediate job offer will accelerate your path toward an interview.

- Be confident, upbeat and optimistic. Contrary to what you may have heard, people like being approached directly—as long as the person doing the approaching is pleasant, outgoing and focused on the positive.

#229: Highlight your experience as a stand-up comic.

Or:

If you want to hear my act, that may be a little bit extra.

Ben was not interested in pursuing a career as a stand-up comedian, (he wanted a job in public broadcasting) but he did prominently feature his stints at a local comedy club on his resume. This unusual element generated instant interest from prospective employers, and also helped spur quite a few good-natured questions during job interviews. It doesn't hurt to put something a little off-the-beaten track on your resume. Ben got two job offers as a result of his unusual experience.

Strategies for success:

- People who schedule interviews have to turn great big stacks of resumes into little teeny tiny stacks representing people who deserve face-to-face meetings. It's a dreary job, but someone has to do it. You'll make it easier on everyone if you offer something unconventional (and unthreatening).

- Given Ben's success, there's probably something to be said for entering the amateur night competition at your local comedy club. Even if you fail spectacularly, you can place the experience on your resume and see what happens.

- Feeling really brave? *On request*, do a couple of jokes from your routine at the interview. But stick with the sure-fire material—and don't tell any jokes that are racist, sexist or in otherwise questionable taste.

- See also #69 and #183.

**#230: Stick out your hand and say "It's a deal"
when offered a package designed to get
you to say no.**
Or:
What do you mean, you'll take it?

According to Andrew A. Lanyi's book *Confessions of a Stock Broker*, an enterprising career-changer with no formal background as a stockbroker used this maneuver and made a go of it at a major New York brokerage firm. The offer had been extended as a courtesy, with a salary significantly lower than that of his previous job. The startled interviewer found himself shaking hands, not quite able to believe that he was agreeing to take the quick-thinking applicant on. But he was, and, as it turned out, he wasn't disappointed; the new broker proved to be a big success, quickly picking up hefty commissions that helped to close the salary gap.

Strategies for success:

- An interesting maneuver that's certainly worth trying if the opportunity arises—and if you've got enough in the bank to tide you over while you prove yourself on the new job.

- Whatever you do, don't hesitate once you decide to try this. The gambit is basically a way of saying, "I've-got-more-*chutzpah*-than-I-know-what-to-do-with." It must be carried off with supreme confidence.

- This can be particularly impressive during interviews for sales positions; it demonstrates confidence, control and strong presentation skills.

#231: Start a rumor campaign against yourself.
Or:
Did you hear the news? I'm dead meat.

A recent article in *The Boston Globe* tells how basketball coach John Calipari landed the job as coach of the University of Massachusetts team by enlisting the help of his buddies in spreading a rumor that he didn't have a chance of winning the position. It all happened during the finals of the 1988 NCAA tournament. Calipari told a reporter, "People were bad-mouthing me. So one morning, I called this 9 a.m. huddle at my hotel room. I asked five of my friends, all assistant coaches, to go to the lobbies of the hotels where all the coaches were staying. I said, 'Tell every coach you can find I'm not gonna get it.' I figured they'd lay off me and start bad-mouthing somebody else. Sure enough, everywhere I went that day, coaches were coming up to me: 'Gee, sorry to hear the news, John.' " Calipari's rivals stopped the assault; the top brass at University of Massachusetts were able to view his candidacy objectively; and within the week Calipari was offered the job.

Strategies for success:

- Politics is a strange thing, especially when a coveted position is at stake. If you find yourself the victim of a smear campaign of some kind, a maneuver like this may well help to silence the voices that have been raised against you. But bear in mind that such techniques represent a toss of the dice, and should probably only be employed when you feel certain your candidacy is strong enough to stand up against a potential backlash.

- After all, there is the very real danger that your message may become a self-fulfilling prophecy and that the decision makers will assume there must be *something* untoward in your background if everyone around them is saying you haven't got a chance.

- If you do adopt Calipari's rather unorthodox approach, be sure you never supply any reason for assessing your candidacy as doomed. Even the most innocuous one will take on staggering dimensions once it's been fed into the rumor mill.

#232. During the construction and remodeling phase, apply to the new business about to occupy the location your old employer once occupied.

Or:

Hey, I remember this place!

Thanks to an incursion by a large national pharmacy chain, the small-town drugstore Jenny once managed had gone under—it had been boarded up for over a year. She'd made ends meet over the months by finding temporary assignments with a local employment agency, but she'd grown tired of this pattern and was eager to find full-time work once again. At about the same time she was preparing to motivate herself to target her resume to a local store for a full-time job, she noticed that a new business—a coffee shop—was remodeling the site the drugstore used to occupy and was preparing to open next month. On a whim, Jenny visited the site and asked to speak with the owner, a genial fellow who was more than happy to talk to her. "I used to work here back when it was a drugstore," she told him. "I was the best manager my boss ever hired, and if you take me on, you'll feel the same way." After asking a few questions about her background, the owner of the new operation asked for her old boss's phone number. Two days later, after her reference checked out, Jenny got the job offer she wanted.

Strategies for success:

- Obviously, this is a scenario that won't apply to everyone. If a business is taking over a spot where you used to work, or has taken the spot over, you may wish to take advantage of this automatic "talking point" in presenting your qualifications. Be prepared to supply appropriate references.

- This method offers an interesting way to overcome the "background problem" you may face in entering a new field, but it depends heavily on the persistence and professionalism of your presentation.

- Do not try to pressure the hiring official into making an immediate decision; calmly, positively outline your contributions in the previous position.

#233: Hang out at a truck stop.
Or:
The networking's great on the interstate.

Brent was eager to get a new assignment as a trucker; when he saw a representative of a competing trucking firm talking to drivers at one of his favorite highway restaurants, he walked over, made his case and was offered a job on the spot.

Strategies for success:

- This sort of thing really does happen, and particularly in this industry, where competition for drivers can be intense. The underlying idea of congregating where the decision makers in your industry are likely to gather can, of course, be translated to any number of fields.

- Keep an eye out for opportunity and be ready, at a moment's notice, to highlight the problems you can solve for the prospective employer.

- For an interesting parallel idea that involves tactful networking *while you're working* at a restaurant your target employers are likely to frequent, see the next entry.

#234: Interview with your boss's competitors as you take their orders.
Or:
And tonight's special is—me.

Terry, a waiter, actually secured a job offer from a competing restaurant while on the job. The management of the other operation had stopped in for a bite to eat—and to get a look at the restaurant's employees, whom they hoped to recruit. (This practice, though not exactly popular among those whose staffs are raided, is apparently quite common in the restaurant industry.)

Strategies for success:

- Be discreet.
- If you don't feel like letting the other employer do the approaching, you may wish to point the conversation in the right direction with a seemingly innocuous business-related remark. ("How's business over at your place? You keeping busy?")
- For other examples of how service-industry encounters led to important career breaks, see #74, #81, #93 and #249.

#235: Use a flattering news clipping as the basis of a targeted mail campaign.

Or:

Did you read the wonderful things people are saying about you?

David Opton of Execunet passes along the story of an out-of-work comptroller who happened to come across a short filler piece in the business section of a major national magazine. The brief "factoid," which mentioned that the majority of chief financial officers at Fortune 200 companies were graduates of a particular university, caught the comptroller's eye because he himself was a graduate of that university. After engaging in a little library research, the comptroller was able to assemble the names of most of the CFOs to which the magazine had referred. He sent each a photocopy of the article, accompanied by a letter that said, in essence, "We share the same alma mater, so you know I've got what it takes; I'm not looking for a Chief Financial Officer job, but I am looking for a job as a comptroller. Please keep me in mind." The letter produced multiple job interviews—and a job offer.

Strategies for success:

- An inventive, instantly memorable way to take advantage of school connections. Locating a similar clipping, a short news piece around which you can design a powerful mail campaign, is probably easier than you think. Check your alumni magazine; ask your local library about a computerized article text search on the name of your alumni.

- Send them a photocopy of the actual clipping; highlight pertinent sentences in yellow.
- Keep the letter brief; enclose a copy of your resume.
- Follow up by phone a week or so after you mail the letters.

#236: Bring food.
Or:
That's the way the cookie crumbles.

A recent account from author Barbara Winter told of an innovative freelance worker in the New York area who found a tasteful solution to the perennial problem of standing out from the crowd. This innovative woman would hand over a small bag of chocolate chip cookies after each in-person meeting with a person considering hiring her. Attached to the bag was her business card and a brief summary of her professional specialty. The result? A dramatic increase in assignments.

Strategies for success:

- This can be an effective technique—if the gift is offered as a small, end-of-meeting thank-you.
- If you take a less discreet route—nervously passing along the bag at the beginning of the meeting, or rambling on about your favorite recipes when the employer clearly doesn't want to hear—you will probably undo any favorable impression this method can create.
- Stay away from exotic, heavy or messy recipes. Your aim is to provide a few snack-sized morsels of a popular favorite that will be easy to enjoy in an office setting. (After all, not everyone likes jalapeno coconut toffee surprise.)

#237: Volunteer to carry groceries at the supermarket.

Or:

Let me help you out with that...here's my card.

Chris, a freelance worker, was eager to get new assignments. His solution? He dressed up in his best suit and tie and headed to the supermarket, where he stood outside and offered to help people transfer the contents of their overloaded shopping carts to their cars. Once everything had been packed away neatly, Chris would shake hands, describe his specialty and pass along his business card. "I got quite a few calls that way," Chris remembers. "And it only made sense; after all, I was offering to pitch in, I dressed like someone who wasn't going to accost anyone and I was really polite. Most of the time, I guess people would keep the card or pass it on to someone who might want to work with me."

Strategies for success:

- Dress very neatly indeed—people may well mistake you for a supermarket employee. Don't claim to be something you're not, but don't be afraid to come across as a conscientious professional, either.

- Do not come across as aggressive or in any way overbearing. If someone declines your offer, smile and wait for the next person.

- Bring plenty of business cards (or whatever other compelling written material you develop).

#238: Wear an abbreviated copy of your resume on your T-shirt.

Or:

The ultimate fashion statement—your own private designer label.

Don, an out-of-work software designer, tried this at the suggestion of his career counselor. He wore his brief career summary to concerts, barbecues, beach parties and anything else he could think of. Guess what? It worked!

Strategies for success:

- Try composing a catchy headline and a brief skill summary (for the front). Put your contact information on the back. Have a friend proofread it carefully.

- If you feel a little silly at first, remind yourself that people are paying good money to wear shirts that advertise shoes, beer, food products and any number of other things. If that's not weird, why is advertising yourself?

- *Don't* wear the T-shirt to a formal job interview.

- T-shirt related techniques were cited by multiple sources during the research for this book. For an intriguing design idea, see #159. For an approach that worked by sending the shirt to the decision maker, see #48.

#239: Track down Human Resources people at industry conferences and corner them.

Or:

Sneaking up on 'em when they least expect it.

Josephine had gotten tired of going through the conventional channels to meet the people who could schedule interviews for her, so she decided to find them where they congregated in large numbers outside of their offices.

She paid to attend a one-day seminar on the Americans with Disabilities act, but not because she needed to know more about that landmark piece of legislation. During the day, she worked the lobbies and lunch tables of the convention center, approaching scores of human resource professionals with a handshake and a confident smile, and briefly outlining her qualifications for the management information services director position she was after. Armed with dozens of copies of her resume, she made more progress in a single day than she had in the previous two months. Interviews, and a job, followed shortly thereafter.

Strategies for success:

- Dress as though you were at an interview for the position you really want—you are.

- Respect the time commitments of the people you approach. They're attending the seminar for a reason. (But do make the most of the "down time" between talks and during lunch hour—making the most of that time is why *you* showed up.)

- Be persistent, tactful and of unfailing good humor.

- Ask for business cards. Follow up by mail and phone as appropriate.

#240: Tee off.
Or:
Bring your qualifications to the fore!

Jim was an out-of-work manufacturing executive who was low on job leads—and cash. Even so, he determined to scratch together the money necessary to join a local country club. It's not that Jim was a rabid golf fan, although he played a decent game. He knew that the networking possibilities on the green and in the lobby of the club were excellent. In a matter of weeks, he'd met dozens of top executives, and gotten several invitations for job interviews—one of which led to a full-time position.

Strategies for success:

- Can't afford to join the club? Consider volunteering to help at charity golf events, which present similarly rich networking possibilities.

- Hate golf? Don't try to fake your way through this technique. Part of the ritual in initiating contacts in this setting is spending a good 15 minutes discussing the intricacies of the game. Poseurs tend to stand out.

#241: Bring a local sports banner to the job interview.
Or:
Go team!

That's what helped to make the difference for aspiring announcer Dick Lutsk, an eternally upbeat radio personality who showed up for his interview with top Boston Red Sox brass bearing just such an accessory—and a matching cap for good measure. They hired him for weekend pregame and postgame work. The story appeared recently in *The Boston Globe*.

Strategies for success:

- Obviously, if you use this technique, you may want to adapt the "team colors" approach to the target company's products, services or logo.

- Warning—Red Sox attire is not recommended for those seeking employment with the New York Yankees.

#242: Hire a boat to cruise the waterfront with a large sign bearing your contact information and job specialty.

Or:

By the sea, by the sea, by the beautiful sea.

An out-of-work remodeler used this to prove that job-seeking really can be a day at the beach.

Strategies for success:

- The more people who can see you, the better your chances.
- Make sure the sign is legible from a good distance.
- Despite their significant logistical hurdles, banner- and billboard-related techniques of one kind or another have delivered results for a good many job seekers. See #42, #62, #205, #242, #253 and #256 for some variations.

#243: Keep a crowbar by your side at all times.

Or:

The conversation piece as employment aid.

Mel, a bartender, always propped a large crowbar by the cash register whenever he came into work. Customers would invariably ask what it was doing there; when his boss was not within earshot, Mel would reply that he was "trying to break into a new field." After a joke or two about the perils of a career in burglary, he would discreetly outline his professional background. He eventually secured a better job as a restaurant manager as a result of a contact he made using this method.

Strategies for success:

- A conversation piece can make initiating contact with strangers a lot easier. If your work involves exposure to many people during the course of your work day, this method may be a good one for unearthing new opportunities.

- Warning: Bosses tend to take a dim view of outright job networking during business hours. If your surroundings make long conversations about career opportunities difficult, consider printing up business cards summarizing your professional aims and passing them discreetly to interested parties.

#244: Memorize a favorite story or poem.
Or:
Wasn't it Shakespeare who said...

Fifteen-year-old Sarah Bernhardt, at her first audition, was very nearly speechless with fright. She had announced that she would be reciting a scene from Racine's *Phedre*—but unfortunately, she had neglected to bring the prompt-book, and thus could not perform the piece. Trembling, she determined on the spot to make the best of a terrible situation by reciting a favorite fable, *Les Deux Pigeons*. The judges were suitably impressed with her technique to award her one of the coveted slots for which she was competing that day.

Strategies for success:

- Forget about acting auditions for a moment. Having a favorite poem, speech or story to recite at any given time shows intelligence, foresight and a sense of direction in life. Consider adding this powerful weapon to your interview arsenal.

- A memorized poem or speech by a great writer yields a refreshing sense of security; you have at least one answer to that infuriatingly vague question, "Tell me about yourself." ("Well, I'm the kind of person who's always been impressed by good poetry. My favorite is probably Auden's *In Memory of W.B. Yeats*. Would you like to hear it?")

- Having *something* profound (or at least not foolish) to say may well be helpful if you find yourself sitting in the middle of an awkward silence during a stress interview situation.
- Memorize the piece *thoroughly* and practice it in front of friends.

#245: Send a message in a bottle.
Or:
Uncorking opportunity.

A corporate trainer in New York tells the story of a freelancer who got more than one assignment by sending each of the decision-makers on his list a targeted cover letter and resume inside a clear, label-free, empty bottle, and then following up by telephone several days later. The technique won attention—and offers.

Strategies for success:
- Develop a cover letter that employs both humor appropriate to the packaging and emphasizes a benefit the prospective employer is eager to hear more about. (For instance, "Do you ever feel lost at sea when you set out to find layout artists who aren't afraid to put in a little overtime?") Remember, the world will little note nor long remember a gimmick employed for its own sake.
- Long-necked glass wine bottles will probably be frustrating for the recipient. Plastic bottles with wide, easy-to-manage mouths are probably a better bet. Just to be on the safe side, experiment with the bottle first. How easy is it for you to extract the paper from the bottle?
- Feeling creative? Design a "label" that addresses itself to the recipient. (If you're not up for this, just scrub the old label off.)
- The bottle must be clean, clear and dry. Send it in a cardboard box with appropriate packing materials.

#246: Bring a slide projector.
Or:
If the machine breaks down, you can always do your shadow puppet routine.

This was used by Sandy, a graphic arts applicant who was looking for an opportunity to show off her work. She'd grown tired of asking prospective employers to use their imaginations in reviewing tiny color slides by holding them up to a window. Sandy made quite an impression (no one else who was applying tried this approach), and she got the job offer. The idea can be adapted with comparative ease to a brief review of the benefits you offer employees.

Strategies for success:

- You can rent the necessary equipment—including a camera to take pictures of signs or samples—for comparatively little money. Considering the added impact you will gain by using the projector, it will probably be money well spent.

- When composing written material for slides in your presentation, focus on success stories from your background, and keep the text brief. One slide can only accommodate a sentence or two.

- Have all your text checked carefully for typographical errors or other mistakes by another person.

- Don't be afraid to use color to liven up the presentation.

#247: Draw up a detailed, customized strategic business plan for the benefit of the company at which you will be interviewing.

Or:

Here's your battle strategy for the next two years.

Sure, it takes a little bit of work, and you always run the risk of having done some free consulting work for the target firm—but is that really a bad thing? Consider the story of Joan, who was applying for a senior executive position at a major financial services firm. On her own initiative, she prepared a detailed analysis of the major competitive and market threats facing one of the company's divisions, complete with strategies for overcoming the problems that would come up. Of course, Joan referred to her work throughout her interview with the firm. When she was informed that she had been passed over for the job in favor of another candidate, Joan decided to send the work she'd done to the president of the company. In a letter, she explained her research methods, offered her thanks for the chance to interview and expressed her hope that the president would be able to put the information to good use. The following week, she received a call from the president's office asking her to accept another position.

Strategies for success:
- Do the very best work you know how to do—and then make sure it's seen by the top people in the company.
- Have a friend or relative review your work carefully for spelling errors or other basic problems.

#248: Tell the people interviewing you that you plan to fire them.

Or:

You're probably all wondering why you asked me here today...

A recent article in *The Boston Globe* told the story of Joseph Bakaleinik, a recent Harvard Business school graduate who took on the daunting task of rescuing the Vladimir Tractor Company, of Vladimir, Russia, from complete collapse. The manufacturing operation, once a powerhouse of the state-controlled economy, had fallen on very tough times indeed. During his interview for the position of director, he told the workers whose votes would determine the outcome of his candidacy that major changes were in order if the plant were to continue operation. He went on to note that, as a result of the restructuring he anticipated, he would almost certainly be forced to eliminate many jobs. The workers of the plant voted to give him the job anyway—with 98 percent of those casting ballots in favor of Bakaleinik's plan.

Strategies for success:

- Bakaleinik's approach—offering the bad news without any apology—is probably a worthwhile one to remember if you're applying for a senior executive position at a troubled company.

- This cut-to-the-chase approach can be adapted to any number of situations, not just reductions in the work force. The key is to deliver the unwelcome news while outlining a clear and compelling vision of the changes that will make current sacrifices worthwhile.

- Before you sound the bell of doom, however, be sure you've researched the company carefully and can make a realistic case for the actions you advocate.

#249: Take a job in the cloakroom of a restaurant where you're likely to meet prospective employers.

Or:

Forget the tip—read my resume.

Christine got a job running the cloakroom at a posh restaurant in her city—and discreetly introduced herself to every customer she could. When she had the chance (and she usually did), she'd mention the courses she was taking at night school and briefly outline her professional goals. As it happened, the clientele of the restaurant was an excellent prospect base. She had a full-time job in the field of her choice waiting for her when she finished up her course work.

Strategies for success:

- Bosses often don't look kindly on overt employment networking on the job. If you try to do this, keep the profile low.
- Write names and numbers down or collect business cards.
- Follow up appropriately by phone or mail.
- For other examples of how service-industry encounters led to important career breaks, see #74, #81, #93 and #234.

#250: Design a promotional display on the spot.

Or:

Don't mind me, I'm just doing a little brainstorming here.

Irene walked into the department store where she wanted to work, asked to see the manager and gave a verbal description of a new approach she'd take with a window display outside. He was intrigued enough by her ideas to grant her an interview on the spot as a retail sales associate. She started that week.

Strategies for success:

- Take your time; develop an innovative new display idea and think it through carefully before you present it.

- Consider supplying visual aids as part of your presentation.

- If, after a few moments, the manager appears intrigued by your ideas, but does not inquire about your employment status, ask for an interview directly.

#251: Offer to work for free.
Or:
Take away the risk and they can't resist.

There were so many instances of this technique resulting in a job offer that space constraints prevent them all from being examined in full here. Suffice to say that the "take-me-now-think-about-paying-me-later" maneuver worked for, among other people, a top-level coaching aspirant at a major professional sports franchise, an eager management trainee at a Fortune 500 firm, a development executive at a nationally-known charitable institution and a special-needs instructor at one of the most prestigious rehabilitation facilities in the country. Typically, these people simply refused to take "no" for an answer, and eventually offered their services at no (or a very nominal) cost to the unfortunate personnel official whose job it was to try to reject them.

Strategies for success:

- Many for-profit firms will cite legal problems with taking on "free" workers, and will insist that only individuals on the payroll be allowed to work for the organization. Your next move is simple: Suggest that the firm pay you a salary of one dollar a month.

- Set up a time-line under which you will provide work in a certain area for a specific period of time (say, 30 days). At the end of that period, draw up a summary of the improvements and contributions you've made, and ask the person to whom you've been reporting for suggestions on how to come aboard as a full-time employee.

- In many cases, of course, some kind of alternate income will be necessary while you prove yourself. Perhaps you can start by working at your target company two or three hours a day, or one or two days a week.

- Ideas based on some form of volunteer work took many forms, and were among the most popular techniques encountered during the research for this book. See #1, #10, #58, #82, #129, #140, #154 and #292.

#252: Surf the Net till you show up at the Online Career Center.

Or:

There must be some reason everyone's logging on here.

Among the most popular career-related sites on the information superhighway is the Online Career Center, which can distribute an online version of your resume and help you reach employers in a bewildering variety of industries. It's a much-visited site, and there's a good reason for that. For a good many job seekers—in high-tech and out—it works!

Strategies for success:

- Think twice before posting your resume in cyberspace if you don't want your current employer to know that you're looking for a job.

- Use the Gopher search function to reach *occ.com*—or, if you're navigating the World Wide Web, head over to *http://www.occ.com/occ/* and check the Center out.

- Successful Internet-related job search stories took many forms. See #21, #26, #35, #128, #136, #142, #151 and #252.

- For a full rundown on the ins and outs of Gopher and the World Wide Web, see John R. Levine and Carol Baroudi's excellent *The Internet for Dummies* (IDG Books, 1993).

#253: Write an ad for yourself on a huge banner and have it hoisted on the building outside your target company's office.

Or:

The power of sending the right signals.

Are you surprised to learn that the person who used this technique was trying to break into the advertising industry? No? Okay. Just checking. (The story is mentioned in David Laskin's fine book *Getting into Advertising*.) Anyway, if an idea like this can work in such a cutthroat field, the method is probably worth considering—but only for those in search of a truly high-profile way to announce a candidacy. Be forewarned that this method will probably entail considerable logistical work. Before taking this stunt on, figure in the time you'll spend checking window angles, renting (or begging for) rooftop space and designing and producing a powerful, attention-grabbing banner. This approach probably represents a significant investment of time, energy and cash. Still, this is a good idea if you're out to show the target company it's not dealing with the average, run-of-the-mill applicant.

Strategies for success:

- Be sure the banner is visible to the decision makers you want to reach.

- Test the banner text you select with friends and associates; listen closely to the critique you receive.

- Use the banner to talk about yourself—and only incidentally (if at all) about the target company.

- Don't load the banner down with lots of text. Keep your message short.

- Feature a phone number where decision makers can reach you or leave a message 24 hours a day. Best bet: A full-time answering service.

- Feeling brave? Change the message every other day until you get the call you're after.

- Do not, under any circumstances, use the banner gimmick to make fun of your prospective employer (or anyone else, for that matter).

- Despite their significant logistical hurdles, banner- and billboard-related techniques of one kind or another have delivered results for a good many job seekers. See #42, #62, #205, #242 and #256 for some variations.

#254: Do an instant market survey of a product you know nothing about.
Or:
Getting beyond "How the hell should I know?"

"How many nonrecyclable batteries are purchased by U.S. consumers each year?" Mike had a feeling that the interviewer's question was meant to be a little intimidating. After all, Mike wasn't trying to get a job at a battery company, but at a consulting firm. Rather than make a number up at random, or admit defeat by shrugging his shoulders and asking for the next category like some befuddled game-show contestant, he thought for a moment about *why* the interviewer would ask him such a question. On the assumption that his ability to think under pressure was being tested, Mike decided to walk the interviewer through the "best-estimate" process. "Well," he said, "before I offered any figures to a client, I'd want to do a little research, but just off the top of my head here, I think I can work up an estimate for you. Now let's see," he continued, "There are about 96 million households in the country, and I'm guessing that maybe three-quarters of them primarily use disposables instead of recyclables. That would be a little over 70 million households. And if you figure that each household purchases, oh, let's say four batteries of all varieties every month—some will purchase a lot more, of course, but some will hardly purchase any—that would give us a rough total of about 280 million batteries every year. That's a ballpark guess, obviously, but it should be in the neighborhood, I'd think." The interviewer smiled. He'd found his man.

Strategies for success:

- Remember: The "right answer" is not necessarily the right answer. In such settings as these, the interviewer is less concerned with the factual details of the question than with your ability to reason your way around unfamiliar circumstances.

- Seemingly impossible questions aren't offered because the interviewer wants to see you crash and burn. On the contrary, he or she is probably hoping to see you rise to the occasion and deliver an answer that shows you to be a clear thinker under fire. Use the opportunity of an arcane or bizarre question, however absurd it may appear, to showcase your ability to set out a rational plan in irrational circumstances.

- Make a point of remembering that figure of 96 million households in the United States. You can extrapolate any number of intelligent estimates using that number as a starting point. (You may even want to weave the figure into the interview when you are asked a question that *isn't* quite as challenging as this one.)

- See also, for comparison, #274.

#255: Swap jobs.

Or:

Two wrongs just might make a right, after all.

David Lipe decided he had to do something about the 120 mile round trip commute he endured each day to get to his job at a power company; he moved to a town closer to the facility where he worked. Not long afterwards, however, he and his wife found that they missed friends and family a great deal, so Lipe determined to keep looking for a position that would take him back to his home town. Nothing surfaced, however, until Lipe came across a listing on a specialized company employment board. The note had been placed by one Barney Craddock, who worked in Lipe's home town and was eager to relocate to improve his own commute. The two halves would fit like the pieces of a jigsaw puzzle...if the two men could arrange permission to swap jobs. That's exactly what they ended up doing, and everyone was better off for the change. (For more information on the innovative personnel practices that allowed the unorthodox switch, see Tawn Nhan's piece on Duke Power in the December 16, 1993 *Charlotte Observer*.)

Strategies for success:

- An innovative approach that can actually help you improve your career prospects, as well as shorten your commute. It requires a little open-mindedness on the part of management, however.

- Once you find a person who's willing to trade positions, make the proposal jointly, in written form, to both of the managers to whom you report.

- Getting the authorization may take some time, and perhaps even some adjustments of hours or compensation arrangements, but for the right job the time and trouble will be good investments.

- If you face a particularly skeptical supervisor, you may want to consider switching on a trial basis for a mutually agreed-upon period of time.

#256: Hire a small plane bearing a banner to fly past the interviewer's window.
Or:

It's a bird! It's a plane! It's Supercandidate!

How it really worked: A recent article in *The Boston Globe* describes how furniture retailer Judy George used this approach to win a position with a major furniture outlet in 1975. The banner read, "Hire Judy George. She'll make you money." (They did. She did.)

Strategies for success:

- George used this gambit when the store refused to give her a shot in the field she knew was right for her. The plane demonstrated nothing if not persistence. That's a quality employers love—and it should go without saying that, if you try this, you'd better be able to deliver that persistence in abundance if you get the job.

- As with all of the stunts in this book that qualify as truly outrageous, you should be sure the company culture is such that you'll win new respect (rather than, say, a harassment citation) for your efforts.

- Schedule the plane to buzz the building when you know your target person will be around, and for long enough to make a real impression. Your aim is not an instant of loud noise and a flash of color, but a series of slow flybys that will bring everyone in the company out onto the parking lot.

- Despite their significant logistical hurdles, banner- and billboard-related techniques of one kind or another have delivered results for a good many job seekers. See #42, #62, #205, #242 and #253 for some variations.

#257: Prostrate yourself before the decision maker.

Or:

Behold, O wise one, your humble supplicant awaits your pleasure.

A recent article in *Success* magazine tells the story of a woman who went by herself to Saudi Arabia in search of a lucrative contract. She was unaware, however, of an important piece of information of interest to any and all women seeking to develop professional contacts in that country. It is, alas, illegal for women to be unescorted in Saudi Arabia. She was arrested as she walked in the door of a government agency. Eventually set free, the woman still faced the dilemma of how to approach the Saudi Arabian men who could give her the contract she was after. Her solution may not have been entirely in keeping with Western standards of equality (or even minimal levels of self-respect), but it got her the assignment. She crawled into the room on all fours, draped from head to toe in a black veil, bearing her business proposal.

Strategies for success:

- This is worth keeping in mind for women who happen to find themselves stranded in Saudi Arabia. As for anyone else—just remember Shakespeare's comment about certain customs being better honored in the breach than in the observance.

#258: Strategically apply correction fluid to the part of the application form that requests information you believe will not support your candidacy.

Or:

I didn't see any box asking about that, did you?

This is how Shannon Faulkner became the first woman accepted to The Citadel, Charleston, South Carolina's elite military academy. She used the white stuff to delete the portion of the form that asked her to identify her gender. The school tried to reverse its decision in Faulkner's favor when it learned of the subterfuge. Not surprisingly, legal action followed; Faulkner's lawyers mounted a long-running challenge to the school's males-only policy. Not recommended.

Strategies for success:

- If you insist on trying this, don't submit the original form, with its layer of white correction fluid—it will probably attract the wrong kind of attention from prospective employers.

- Be prepared for some fireworks if anyone notices your inventiveness with the application.

- Don't lie when asked directly about your background.

#259: Take a maintenance job, then pay someone else to perform the cleanup duties so you can pitch in full-time in the area you want.

Or:

What do you mean, you didn't hire me?

A story in *The Milwaukee Journal Sentinel* (January 22, 1995) tells how Corrine Burnett worked as a chambermaid at a resort in the Catskills to help pay tuition at the nursing school she attended in the fall. Burnett, a major tennis enthusiast, heard that the overburdened tennis pro at the resort was in desperate need of someone to help out. She decided to pay a friend of hers to handle her cleaning duties; during the time she was supposed to be working as a chambermaid, she became the resort's newest tennis instructor. "The money was much, much better," she told the *Journal Sentinel*. "The tips were great."

Strategies for success:

- Asking for formal permission to execute such a maneuver seems a little cumbersome, doesn't it? Who needs paperwork? In all likelihood, if you're determined to try something like this, you're better advised simply to execute the shift with lightning speed and see what happens. If you do so, however, you should be prepared for the possibility of a heated exchange with some disgruntled superior in the organization. That's why it's good to have an ally (as Burnett did) who is eager to help you succeed in the area you really want to work in.

- Make sure all the obligations are fulfilled and you'll stand a pretty good chance of pulling this off.

#260: Show up at 6:30 every morning with coffee and doughnuts; keep it up for three weeks.

Or:

Care for a napkin? Some cream and sugar? How about a top-notch employee?

Jon was after a shipping mate's job on a merchant marine ship that was scheduled to put to sea in about a month. After having gotten a standard "thanks, but no thanks" from the man in charge of hiring for the voyage, he decided to demonstrate his persistence by bringing his contact coffee and doughnuts each morning as he began his work day. That meant getting up at the crack of dawn and waiting in the parking lot, but that's just what Jon did. With a smile on his face, and bearing gifts from Dunkin' Donuts, he beat the hiring official to the front door of the building every morning for three weeks. By the time the ship put to sea, Jon had his job.

Strategies for success:

- As with all the "see-how-persistent-I-can-be" techniques discussed in this book, this approach requires considerable tact, unfailing good humor and a positive attitude if it is to result in a job offer.

- The aim is to be unbelievably polite and committed, not overbearing and bull-headed.

- Your best bet is to try this from a "home base" that is considered a public or quasi-public area, such as the lobby of an office building or a public parking lot. Trying to invade the prospective employer's office each day is probably not a good idea. (By the way, if you are ordered to leave private property, you must do so. If you don't, you will invite unpleasant legal proceedings.)

- Don't turn the coffee-and-doughnuts campaign into a contest; don't think of yourself as trying to "wear down" the prospective employer. Think of yourself as an unfailingly thoughtful colleague eager to help out in the morning.

- This gambit is not right for every prospective employer. Before you commit yourself to this approach, stop and think: Is the person you're targeting likely to react well to your morning offerings, or is he or she the type to become antagonistic to any perceived outsider, no matter how pleasant you make your visits?

- Is the culture of the organization staid, conservative and rigidly hierarchical—or is it more creative and open to new ideas? If the operation you're trying to gain entry to falls into the first category, the coffee-and-doughnuts routine may not be the best idea. If the prospective employer falls into the second group, however, the morning wake-up service may be worth a shot.

#261: Simply report for work without being offered the job.
Or:
At least they won't wonder about whether you're a self-starter.

Whether or not the incident was inspired by a plot line on a recent *Seinfeld* episode is hard to say, but one of the people interviewed for this book insists that an acquaintance of his simply walked into a company at which he wished to work and declared himself to be the new marketing director. He proceeded to set up shop in the vacant office intended for the new director, and worked like a dog initiating innovative promotions for the company's products. When the fellow hiring for the marketing position finally got wind of what was going on and demanded an explanation, our hero informed him that he was interested in making a formal application for the job, and cited his efforts of the past week as evidence of his suitability for the job. After a period of adjustment that must have been fascinating to watch, the hiring manager resigned himself to the impossible logic of the situation, conducted a formal interview of the trespasser and, eventually, offered him the job.

Strategies for success:
- Don't do this unless you're feeling extraordinarily lucky, are confident beyond words of your ability to avoid legal prosecution, and have more guts than F. Lee Bailey, Ross Perot and Bill Gates put together.

- Those few conditions having been outlined, please do drop a line if you, too, feel the call of the wild and are foolhardy—er, courageous enough to give this method a whirl.
- For the record, this correspondent wouldn't try it on a bet, and wouldn't advise you to, either.
- See, for comparison, #283.

#262: Drive into the middle of a riot zone.
Or:
Out of my way!

That's what one enterprising California freelance bicycle delivery man agreed to do in order to win an assignment. At the height of the chaos following the Rodney King verdicts in 1992, he delivered a packet of promised materials on time and as advertised to a spot that happened to be located very near the heart of the uproar. Yes, it impressed people. Yes, he got a lot of work in the long term from the organization he won as a client. Yes, he came away without injury. No, we don't recommend trying this. The story appeared in the Sacramento *Business Journal*.

Strategies for success:
- Check to see whether there's an armored car handy and plenty of protection from your local National Guard outfit. If not, don't bother.

#263: Place a listing in an international lonely hearts club letter.
Or:
Objective: Employment.

A recent article in *The Denver Post* describes how some women in the countries of the former Soviet Union are using pen-pal services and lonely-hearts organizations to contact prospective U.S. employers. Interested American men must pay a fee to contact women on agency lists, which feature photos, lists of potential common interests and marital histories. Even with such dating-service trappings, many of the women use the services as a means of presenting their career and educational backgrounds to American businessmen. Some women actually do find romance with the men who contact them through the network, but one businessman who used the lists as a means of recruiting bilingual Ukrainian workers found that most of the responses he got as a result of using the services were employment-related rather than romantic in nature.

Strategies for success:

- The women who used this method faced an economy very near the meltdown stage and a barrage of restrictive visa regulations. Unless you face the same problems (and here's hoping you don't), don't take the gamble of mingling your personal life with your professional aspirations.

#264: Tell the government you want to deal drugs.
Or:
Button, button, who's got the button?

That's the only way to get a license to sell peyote buttons to members of recognized Native American tribes, who incorporate the edible hallucinogenic plant into their religious ceremonies. Salvator Johnson, a West Texas man who wanted to become a legally authorized peyote harvester, decided to cut through the mountains of red tape necessary to win the right to sell the buttons legally. He had to submit notarized letters of referral from local law enforcement officials to the Texas Department of Public Safety and the federal Drug Enforcement Administration. Then he had to cough up some hefty fees. But he got the work he wanted, which is solitary in nature and, not too surprisingly, off the beaten track, both literally and figuratively. Peyote only grows wild in northern Mexico and in the Rio Grande Valley. Johnson's story appeared recently in the *Los Angeles Times*.

Strategies for success:

- Don't bother unless you like solitary work and a good deal of sagebrush in the workplace.

#265: Have yourself shipped to the employer's office in a crate.
Or:
Watch that hammer, buddy.

This apparently did the trick for an intrepid applicant who was eager to enter the advertising industry. The incident was mentioned in a recent Bill Corbin article in the *National Business Employment Weekly*.

Strategies for success:

- If you want to give this truly exotic method a whirl, you do so at your own peril; this book doesn't recommend it.

- See also, for similar sheer ridiculousness, #281.

- Do the words "Handle with Care" and "This Side Up" seem more essential now than they did a few moments ago? Thought so.

#266: As a switchboard operator, keep an ear open for opportunity.
Or:
One ringy-dingy...two ringy-dingies...well, perhaps you'd be interested in speaking to me.

Miriam, a phone operator, was preparing to connect a call one day when she heard the caller, a real estate developer, mention to someone in his office that he was hiring for positions at his new hotel. She offered her services as a switchboard operator and got the interview and the job.

Strategies for success:

- Keep it discreet; supervisors who find that you're networking for job offers during work hours probably won't react well.

- For a slightly less perilous approach to using information gleaned as a result of work as a telephone operator, see #57.

- A reminder: Listening to private conversations without the knowledge of those involved is illegal.

#267: Hop into a cab at the same time your target decision maker does.

Or:

No, I'm not kidnapping you; I want a job interview.

Denny had attended a speech at a trade organization by a top shipping executive because he'd hoped to get a chance to interview at the man's firm; at the end of the event, however, he'd been unable to muscle his way through the crowd of admirers to introduce himself. No problem. He simply left the building, stepped behind a pillar near the door he knew the executive had to use in order to leave, and waited. When the executive stepped through the front door of the building, Denny made his move and strode from behind the pillar confidently, ready to introduce himself. When his man stuck out his arm and hailed a passing cab, however, Denny had to think fast. As the executive opened the rear door of the vehicle and got in, Denny grabbed the handle. "Where you headed?" Denny asked. "Fifteenth street," the puzzled executive answered. "Why?" "I'm headed up just a few blocks beyond Fifteenth myself," Denny said, showing impressive improvisational skills. "Let's share the fare." The shipping executive agreed, and Denny sat down next to him and slammed the door. In the 10 minutes that followed, Denny complimented his riding companion on an excellent speech—and offered up his own pitch for a job interview at the firm. He got the executive to agree to see him, and their second meeting led to a job offer.

Strategies for success:

- It's hard to imagine you couldn't put this approach to good use at industry shows and trade fairs, where top-level people are usually identified by name tags and in constant search of cabs.

- Residents of some cities (Washington, D.C., for example) react more favorably to the idea of sharing a cab than residents of others (Boston, for example).

- Do the research. The more you know about your fellow traveler's background, company and industry, the better your chance of landing an interview through this method.

#268: Break into the target organization's computer.

Or:

What do you think this "missile launch" option does, and why does it keep calling me "Mr. President"?

A recent article in *The Record* (Hackensack, N.J.) tells how Discount Telecommunications, a local high-tech firm, sought out the security system programmer it needed by holding a contest: Whoever could successfully break into the company's internal computer would be considered for the job. No better way to gauge the available talent, right?

Strategies for success:

- *Don't* try this on your own initiative. You'll spend time in jail. Wait for a contest.

#269: Demand an answer within 48 hours.
Or:
You think I'm going to wait forever to hear from you guys?

The day after his interview for an executive position at a high-powered financial institution, David called the hiring manager and informed her, coolly and professionally, that he'd appreciate a decision on his application within 48 hours. She called back the next day with the job offer.

Strategies for success:

- Clearly, this is not for the faint of heart. You should only try this if you are more or less certain that you are in strong contention for the position after an excellent performance at the interview—and you know that the employer is looking for evidence of a take-charge, make-things-happen outlook.

- Trying this at an organization where the culture frowns on "breaking the rules" won't get you very far. Be sure you know the company's general world outlook before you opt for this approach.

- Don't come off as officious or overbearing; deliver your ultimatum in cool, reasoned, nonconfrontational tones.

- See, for comparison, #216.

#270: Act quickly when you hear the proprietor of a favorite shop has recently died.
Or:
Picking up the pieces

In his book *The Career-Changer's Sourcebook* (Facts on File, 1986), Gene R. Hawes tells the story of Joanna, an executive on the lookout for new opportunity who visited her favorite antique shop one day and encountered a strange change in the environment. She found the usually amiable employees to be grim-faced and edgy. The problem, she learned, was that the store owner had died suddenly, and the shopkeepers were uncertain about their futures at the store. Joanna arranged for a series of meetings with the store's senior employee, an accountant and a lawyer; before long she had made arrangements with the late owner's estate to assume control of the shop, which flourished under her direction.

Strategies for success:

- Don't laugh; unexpected developments like this, when handled with tact, authority and decisiveness, may indeed be managed to your benefit.

- For another example of using your status as a long-term customer to your advantage, see #201.

#271: Sneak into the decision maker's home while her security people are distracted with something else.
Or:
The stealth applicant.

Millie wanted to obtain an on-air opportunity with a major syndicated television program. She'd tried just about everything to reach the top woman at the program, but couldn't seem to get through. When she heard that her contact (who lived in the same county Millie did) was having her patio renovated, Millie saw her chance. She waited until the security guards at the woman's home were busy discussing something with the carpenters, then strode confidently into the decision maker's house and left a package of materials for her on the kitchen table. Millie left the house without incident—and, a short while later, got a call from her contact. Not long afterwards, she won a spot on the show. Not recommended.

Strategies for success:

- This approach may win points for inventiveness and serious guts, but the fact remains: trespassing is illegal and very likely to land you in jail. Don't do it.

#272: Look 'em in the eye, take a deep breath, and simply let 'em know you've made up your mind to work for the firm.

Or:

Let me tell you how it will be...you're going to give this job to me.

Napoleon Hill's classic *Think and Grow Rich* tells the story of Edwin C. Barnes, who got a job as a result of using this technique with Thomas Edison!

Strategies for success:

- Not for the easily intimidated, this straightforward approach requires an iron will, the ability to stand one's ground, and, perhaps most difficult of all, a commitment, once the statement has been made without equivocation, *not to say anything until the prospective employer does.*

- Although it seems very daunting, this approach can save you a good deal of time and help you find out exactly where the decision maker stands in short order. It is appealingly direct—and what's the worst thing that can happen if you try? You might get rejected. That's already part of the equation, right?

- Save it for the end of the interview. Say it before you stand up.

- Remain seated while you wait for a response.

#273: Without any preparation, get your U.S. Senator on the line for an instant taped interview.

Or:

No, I'm afraid I can't hold.

The news director at the station where Mike secured an internship gave him this task his first day in the office! Mike dutifully made the call, confidently identified himself as a reporter at the station (which, as an intern, he was), and got through in a matter of minutes. Shortly thereafter, the news director, impressed with Mike's poise, offered him a full-time job.

Strategies for success:

- This is actually not that difficult to do if you are a legitimate representative (paid or unpaid) of a news organization your legislator's office will recognize.
- Do not misrepresent yourself when trying to arrange an interview.
- If you've secured an internship at a newspaper or broadcast station, you may want to give this a try on your own initiative. Prepare five or six intelligent questions related to local or national events.

#274: Ask the interviewer if she wants you to lie.

Or:

Yeah, I've read *War and Peace*...twice!

In her excellent book *Interviewing*, Arlene S. Hirsch tells the story of a strange interview exchange in which the applicant was asked an innocent-sounding question: whether or not she'd seen the film *Batman*. After replying that she hadn't, the applicant was astounded to hear the interviewer ask a barrage of overbearing, aggressively phrased questions. How could she have missed such a phenomenal movie? Didn't she know *Batman* was the biggest blockbuster of the year? Was she completely out of touch? Instead of losing her cool or changing her position (either of which would have been a serious mistake), she simply restated her answer and waited for the storm to pass. After being pressed further by the interviewer, the applicant gave a calm but firm response: "I didn't see it. What do you want me to do, lie?" With that, the interviewer's assault stopped; the applicant eventually won the position.

Strategies for success:

- The *Batman* inquisition is an illuminating, if not particularly pleasant, example of the stress-interview method of evaluating applicants for high-tension positions. Prospective employers who pull this sort of thing (usually) aren't insane or inherently belligerent; they're simply trying to duplicate the conditions of particularly challenging jobs. In this case, the interviewer was eager to learn how the applicant might react to a particularly demanding supervisor. The poise, consistency and confidence she showed should serve as a model for a besieged applicant.

- If you find yourself in the midst of a stress interview, take a deep breath, remind yourself that no one would launch such an absurd assault without thinking you were worth checking out closely and beware of reversing yourself from a common-sense answer to a simple question.

- In other stress interview settings, your ability to think coolly, even when under pressure, may be being tested. See #254.

#275: Dive into the path of a mechanical sea monster.
Or:
Yes, you could say I made a splash.

An eager applicant interviewing for a theme park tour-guide job pulled this stunt during a water-borne trial run on a new thrill ride. Apparently, he made quite an impression. Not recommended.

Strategies for success:

- If you insist on trying something like this, do it safely.
- Don't douse the interviewer.
- Keep away from moving parts.
- Mediocre swimming skills—and you still want to try this? Have you considered seeking professional help?

#276: Pretend to be a window-washer, enter a producer's office with squeegee in hand, and do your audition piece.
Or:
Talk about making the most of an opening at the organization!

Yet another wild-and-wooly technique from the world of the performing arts. Sources assure the author that this method has been successfully appealed to not only among the more determined aspiring actors (from whom you might expect such shenanigans), but also, with some variations, by those eager to break into the disc-jockey game. Not recommended.

Strategies for success:

- Trespassing is against the law; you are not advised to try this technique, which is included here for the sake of completeness only. But if you are foolhardly enough to want to try to pull this off...

- Feel lucky.

- Be really, really charming.

- Work through that whole fear-of-heights thing before you give this a go.

- Time in the slammer for trespassing is a real possibility here. Arrange for bail ahead of time just to be on the safe side.

#277: Wait near the elevator until the organization's head honcho gets ready to step in.

Or:

If you can't get a meeting, schedule one yourself.

For four mornings, Ross waited in the lobby of the building where the chief executive officer of the organization he'd targeted worked. When he finally spotted his man stepping into an elevator, Ross dashed in too—and made his pitch. Four minutes later, he had a handshake and a promise to "look into things" that eventually paid off.

Strategies for success:

- You won't have much time. Conversations with top decision makers tend to be very short, so practice your pitch thoroughly.

- Emphasize what you have to offer, not what you want from the organization.

- Feeling brave? Ask directly: "Mr. Smith, what do I have to do to make a contribution to your organization?"

- Nervous? That's normal. You probably wouldn't be alive if you didn't have a few butterflies while trying something like this.

- Bear in mind that top-level officers *like* people who take responsibility and show personal initiative.

#278: One by one, challenge the performance and results of each of the members of the group interviewing you.
Or:
Ladies and gentlemen, you're in a heap of trouble here.

An embattled public utility, in search of a new leader to turn the company around, made a point of asking the applicants for the vacant job of president a simple question: What do you think is wrong with our firm? Most of the applicants offered vague generalities based on recent news reports and concluded by outlining a few comforting visions of the future. One showed that he had done his homework—and that he knew how to look bad news straight in the eye. This applicant stood up, walked to each member of the interview panel, methodically outlined the recent problems and miscues in that person's department and offered specific advice on how best to remedy the situation. The lecture continued until every member of the interview team had received a personal critique! It was a daring maneuver, but because it was executed with confidence, poise and a sense of long-term direction, it won the upstart candidate the president's job.

Strategies for success:

- No, launching an unrelenting attack on the company (or your interviewer) is not, as a general rule, a solid bet for career success. This highly risky approach should only be employed *after* you've conducted extensive research on a firm that is in deep trouble and knows it.

- An argument can be made that this method should only be used when applying for the top job at a company. If you decide to mount such an assault when applying for another management job, you may get some strange looks. Some of them may be admiring and some of them may not.

- Keep the assessments thorough, polite and professional in nature. Do not engage in personal attacks.

#279: Refuse to submit a resume when asked directly to do so.
Or:
I'm terribly sorry, it's at the printer's. And being retypeset. And stuck in the garage door opener.

A placement official at an Ivy League university always offered the students he met with some surprising advice. "Never give the prospective employer a resume before a face-to-face interview," he'd say. "Make any excuse you have to, but don't do it." He went on to explain that resumes tend to screen you out, rather than in—unless they offer evidence of a perfect or very-nearly-perfect fit between the job and the applicant. The best course, he maintained, was to win an interview with a tantalizing cover letter and superior, persistent telephone follow-up. During the interview, he advised, you should find as many points of contact between your background and the position's requirements as possible. Once the interview has concluded, you should head home and write, from scratch, a resume targeted *specifically for that position.* The students who followed his advice over the years never regretted doing so.

Strategies for success:

- The trick, of course, is coming up with an excuse for not providing your resume at the outset. Sometimes, thankfully, this won't be necessary. High-level decision makers (presidents of companies and the like) may respond well to the idea of meeting with you after you've followed up a compelling one-page letter by telephone. Lower-level people (human resources professionals, for instance) may be a bit bewildered at the prospect.

- With such contacts, you may have to be persistent, yet studiously evasive. ("Actually, I'm having my resume redone right now; why don't I come in to talk with you on the 13th, and I can get a copy of it to you once it's finished.")

- In place of a resume, it's probably a good idea to offer something on paper for the contact to review and file: a strong recommendation, perhaps, or a good writing sample.

- Remember, your resume is an advertisement for your candidacy for a particular position at a particular firm. To the extent that it suggests a strong likelihood of a good match to the employer, it works. To the extent that it doesn't suggest a good match, it fails. Customizing it to the specifics of the job you're after can only help your cause.

#280 Break your ankle.
Or:
My lawyer really thinks you ought to hire me.

Shortly after an interview for a public relations position at a large museum, Laura slipped and fell on an unshoveled, icy staircase leading out of the building. The department manager who'd interviewed her saw what had happened from her office window and rushed down to help. As it turned out, Laura had broken her ankle in the fall, and the manager had to call an ambulance to transport her applicant to a nearby emergency room. Eager to avoid a lawsuit, the manager offered Laura the job on the way to the hospital. She accepted. Not recommended.

Strategies for success:
- It really hurts—avoid this.

#281: Have yourself delivered to the decision maker's office concealed in a large, bushy houseplant.

Or:

Hey, is it my imagination, or is everyone in the office watering me?

This probably involved significant amounts of mulch. But someone tried it with good results, or so a source leads this correspondent to believe. This entry appears here for reasons of thoroughness, but honesty compels the observation that actually *shipping* yourself anywhere in pursuit of a job opening is a good way to prove yourself, well, a little green. Not recommended.

Strategies for success:

- You will need to get plenty of direct sunlight and rotate yourself regularly.
- As though this weren't absurd enough, see also #265.

#282: Walk in off the street and ask to see the president.

Or:

Trust me; he needs to take a break for a minute.

Alan made this work by asking the receptionist to pass along that he had a strong background in retail auto parts sales—an area which he knew the newly-appointed chief executive had no background to speak of. He got the meeting he was after—and an on-the-spot job offer as a special assistant—because he knew the experience gaps the company head was eager to fill and demonstrated his ability to fill them.

Strategies for success:

- Presidents are people, too, and they're probably more concerned than most of us about screwing up because of a "blind spot." If you can help fill a gap, you may well find an eager listener.

- Dropping in for an instant meeting may be a bit of a longshot, but by concisely outline what you have to offer, you may just be able to schedule a face-to-face meeting if you make a compelling case for being able to help out in a key area.

- Research the company, and the president, thoroughly. Focus on areas of expertise you offer that are not part of the president's personal background.

- Don't be rude to any receptionist or administrative support person. Be particularly careful about building a good relationship with the president's secretary or assistant; he or she is often among the most powerful players in the organization.

- Direct appeals to the head of the target organization, whether in person (as in this example) or through indirect means, were among the most frequently cited methods by those interviewed for this book.

#283. Claim repeatedly that the company has already hired you in order to win your first assignment.

Or:

You've got a lot of nerve forgetting my name.

Ray Wax, like many young men in New York City during the depths of the Great Depression, was out of work and out of cash. In the subway one day he spotted a newspaper advertisement seeking experienced florists. The paper was a day old, and Wax was no experienced florist, but he decided to give the job a shot anyway. When he arrived at the company's offices, a crowd of men was gathered around the front door—all of them, apparently, reporting for work. Wax asked one of them if the firm was still hiring, and was told that all the florist positions had been filled the day before. Another man, however, told him to walk in with the rest of the group, because the company's managers had no idea who had been hired and who hadn't. The ruse worked—although Wax was challenged on the way in, he earnestly maintained that he'd been hired the day before and was allowed to pass through. (See the compelling *Hard Times* by Studs Terkel, where this story appears in Wax's own words.)

Strategies for success:

- Cattle-calls for flower-selling jobs may not be quite as common these days as they were in the early 1930s, but the story does illustrate the value of good old-fashioned determination in the face of tough times. It was an appealing quality then, and it's an appealing quality now.

- That having been said, a subterfuge of this kind should fall into the "don't-try-it-unless-you-have-absolutely-no-alternative" category.

- See, for comparison, #261.

#284: Bring your own plane.
Or:
The runway to success.

In 1920, 17-year-old Phoebe Jane Fairgrave walked into the offices of the Fox Moving Picture Company, which was developing a soon-to-be-famous serial attraction called *The Perils of Pauline*, and announced that she was a stunt flyer with her own plane. Fairgrave, who had bought the plane with the proceeds of an inheritance from her grandfather, had no license and no formal training. The plane apparently put her at an advantage, however; the company hired her for stunt shots, and by the time she had finished shooting she had earned $3,500 for her aerial work on the project. She was better known in later years as Phoebe Omlie (her married name), one of the most popular aviators of her era.

Strategies for success:

- The plane is optional. An unshakable sense of purpose, however, is mandatory.

#285: Call the decision maker at home at two in the morning.

Or:

Did I reach you at a bad time?

You wouldn't *think* this would win too many points, but a talented musician eager to leave a Communist country won a spot in an American orchestral program by just such persistence. (The caller had apparently forgotten about the time difference, a fact that was probably of little comfort to the besieged party on the other end of the line.)

Strategies for success:

- Not recommended unless you can definitely appeal to extraordinary circumstances.
- Bear in mind that people usually aren't at their best when roused from a sound sleep. "Networking" with someone who's incoherent, furious or both probably won't get you too far.
- For a more promising approach that targets decision makers *at the office* at odd hours, see #109.

#286: Commandeer the interview and start asking tough questions yourself.

Or:

How can I get your job?

Ariel, a recent law-school graduate, did her research; she knew the law firm at which she was applying was facing a particularly tricky case in an area with which she was familiar. Before her interview got started in earnest, she used the customary period of small talk initiated by her interviewer to ask specific questions about the case, and to provide some possible approaches to the thorny technical issues faced by the attorneys at the firm who were working on the case. The "pre-interview chat" extended for quite some time. Before she'd been asked a single interview question, Ariel had a feeling she'd already won the job. She was right.

Strategies for Success:

- Warning: Some interviewers may react badly to this. A delicate balance of confidence and tact is required from those attempting to duplicate Ariel's feat.

- If you do the right preparatory work and deliver sound advice in a direct, professional manner, you'll leave the interviewer with an interesting dilemma. If she passes on what you have to offer to the appropriate people in the organization (or uses your advice herself), how can she possibly convince herself you're not the right person for the job? If she doesn't, how can she justify ignoring a possible solution to a pressing company problem?

- Don't wing it! Extensive preparation is necessary if you hope to pull this off. Unfortunately, poorly thought-out, incomplete or otherwise ill-conceived suggestions on a current problem facing the organization will probably cripple your candidacy.

- Best bet: Sit down with a trusted friend with some experience in the industry and outline the advice you intend to give. Pay close attention to the critique you receive.

- Be sure you don't come off as overbearing, abusive or demanding. Show poise, purpose, and tact as you begin your questioning.

#287: Disassemble and reassemble a piece of equipment on the spot—even though you've never seen it before.
Or:
Sure, I know how to do that.

In need of a job, Herb watched from the factory gates as a pair of factory workers disassembled a large drill press. After half an hour of observation, he walked into the factory manager's office and declared himself to be an "experienced drill press operator." Asked for his references, he explained that he wanted to get to work immediately and offered to take apart the factory's drill press machinery and put it back together again. The manager took him up on the offer, led him out to the factory floor and put Herb in front of a drill press. He passed the audition and started work that day.

Strategies for success:

- Feeling brave? If you can pull off something like this, more power to you.
- Don't be surprised if your first few days on the job are, well, interesting.

#288: Get a janitorial job that allows you to mop the floor in front of the head of the organization's office.
Or:
If it's good enough for a future president...

The tactic worked for a young college student named Lyndon Johnson, whose cleaning efforts always seemed to bring him to the door of the head man's office. Johnson never tired of striking up conversations with the gentleman. In no time, the tall young Texan had convinced the college president that he needed a personal assistant—and that Lyndon himself was the very fellow for the job.

Strategies for success:

- If the aim is to win repeated exposure to the person who makes the most important decisions in the organization, this method probably has a greater likelihood of succeeding than, say, phoning repeatedly and getting sidetracked by gatekeepers. (Especially if you work the early-morning or late evening shifts. Not surprisingly, a good many top executives are workaholics whose hours extend beyond the standard office day.)
- Tell the truth.
- Demonstrate a tangible benefit you can bring to their day.

- Don't be put off by short conversations; be persistent.
- Finally, don't screw up the job you were hired to do. Great shmoozing skills but lousy mopping ability will probably lose you points.
- For another intriguing idea employed by the young Johnson, see #184.

#289: Show up during a paralyzing blizzard.
Or:
Weather advisory? What weather advisory?

Gina heard on the early news that the sudden winter storm that had taken her city by surprise was likely to tie up traffic for miles, so she left an hour or so early and took the subway to her interview. When she arrived at 9 a.m., as promised, despite the worst traffic jam in years, she impressed her interviewer mightily. After all, the interviewer had only shown up to tell everyone in the department that the company was giving its employees the day off! The building emptied quickly, and Gina and the interviewer met for over an hour at a local restaurant. Impressed as much by her commitment as by her background and interviewing skills, the interviewer offered Gina the job.

Strategies for success:

- Showing up during severe weather warnings or other natural mishaps can put you at an advantage over those other, wimpy applicants for the job who think six-foot snowdrifts and driving gales somehow constitute a reason not to show up.
- Do not risk life and limb to reach a job interview; do keep an open mind to the idea of using lousy weather as an opportunity to show the employer your level of commitment to the job.

#290: Sue the pants off them.
Or:
Let Judge Wapner be your headhunter.

Marilyn had spent seven years at the same consumer products company as an executive assistant for a top brand manager. During a company reorganization, her boss was demoted and then discharged. Marilyn, too, was let go—simply because she had worked for someone whose career was over at the firm. Although her work record was excellent and there were many other areas in the firm where she could make contributions, the company's policy was to release employees in administrative positions when such management firings took place. Marilyn was let go not because of the quality of her work, but because she was a reminder of an executive who had become *persona non grata*. Marilyn filed a complaint, and won a ruling that the company's policy had a severe impact on other workers at the company. She was granted the right to sue—and eventually reinstated at the firm.

Strategies for success.

- Be sure you have a case. The legal system is expensive and time-consuming; a good attorney will let you know when you stand little chance of winning back your job.

- Be prepared to wait for several years for the outcome of your case.

- Be certain that you will be comfortable working at a company you have targeted for legal action. Even if you do get your job back, stunted career growth is a real possibility. (Outright hostility or recrimination may be less likely, however, since employers will take a dim view of the prospect of being hauled into court again.)

- This plan of action is worth examining if you are part of a particular class of people (i.e., a woman or a member of a minority group) that can be demonstrated to have been adversely affected by a company policy.

- See also #181 and #192.

#291: Tell Patrick Ewing you're going to dunk on him.

Or:

Talking trash can pay off...sometimes.

Back when his job was offering token opposition during team training sessions, a recent grocery store worker by the name of John Starks talked a little too much trash to New York Knicks megastar Patrick Ewing. But it got him a shot in the NBA, and the enterprising Starks made the most of that shot. As the story goes, Starks, a former NBA player was invited to the Knicks' training camp for the express purpose of providing the big guys with some undramatic competition during practice. Starks had other ideas; he boasted to Ewing that he was determined to dunk on him. When Starks made his move, he was promptly hammered by the huge center. The overconfident Starks messed up his knee pretty badly when he hit the floor, and consequently couldn't be cut from the Knicks' roster. (NBA rules prohibit a team from releasing a player who's on the injured list.) By the time he was back to 100 percent, the Knicks had a hole in the roster to fill. Starks got the call and eventually won a starting job.

Strategies for success:

- A good example of how a certain amount of bravado, coupled with a certain engaging willingness to take a few lumps, can lead to opportunity.

- That having been said, the following principle is worth reviewing closely: Don't tell Patrick Ewing you're going to dunk on him unless you're feeling really, really lucky.

#292: Volunteer to coach the Little League team the Big Cheese's kids play for.
Or:
That winning spirit.

Marc did some intensive research on his target company, one of the biggest entertainment conglomerates on the East Coast. He found out everything he possibly could about the CEO. (Note: you can research other top officers in the organization, too.) He did a little more digging. He found out that the CEO's children competed in a local Little League. He volunteered to coach the team. On the weekends, when the CEO showed up for the games, Marc asked intelligent questions about the industry. Eventually, the CEO called him in for an interview—and gave him the job he wanted.

Strategies for success:

- This approach is worth considering if you really can coach the team and you have a strong employment background that is applicable to the field you're trying to enter. Don't try it, though, if the industry or position you're targeting is one for which you do not have a relevant professional background. That doesn't mean you have to have professional experience in the same industry, but you should be able to cite compelling parallels at a moment's notice.

- Honest, intelligent assessments of the child's skills, delivered tactfully and with confidence, are almost certainly in order. Don't make an effort to flatter the Big Cheese, but don't be afraid to make honest assessments of the good points of his or her child's game, either.

- Don't say anything along the lines of, "I've always wanted to work at MediaGiant." You're building a relationship slowly; Let the Big Cheese make the offer.

- Remember, when dealing with very important executives, you must let them control the conversation. It's what they're used to. When appropriate, ask brief, intelligent questions about the direction of the industry in question, and listen carefully to the answers you get. That's a far more effective way to demonstrate your fitness for the organization than reciting your own accomplishments.

- Finally, always tell the truth. That's good advice for anyone you meet in a business context, of course, but it's absolutely essential here.

- Ideas based on some form of volunteer work took many forms, and were among the most popular techniques encountered during the research for this book. See #1, #10, #58, #82, #129, #140, #154 and #251.

#293: Find a high-ranking contact in your target industry who happens to have the same last name as yours; get past the gatekeepers by giving your own last name with a ring of authority.

Or:

Just tell him it's...

Larry learned of a top-level decision maker in the telecommunications industry who happened to have the same last name he did. When he tried to initiate contact, he found that getting through the switchboard and the other gatekeepers was a breeze. He never came out and lied about his relationship with the contact...but, then again, he never volunteered that he was no relation, either. The contacts led to a series of consulting jobs with the telecommunications firm—and, eventually, a full-time job offer.

Strategies for success:

- Admittedly, this one depends on a little bit of luck. You need to point yourself toward a decision maker in a target industry that is a good match for you...and happens to have the same last name. But hey, it's worth a look in a few directories, especially if your last name is a common one.

- Research the target firm thoroughly. Write a brief, compelling single-page cover letter, and then follow up by phone.

- Never lie. (You may, however, wish to try out this line on an earnest gatekeeper: "This is a matter I need to discuss with him/her directly.")

- Once you do make it through to the person you wish to speak to, do not attempt to make too much of the "coincidence" of your shared name. Get straight to the point by highlighting your past problem-solving and revenue-generating successes. (The shared name may, of course, make for an interesting point of conversation to start off the exchange.)

- You will probably have the best luck if you do not ask directly for a job, an interview or even a meeting, but focus instead on your past successes in related work environments. Then ask how you could "learn more about how XYZ company has come so far so fast." Your aim is to get the person to *tell you* to come in for a meeting.

#294: Bluntly tell the president of the firm, "Your customers are having as much trouble getting in touch with you as I am."

Or:

When in doubt, appeal to the bottom line.

Catherine wanted an executive assistant position at a fast-growing entertainment firm; she knew that the head of the company did not have such an assistant, and she knew, after only a little bit of digging, that he was up to his armpits in work. She called at all hours of the day (and even a few of the night), but whenever she reached the head of the company, she was given a polite brush-off. Finally, after more than a month of persistent calling in search of an interview, she told him, "Listen, this is costing you money. Your customers are having just as tough a time getting in touch with you as I am." A long pause followed, after which Catherine heard herself being asked to come in to talk. She got the job.

Strategies for success:

- Persistence pays off, and so does a little plain speaking directed toward the top banana—if you can do it politely and without the slightest hint of rancor.

- Adapting this line to hard-to-reach decision makers may give you a leg up on the competition if the job you're after really will simplify the head honcho's life.

- If you come off as arrogant or ill-informed, however, you'll needlessly antagonize the person to whom you're speaking.

#295: Corner local government officials at the grocery store and start talking.
Or:
Pleased to meet you, Mr. Mayor.

How it really worked: Frank ran into the chairman of the local board of selectmen in the supermarket one day. He told him that their town needed some help getting out the word about the local library's snazzy new text retrieval system, which could access articles from hundreds of publications nationwide. Frank offered to write a newsletter trumpeting the virtues of the new system, which he had discovered on a recent visit. As a result of the meeting, the selectman saw to it that Frank got the supplies he needed. The newsletter was such a rousing success that the board of selectmen eventually authorized funding for Frank to join the library staff as Coordinator of Information Services.

Strategies for success:

- Solving problems in your community is a wonderful way to go about demonstrating your proficiency in a certain area. If you have a *clear plan* that you can outline briefly for a municipal official, tracking that person down in the local market, library or laundromat may pay off.

- Be prepared to demonstrate your idea and track the results of a small-scale version of your proposed solution.

- Be patient and persistent. Local governments usually aren't speed demons.

- Quantify your results and, if necessary, submit a written proposal to town officials about what you'd like to do.

#296: During the interview, ask the president of the company what will happen if he dies.
Or:
Yes, as a matter of fact, I do have a question.

How it really worked: An applicant for the job of CEO at one of the nation's best-known business products firms took the direct approach when it came to assessing the problems he might face during a succession crisis. He asked the outgoing president directly about the possibility of challenges to his leadership by members of the president's family in the event the president passed on. The president, impressed by the courage and the long-term thinking the question displayed, decided he'd found the right man for the job.

Strategies for success:

- While this particular question might be a little too touchy for those of us who aren't auditioning for the top job in the company, a similar query about potentially difficult future obstacles might just stand you in good stead.

- You might consider asking: "In the event of a natural disaster of some kind, would I be allowed to make the best decisions I could in area X if I couldn't reach my superiors for a time?"

- Demonstrate long-term thinking and a profound concern for the best interests of the company.

- Asking one or two thoughtful, tactfully presented "toughies" that show you have thought the job through carefully is a very good way to score points during the interview.

#297: Apply using a pseudonymous last name that is identical to that of the interviewer.
Or:
Keep it in the family.

A woman seeking to enter the advertising industry used this ruse to get a job many years back—both in order to avoid the effects of anti-Semitism and, presumably, as a talking point with the person interviewing her. These days, it's not recommended.

Strategies for success:

- The gambit would be a good deal trickier these days, given most employers' insistence on seeing materials verifying the identities of prospective employees. (The law requires them to ask for these documents.)

- Nevertheless, you may feel that your current name is a significant career handicap—and what's more, you may be right. The fact is, formal name-changing for professional reasons has a long and illustrious list of adherents. (It's not Robert Zimmerman's and Marion Morrison's deeds we remember, after all, but Bob Dylan's and John Wayne's.)

- Perhaps a formal, legal change to a name you select carefully may be worth considering.

- See also, for comparison, #293.

#298: Say you know Mr. A, who has referred you to Ms. B with regard to a position, when in fact you have never met Mr. A.
Or:
Trust me. He thinks I am great!

It wasn't exactly *honest*, but it did get Peter an interview with a vice-president at a major consumer products firm. The VP eventually found out about the subterfuge, but was impressed enough with Peter's background—and his performance the first few weeks on the job—to let the indiscretion slide. Not recommended.

Strategies for success:

- This is not a recommended strategy, especially considering the growing trend toward reference checks among employers. Why should the employer trust anything else about your background if you lie about a referral?

- A major brouhaha in the publishing world erupted recently when a writer tried this and very nearly got away with it, citing endorsements from a raft of top-level authors who had, as it turned out, never heard of him.

- If you do try to pull this off, despite this book's advice not to, be sure you do an amazing (nah, better make that *indispensable*) job from day one, and impress everyone in sight. If (when?) your ruse is discovered, you will need more than a charming smile to appeal to.

#299: Promise that you'll attain a particular goal by a certain date—or expect to be fired.
Or:
Behold the latest advance in human resource technology: The self-terminating employee.

Master stock broker Andrew A. Lanyi used this method to get a job early in his career. The brokers in the office where he wanted to work were supposed to be generating enough revenue to be completely self-supporting within about three years. Lanyi promised either to hit this mark within six months or hit the road. He got the offer and hit his target.

Strategies for success:

- This promise can be particularly effective when delivered in person at the end of an interview.

- Don't talk the talk unless you are sure you can walk the walk. Executed confidently and with considerable charm, this will probably work—once. After that, you're on your own.

#300: Patiently sit in the lobby of the president's office until you're granted an interview.
Or:
Turn off the lights when you leave, will you, son?

This strikes the author as extreme, but apparently more than one courageous soul has successfully appealed to this technique, perhaps the ultimate entry in the "you-have-to-hire-me-because-I-won't-go-away" sweepstakes. (Richard Bolles mentions the method briefly—but not enthusiastically—in his classic *What Color Is Your Parachute?*) The drawback to this idea? In today's security-conscious workplace, any approach that smacks of civil disobedience is as likely to get you arrested as hired.

Strategies for success:

- Alternatively (and this would be the first choice by an easy margin), try something else.
- Have a good attorney handy and bring plenty of money for bail.
- For a slightly less hazardous, but still courageous contact method, see the next entry.

#301: Outside the building, stand right next to the head of the company's parking space each morning.

Or:

Why would they mark the spaces with the person's name if they didn't want you to know where to wait?

Reliable sources indicate that this straightforward technique was the basis of a successful appeal for an administrative job in an educational institution. It wins points for forthrightness, right?

Strategies for success:

- All the gall in the world may be for naught if you don't offer the prospective employer persuasive evidence of your ability to solve the unique problems of his or her organization. Do your research; target your resume to a specific opening.
- Feeling brave? Try showing up on subsequent mornings to ask whether or not the decision maker had a chance to review your materials. However, if you try this, *don't harass*! Keep a respectful, professional but persistent demeanor in evidence at all times.

- Carried off properly, this approach should win you an admiring smile. If a harried scowl comes your way, however, back off. If you are asked to leave, you should do so.

- Do not trespass on private property.

#302: Highlight your kung fu skills.
Or:
Would you mind holding up this board for a minute, sir?

Fred, an applicant for a position at a private security firm, mentioned his twice-weekly kung fu classes to his interviewer because he thought it might add some color to his presentation. After he got the job, he found out that the martial arts skills he'd acquired had been what put him over the top. (The job he was after required occasionally intense interaction with some pretty shady characters.)

Strategies for success:

- If the position you're applying for requires any time out on the road or interacting with the public in an unstructured setting, appealing to martial arts training can serve as a powerful incentive to an employer. Researchers who must travel regularly for the firm, road salespeople and other itinerant company representatives often cause their managers to worry that they'll be accosted while on the job. Proof that you can take care of yourself may just make the difference.

- Special note for women applying for "high-risk" positions: More than one woman's career (and overall self-image) has benefited from taking karate, kung fu or judo classes. Consider enrolling in such a class. Listing martial arts skills on your resume may help you overcome stereotypes on the part of male employers about your suitability for the job.

- Don't try to fake your way through this one. If you say you can smash a two-by-four in two with your bare hand, you'd better be able to back it up. They just might ask for a demonstration.

#303: Send a personal letter out over a national news wire.
Or:
What does that button do again?

Reporter Linda Ellerbee was working for the Associated Press in Dallas in 1972; one day she wrote a long, revealing letter to a friend of hers in Alaska on the office computer. The letter offered chatty, nonchalant assessments of a couple of Texas news organizations, a current boyfriend and the Dallas city council. Ellerbee also shared some candid observations about the Dallas bureau chief (her superior), and made a few colorful, not-for-general-circulation suggestions about how he might fill a recent staff opening. (Her suggestion was something to the effect that hiring a Hispanic, African-American, lesbian writer who could master the news organization's style manual would help the bureau chief overcome any guilty feelings he might have about the AP's hiring practices.) She printed out the hilarious, obviously private document— but left it on the machine's memory. The next morning, during a demonstration of the new computer system, someone at AP inadvertently sent the letter out over the wire. The soon-to-be-legendary epistle churned its way through newsrooms in four states. As Ellerbee recalled later, she got fired for one reason and one reason alone: The legal people at AP convinced the top brass that having her executed would be a clear violation of current law. The kicker, though, was that she got a number of job offers as a result of the blunder, eventually securing a better job at a Houston station that thought her letter showed real talent. Not recommended.

Strategies for success:

- The story does illustrate the potential of a good guerrilla distribution network (even, perhaps, one you didn't intend to use), an appealingly funny page or two of copy and a little openness to the machinations of powers that be of which we may be, for the moment, unaware.

- On the other hand, commandeering your company's e-mail system in order to make elaborate fun of your boss isn't the best way to enhance your career prospects.

- Sometimes, as in this story, the worst news you could possibly hope for leads, almost without effort, to the best news you could possibly hope for. Keep your sense of humor and your eye out for opportunity and you never know what might happen. As William Shakespeare put it, "Ripeness is all."

- When it comes right down to it, people are more interested in *who you are* and *what you have to offer* than with whether or not they heard of you in the way they expected to.

Here's to pleasant surprises and the neglected art of making your own breaks!

Appendix

Organizations you may wish to contact

Most of the ideas in this book put you in front of the prospective employer in a dynamic and exciting way...but coming up with what to say once that employer is listening will depend on your commitment and research efforts. In addition to being able to convey the high points of your own background to the prospective employer (see Section 1), you will need to have some knowledge of your target industry.

One great way to gather that kind of information is to read your industry's trade magazines regularly. If you don't have a subscription, you should check in at your local library.

Another essential step is to contact the professional or trade organization that represents the field or industry you want to enter. Here is a sampling of the most important groups, and the contact information you'll need. Also included: Non-industry-related groups that may provide employment information or other important support functions.

AARP (American Association of
Retired Persons)
601 E Street
Washington, DC 20049
202-434-2277

Actors Equity Association
165 W. 46th Street
New York, NY 10036
212-869-8530

Air Line Pilots Association
535 Herndon Parkway
Herndon, VA 22070
703-689-2270

American Academy of Mechanics
c/o Dr. Dean Mook
Dept. of Engineering, Science and
Mechanics
Virginia Tech.
Blacksburg, VA 24061-0219
703-231-6841

American Association of
Community Colleges
One Dupont Circle NW
Suite 410
Washington, DC 20036-1176
202-728-0200

American Bar Association
750 N. Lake Shore Drive
Chicago, IL 60611-4497
312-988-5000

American Booksellers Association
828 South Broadway
Tarrytown, NY 10591
914-591-2665

American Chiropractic Association
1701 Clarendon Boulevard
Arlington, VA 22209
703-276-8800

American Hospital Association
1 North Franklin
Chicago, IL 60606
312-422-3000

American Institute of Architects
1735 New York Ave. NW
Washington, DC 20006
202-626-7300

American Institute of Aeronautics
and Astronautics
370 L'Enfant Promenade SW
Washington, DC 20004-2518
202-646-7400

American Institute of Certified
Public Accountants
1211 Avenue of the Americas
New York, NY 10036
212-596-6200

American Institute of Chemical
Engineers
345 E. 47th Street
New York, NY 10017
212-705-7338

American Institute of Chemists
501 Wythe Street
Alexandria VA 22314-1917
703-836-2090

American Institute of Mining,
Metallurgical and Petroleum
Engineers
345 E. 47th Street
New York, NY 10017
212-705-7695

American Library Association
50 E. Huron Street
Chicago, IL 60611
312-944-6780

American Management Association
135 West 50th Street
New York, NY 10020-1201
212-586-8100

American Nurses Association
600 Maryland Avenue SW
Suite 100
Washington, DC 20024-2571
202-554-4444

American Society of Appraisers
P.O. Box 17265
Washington, DC 20041
703-478-2228

American Society of Civil
Engineers
345 E. 47th Street
New York, NY 10017-2398
212-705-7496

American Society of Clinical
Pathologists
2100 W. Harrison Street
Chicago, IL 60612-3798
312-738-1336

American Society of Heating,
Refrigeration and Air-Conditioning
Engineers
1791 Tullie Circle NE
Atlanta, GA 30329
404-636-8400

American Society of Journalists
and Authors
1501 Broadway
Suite 302
New York, NY 10036
212-997-0947

American Society of Magazine
Editors
919 Third Avenue, 22nd Fl.
New York, NY 10022
212-752-0055

American Society of Mechanical
Engineers
345 E. 47th Street
New York, NY 10017-2392
212-705-7722

American Society of Newspaper
Editors
P.O. Box 4090
Reston, VA 22090-1700
703-648-1144

American Veterans Committee
6309 Bannockburn Drive
Bethesda, MD 20817
301-320-6490

Association for Investment
Management and Research
5 Boar's Head Lane
P.O. Box 3668
Charlottesville, VA 22903
804-977-6600

Association of Conservation
Engineers
Alabama Dept. of Conservation &
Natural Resources
Engineering Section
64 N. Union Street
Montgomery, AL 36310
334-242-3476

Association of Consulting Chemists
& Chemical Engineers
The Chemists Club
40 W. 45th Street
New York, NY 10036
212-983-3160

Association of Energy Engineers
4025 Pleasantville Road
Suite 420
Atlanta, GA 30340
404-447-5083

Authors League of America
330 W. 42nd Street, 29th Fl.
New York, NY 10036-6902
212-564-8350

Exec-U-Net (employment networking organization for executives)
25 Van Zant Street
Norwalk, CT 06855
203-851-5180

Federal Research Opportunities
(publishes Federal Career
Opportunities newsletter)
Box 1059
Vienna, VA 22183
703-281-0200

Forty Plus Club of New York
(helps job seekers over age 40)
15 Park Row
New York, NY 10038
212-233-6086

Gray Panthers Project Fund
2025 Pennsylvania Avenue NW
Suite 821
Washington, DC 20006
202-466-3132

Institute of Industrial Engineers
25 Technology Park
Norcross, GA 30092
404-449-0460

Institute of Management
Consultants
521 Fifth Avenue, 35th Fl.
New York, NY 10175-3598
212-697-8262

National Aeronautic Association
1815 N. Fort Myer Drive
Suite 700
Arlington, VA 22209
703-527-0226

National Association for Female
Executives
30 Irving Place
New York, NY 10003
212-477-2200

National Association of
Broadcasters
1771 N Street NW
Washington, DC 20036
202-429-5300

National Association of Legal
Secretaries
2250 E. 73rd Street
Suite 550
Tulsa, OK 74136-6894
918-493-3540

National Association of Life
Underwriters
1922 F Street NW
Washington, DC 20006
202-331-6000

National Business Women's
Association
9100 Ward Parkway
P.O. Box 8728
Kansas City, MO 64114-0728
913-432-7755

National Cartoonists Society
2676 Gerritsen Avenue
Brooklyn, NY 11229
212-627-1550

National Education Service Center
P.O. Box 1279, Dept. PB
Riverton, WY 82501
307-856-0170

National Federation of Federal
Employees
1016 16th Street NW
Washington, DC 20036
202-862-4400

National Society of Professional
Engineers
1420 King Street
Alexandria, VA 22314
703-684-2800

Professional Photographers of
America
57 Forsyth Street NW
Suite 1600
Atlanta, GA 30303
404-522-8600

Screen Actors Guild
5757 Wilshire Blvd.
Los Angeles, CA 90036
213-954-1600

Society of Actuaries
475 N. Martingale Road
Suite 800
Schaumburg, IL 60173-2226
708-706-3500

Society of Exploration
Geophysicists
Box 702740
Tulsa, OK 74170-2740
918-493-3516

Society of Illustrators
128 E. 63rd Street
New York, NY 10021
212-838-2560

Society of Motion Picture and
Television Engineers
595 West Hartsdale Avenue
White Plains, NY 10607
914-761-1100

Society of Plastics Engineers
14 Fairfield Drive
Brookfield, CT 06804
203-775-0471

Society of Professional
Journalists
16 South Jackson
Greencastle, IN 46135
317-653-3333

Women's Educational and
Industrial Union
356 Boylston Street
Boston, MA 02116
617-536-5651

Appendix

A few pointers on networking

The standard advice on networking goes something like this: Identify an important decision maker in your target industry, preferably on the referral of someone you both know; call him or her and ask for a "a moment or two" to drop by and discuss "current events in the industry"; repeat the calls as necessary until you schedule a meeting; drop by for your one-on-one session, but studiously avoid asking directly for the opportunity to work for the decision maker's firm; at the end of the meeting, outline your broad professional objective and ask whether the decision maker knows of anyone else with whom you might meet.

That's more or less the approach that's been advocated by any number of career experts, and you can follow it as laid out above if you want. This method, applied persistently and for a long span of time, may well help you get closer to your employment goal, but bear in mind that it does carry a number of drawbacks. First, overworked key people usually have more requests for "informational meetings" than they know what to do with. Second, it's not quite on the level, because even though you don't come out and say you're looking for work, the decision maker knows you are, and knows that you probably wouldn't be wasting your time meeting with him or her if you didn't consider the organization to be a likely target employer. Finally, the method is pretty time-consuming.

The ideas passed along in the main section of this book should provide you with ample material for bringing a new approach to your networking efforts. Once you've had the chance to see some of the inventive methods others have used to get to know people who can get them closer to a job, you can use the time-honored method above as a starting point and add your own refinements. A few additional suggestions on making the networking visit seem less run-of-the-mill are offered below.

One of the people interviewed for this book reported good results after asking to meet with prospective employer for the express purpose of critiquing his resume. The critique went on for some time until, after the second or third meeting, a job offer resulted. The story illustrates that there is indeed an advantage in maintaining a neutral, I'm-not-asking-you-for-a-job posture during some meetings. The appeal for help on the resume, however, has the advantage of acquainting the prospective employer with your background and issuing a flattering compliment: You trust the person enough to place your career advertisement in his or her hands.

This probably doesn't qualify as a news flash, but people in the target industry will tend to be more willing to meet with you if you are referred by a mutual friend or colleague than if you call cold. You should, of course, make a point of contacting anyone and everyone you know who has even the vaguest connection to the target industry. Ask whom you should contact; ask for permission to use your friend's name in doing so. In addition, you should consider putting the same questions to:

- Your (or your family's) attorney.
- Your (or your family's) accountant.
- The head of the local chamber of commerce.
- Representatives at your target industry's trade organization.
- Salespeople at a target company.
- Customers of a target company.

Finally, keep an eye out for ways you can establish a common bond with someone before you ask for a referral. This may come about in any number of ways, but it's easiest to envision strong employment-related referrals coming about through your involvement in social, fraternal or charitable organizations.

Appendix

References/bibliography

#6: Gardner, Bruce, "Buffalo Guys," *The Paducah Sun* (Kentucky), October 23, 1994.

#8: Associated Press, "Cohane—a Master of the Trade," *The Boston Globe,* December 12, 1993, p. 63.

#14: Gruley, Bryan, "Stardom Faded Quickly at Chrysler for Creator of Cirrus and Stratus," *The Detroit News,* January 6, 1995, p. E1.

#19: Goldberg, Robert, *Anchor,* Birch Lane Press, 1990.

#20: Davis, Scott E., "A Little Instruction Book for Job Hunters," *National Business Employment Weekly,* May 7, 1995, p. 4.

#22: Youngblood, Dick, *Minneapolis StarTribune*, February 5, 1995, p. 2D.

#26: Davis, Jessica, "Ex-Scott Paper Employees On-line for Work," *Philadelphia Business Journal,* October 21, 1994, p. 5.

#35: Gugliotta, Guy, "Going On-Line to Get Out of the Bread Line," *The Washington Post,* December 29, 1994, p. A23.

#53: Corbin, Bill, "Who's Afraid of a Creative Resume?" *National Business Employment Weekly,* May 28, 1995, p.16.

#55: Laskin, David, *Getting Into Advertising*, Random House, 1983.

#58: Sicherman and Green, editors, *Notable American Women: The Modern Period,* Belknap Press of Harvard University Press, 1980.

#62: McGrory, Brian and Betsy Q.M. Tong, "Secret Santa Shelling Out $50s May Really Be a Shill," *The Boston Globe,* December 13, 1993, p. 19.

#70: Corio, Gregory, "Why Not Take All of Me," *People* magazine, November 21, 1994, p. 145.

#72: Riesse, Randall, *Her Name Is Barbra,* Birch Lane Press, 1993.

#74: Gliatto, Tom, "No Pain, No Fame," *People* magazine, May 31, 1994, p. 47.

#76: Brooks, Kim, "Theater Director Prepares for Act 2," *News & Observer* (Raleigh), April 17, 1994, p. C1.

#78: Dyer, Richard, "How Dubravka Tomsic Got to Carnegie Hall," *The Boston Globe,* February 21, 1995, p. 27.

#79: Riesse, Randall, *Her Name Is Barbra,* Birch Lane Press, 1993.

#83: Chapelle, Dickey, *What's a Woman Doing Here?* William Morrow and Co., 1962.

#92: Corbin, Bill, "Who's Afraid of a Creative Resume?" *National Business Employment Weekly,* May 28, 1995, p.16

#93: Reidy, Chris, "The Making of Dr. Katz Computer Breakthrough?" *The Boston Globe,* May 29, 1995, p. 1.

#94: Gonzalez, Fernando, "Mario Bauza Married Jazz to a Latin Beat," *The Boston Globe,* July 12, 1993, p. 30.

#96: Corbin, Bill, "Who's Afraid of a Creative Resume?" *National Business Employment Weekly,* May 28, 1995, p. 16.

#99: Rosen, Marjorie, "Dead Ringers," *People* magazine, March 28, 1994, p. 91.

#103: Levine, Michael, *Guerilla P.R.,* HarperCollins, 1993.

#113: DeVoss, Lishka, *How to Be a Professional Waiter (or Waitress),* St. Martin's Press, 1985.

#114: Carton, Barbara, "A Car Salesman's Perfect Pitch," *The Boston Globe,* November 5, 1993, p. 33.

#117: Arnett, Allison, "Fusion, American-style," *The Boston Globe,* June 22, 1994, p. 29.

#118: Corbin, Bill, "Who's Afraid of a Creative Resume?" *National Business Employment Weekly,* May 28, 1995, p. 16.

#119: Savage, Mark, "Car Sculptor," *The Milwaukee Journal Sentinel,* May 12, 1994.

#123: Bickelhaupt, Susan, "DJ Dorman's Long-Playing Career," *The Boston Globe,* November 24, 1993, p. 50.

#131: Kroeger, Brooke, *Nellie Bly: Daredevil, Reporter, Feminist,* Times Books, 1994.

#133: "Kenneth Leibler: Man of Options," *Boston Business Journal,* February 3, 1995, p. 22.

#137: Corbin, Bill, "Who's Afraid of a Creative Resume?" *National Business Employment Weekly,* May 28, 1995, p. 16.

#151: Kitchen, Patricia, "Where the Jobs Are: Strategies," *New York Newsday,* April 17, 1994, p. 21.

#162: Cullen, Kevin, "The Cal Zone," *The Boston Globe,* March 21, 1993, p. 12.

#165: Corbin, Bill, "Who's Afraid of a Creative Resume?" *National Business Employment Weekly,* May 28, 1995, p. 16.

#166: Mele, Linda, "His Success Is No Joke," *Connecticut Post,* April 7, 1994.

#167: Angelelli, Cheryl, "Woman Wants Employment for Disabled Enhanced," *The Detroit News,* January 12, 1995, p. B5.

#168: Simon, George T., *The Best of the Music Makers,* Doubleday and Co., 1979.

#171: Morris, Linda Lowe and Ted Shelsby, "The Ballgame's Over, But Anita Dunham and Grace Blackstone Have Their Team Psyched," *The Baltimore Sun,* May 23, 1993.

#173: Hodges, Jill, "State Trucker Receives Federal Waiver After Long Fight Over Vision Impairment," *Minneapolis StarTribune,* February 11, 1995. p. 1.

#175: Hadley, Mark, "From Vacuum Cleaners to Insurance to Luxury Liners: Cicero's Falcone Finds the Cruise Business is Booming," *Central New York Business Journal,* September 5, 1994.

#177: Sege, Irene, "Demothed T Workers Battle Reading Handicap," *The Boston Globe,* February 5, 1995, p. 1.

#179: Sicherman and Green, editors, *Notable American Women: The Modern Period,* Belknap Press of Harvard University Press, 1980.

#181: James, Robert P., "Court Lets Lying ABF Freight System Worker Keep Job," *Traffic World,* February 7, 1994.

#184: Caro, Robert A. and Alfred A. Knopf, *The Years of Lyndon Johnson: The Path to Power,* 1982.

#192: Swisher, Kara, "At the Checkout Counter, Winning Women's Rights," *The Washington Post,* June 12, 1994, p. H1.

#199: O'Connell, Sinara Stull and Raymond R. Cech, "One New Year's Resolution You Must Keep," *National Business Employment Weekly,* January 22, 1995, p. 7.

#201: Amidor, Abe, "The Yo-Yo Keeps Coming Back," *The Indianapolis Star*, June 11, 1994, p. E1.

#202: Craig, David, "Glickenhaus: Maverick Money Manager at 80," *USA Today,* December 12, 1994, p. 5B.

#205: Wallach, Ellen J., "How to Become Lucky With Job Hunting," *National Business Employment Weekly*, January 22, 1995, p. 7.

#209: Long, Sheila, "Want a Job? Call Automated Interviewer," *News & Record* (Greensboro, NC), June 6, 1994, p. 9.

#212: Fitzpatrick, Doreen, "Speeding Up the Distribution Cycle Fulfills Market Demand," *Westchester County Business Journal,* January 30, 1995, p. 7.

#220: Hirsch, Arlene S., *Interviewing,* John Wiley and Sons, 1994.

#222: Robbins, Anthony, *Awaken the Giant Within,* Fireside/Simon & Schuster, 1991.

#223: McBucklin, Brad, "Mr. Employer, I'm a Great Catch," *National Business Employment Weekly,* March 28, 1995, p. 19.

#224: Hemp, Paul, "An Inn of Their Own," *The Boston Globe,* September 25, 1994, p. 12.

#230: Lanyi, Andrew A., *Confessions of a Stock Broker,* Prentice Hall, 1992.

#231: Cullen, Kevin, "The Cal Zone," *The Boston Globe,* March 21, 1993, p. 12.

#236: Winter, Barbara J., *Making a Living Without a Job,* Bantam Books, 1993.

#241: Craig, Jack, "Lutsk a Real Go-Getter—and It's Paid Off," *The Boston Globe,* September 17, 1993, p. 86.

#248: Kaplan, Fred, "The Toughest Job He'll Ever Have," *The Boston Globe,* May 29, 1994, p. 73.

#253: Laskin, David, *Getting into Advertising,* Random House, 1986.

#255: Nhan, Tawn, "Duke Power's Job-Swap Program Helps Meet NC Employee Needs," *The Charlotte Observer,* December 16, 1993.

#256: Reidy, Chris, "In Her Eminent Domain," *The Boston Globe,* June 22, 1994, p. 69.

#257: "Grovelers Wanted?" *National Business Employment Weekly,* May 7, 1995, p. 26.

#259: "Three Businesses Aren't Enough," *The Milwaukee Journal Sentinel,* January 22, 1995, p. 1.

#262: Pulley, Mike, "Bike Couriers Keep Pedaling," (Sacramento) *Business Journal,* May 24, 1993, p. 1.

#263: Brimberg, Judith, "From Russia With Love," *The Denver Post,* February 17, 1994.

#264: Sahagun, Louis, "Peyote Harvesters Face Supply-side Problem," *Los Angeles Times,* June 13, 1994, p. A-5.

#265: Corbin, Bill, "Who's Afraid of a Creative Resume?" *National Business Employment Weekly,* May 28, 1995, p. 16.

#268: Stolzfus, Duane, "A Few Good Hackers," *The Record* (Hackensack, NJ), January 21, 1994.

#270: Hawes, Gene R., *The Career-Changer's Sourcebook,* Facts on File, 1986, p. 55.

#274: Hirsch, Arlene S., *Interviewing,* John Wiley and Sons, 1994.

#283: Terkel, Studs, *Hard Times,* Pantheon Books, 1970.

#284: Sicherman and Green, editors, *Notable American Women: The Modern Period,* Belknap Press of Harvard University Press, 1980.

#288: Robert A. Caro, *The Years of Lyndon Johnson: The Path to Power,* Alfred A. Knopf, 1982.

#297: Polykoff, Shirley, *Does She...Or Doesn't She?,* Doubleday & Co., 1975.

#299: Lanyi, Andrew A., *Confessions of a Stock Broker,* Prentice Hall, 1992.

#303: Ellerbee, Linda, *And So It Goes*, G.P. Putnam's Sons, 1986.

Index of topics

Cover letters, resumes and job applications

Finding a job after being fired

Finding a job after being laid off

Finding a job in advertising

Finding a job in broadcasting

Finding a job in music

Finding a job in public relations

Finding a job in publishing

Finding a job in sales

Finding a job in the performing arts

Finding a job in the restaurant business

Finding a job in visual arts

Finding job openings

Finding your first job

Follow-up calls

Interviewing

Networking

Overcoming lack of experience

Salary negotiations

Turning rejections into job offers